Little Boy Lost
-A Dose of Reality-

Scott Weidle

Edited and coauthored by
Wes Weidle PA-C, CAQ-PSY

Library of Congress Control Number: 2019912482

ISBN (paperback): 9781686220067

Front cover image by Scott Weidle

Book design by Wes Weidle

Disclaimer

While all of the stories in this memoir are true, the content has been recreated from memory, and therefore is not immune to inaccuracies. In a few cases, minor details, such as the timeline of events, names of individuals and places, as well as identifying characteristics of individuals and places, have been changed to respect the privacy of those involved.

Dedication

This book is dedicated to my three grandsons –

Dylan Zachary Weidle,

Landon Daniel Weidle,

and

Gavin Cruz Weidle

– and is in memory of their father, Daniel Allen Weidle.

Little Boy Lost
A Dose of Reality

Foreword

Introduction

Chapters

Foreword

On March 15th, 2011 I participated in a town hall with newly elected Governor John Kasich and several other recently appointed members of his cabinet. The Governor asked me what we were doing about the opiate epidemic. I discussed our preliminary plans and confidently stated that 2011 would be the year Ohio turned the corner on the overdose epidemic. I was wrong. Over the next seven years, a staggering 214% increase in Ohio overdose fatalities ensued.

It is important for us to look beyond this horrific statistic. Each of us must understand that every overdose death represents the son, daughter, mother or father of an Ohio family. Lives cut short in this manner steal our most precious commodity and cause unbearable pain for those left behind.

Little Boy Lost is a window into the experience of an Ohio family that has borne more than its share of profound trauma. Scott Weidle and his son Wes recount the story of their son and brother, Daniel who lost his struggle with addiction on December 26, 2015. They chronicle in meticulous detail the complex family dynamics and environmental factors that shaped Daniel's young and tragically short life.

Daniel was a bright, sensitive and caring young man, fully supported by a family who loved him deeply and worked tirelessly to keep him safe. The Weidle's approached this life-threatening challenge with a sense of urgency. Along the journey, they confronted family demons, drug dealers and indifferent treatment professionals.

It is now common knowledge that the overuse of prescription opioids and the systematic indoctrination of our healthcare system and general public regarding the safety of opioids to treat chronic and routine pain was the major catalyst for the overdose epidemic. State and federal courts are in the early stages of awarding vast sums of Big Pharma profits to mitigate the willful damage caused by a callous and profit motivated industry indifferent to the carnage caused by their profit seeking behavior.

We must also acknowledge that well-intended but ineffective policies may have also contributed to and prolonged the opioid epidemic. In our search for final causes, we must ask ourselves did we do everything possible to resolve this terrible tragedy? Were there unintended consequences to our actions? There are important lessons to be learned from Ohio's opioid epidemic. If we lack the commitment to ask the questions and learn the hard lessons, we will not be prepared for the next public health crisis that awaits to claim our most precious commodity.

Orman Hall, former Director
Ohio Department of Alcohol and Drug Addiction Services

Introduction

The day I will never forget…

The sun was just beginning to rise over the gulf. It was already hot, even by Florida standards for late December. The water was relatively calm, and I was sitting alongside my wife on the beach listening to the gentle sound of the small waves breaking against the shore. This is what people work all their lives for - retirement on a resort in southern Florida. It all seemed surreal. *What am I doing here?*, I thought. Inside, I felt so out of place. My body was here, my wife was here, my dog and Harley Davidson were here, but my heart and mind were 1,000 miles away, back home in Ohio.

Then it happened. The phone… and not even a call, but a one line text message.

"I'm so sorry, Daniel was my best friend."

"Was!?," I said aloud.

At that very moment, everything in my world stopped. Everything I had worked for, everything I wanted for my future - from passing the family business to the next generation to the faux retirement - all of it, gone in a split second.

Nothing could have prepared me for this pain. Daniel had relapsed and even overdosed before, but I had always been there to help pick up the pieces and get him back on track. Not this time; not when it mattered the most.

Addiction is a disease of the brain. Through modern medical imaging, researchers can now pinpoint critical areas of the brain that are severely affected in a person suffering from this disease. Daniel was winning his battle with addiction, but now it was over.

What contributed to this final defeat? Who or what, had triggered him to use again?

How would I go on? Could I go on? The answers were a 24-hour drive away, back home in Ohio. The opioid epidemic had ravished our home state, and this was definitely a factor. How much of my family history and genetics also contributed to this tragedy, though? I had to get home and I had to try to make sense of all this. Past, present, and future.

The little boy I loved with all my heart was gone, and finding a reason to go on had just begun.

This is a father's story. It's also a son's story and a family's story. Life is filled with joys and heartaches, and every family experiences both. For some families, the joys outweigh the sorrows, but for many, tragedies seem to be the underlying tale. As I write this, it's my wish that this story will provide hope; and for those of us who find the balance tipped to the side of heartbreak, purpose. I have personally known great joy and have achieved many goals, but the pain and losses have been overwhelming.

I invite you to walk with me, Scott Weidle, through my story, and the story of my beloved son, Daniel. You will also meet some deeply loved family members and friends, as well as some not so favorable individuals, all of whom played a part in this story. This book is intended to educate you on the realities of the disease of addiction, expose the truth about opioid abuse, pull back the curtain on our government's lack of willingness to do the right thing in the war on drugs, and finally, to touch your humanity as we share our journeys.

May you find knowledge, comfort, hope, motivation, and relevance in these pages.

Chapter 1

Humble Beginnings

"It's not where you come from that makes the most difference. It's who you come from that often deals the greater blow - either to propel us forward, or to keep us trapped." – anonymous

I'm a simple man, there's no getting around it. Growing up in a tiny rural community in southwest Ohio was about as typical as it sounds. Germantown, Ohio is a sleepy little place populated by blue-collar families and farm land. At the time of my childhood in the seventies and eighties, most residents were either farmers, factory workers at the local steel mill, or assembly line workers for one of the many manufacturers in the area. Along with my mother, father, older brother Ron, and my little sister Jamie, we grew up living the life of an ordinary family in rural small town USA. Although this part of our story is shared by millions of other Americans, the way our life would end up panning out would prove to be far from typical.

The story of my father, Ronal Weidle Sr., is quite extraordinary, and it only seems fitting that we start this journey from his beginning. My dad was very much an average Joe, yet the man he would become is quite the antonym to the word average. He went straight from high school into a third shift position at a local factory, Frigidaire, where he became a tool and die maker. At the time, he was paid well and enjoyed his work, but had visions and dreams of becoming and doing more. Dad quickly grew bored with the life of a factory worker, and decided to take life by the horns to make something of himself – to bust out of the Midwestern molds and create a better world for he and his family.

My mother, Nancy Wills, grew up in a neighboring town, and went to college to become a nurse. Mom flourished in the field, and thoroughly enjoyed her work caring for patients. It was just in her nature to be that way. She was kindhearted, generous, and didn't know a stranger. While finishing her degree, she met my father at the local skating rink. A few laps around the rink later, they quickly fell in love and would later marry on July 24th, 1954.

My dad had always been one to take chances, and usually would do so against the wishes of my mother. One of these moments came when the two of them had only been married for a couple of years. Dad decided to sell mom's car and with the money, buy a brand new backhoe. He had never even been on a piece of heavy equipment in his life, but that didn't deter him. He saw an opportunity to use this tool to make money, and jumped head first into the venture without seeing the destination. He started doing various odd jobs with the backhoe on the side, digging ponds and septic tanks mostly. Within a year, he was able to quit his night shift job at the factory, and begin working full-time excavating land. It wasn't long before this went from a one-man operation to a full-fledged thriving business, employing several other people.

By the time I was born in 1959, my father was busy building an aggregate/gravel plant along with operating his excavation business. At the time, we lived in a very typical middle-class, 1800 square-foot, three bedroom home that my dad had built on one acre of farmland, just outside the little village of Germantown.

From the time I was a little boy, I have always enjoyed being outdoors. My mom would often say, *"Scott, you do have a room inside the house, ya know!,"* but I didn't care. I thrived being outside - exploring, working, and finding things to get into. Since my dad was always out on a job, and my brother, who was a few years older than me, was usually off doing his own thing, most of the chores fell to me. That didn't bother me at all because it meant more time outdoors.

Amongst the many activities that living on a farm provided, riding horses was without a doubt at the top of my list. In the area where I grew up, most of us had horses and would ride just about anywhere and everywhere. During my early teens, usually in the summer, it was a normal weekday activity to hop on our horses and ride around town with my childhood friends, Johnny and Eddie. On one summer day in particular, I remember riding several miles down a country road with my buddies, ending up at a location where our new high school building was in the process of being constructed. The building was 80% complete and on that specific day, there was no construction crew on site, so we did what most typical 13-year-old boys would do. We went inside to investigate, trotting through the hallways on our three horses. Clear as day, I still remember sitting atop of my horse in the middle of the gymnasium, where we would soon become students just two short years later.

Around this same time, my mother was working part-time as a registered nurse and part-time helping my father at the office, mostly with bookkeeping duties. Although my dad is credited with building such a successful business in our hometown, my mom was really the glue that held the place together. She was truly instrumental in the overall success that my dad was able to achieve. She made sure we never lost sight of what it meant to be a family while embarking on the endeavor of building what was to become a family business, which is still in operation today. No matter how busy we became, Sundays were

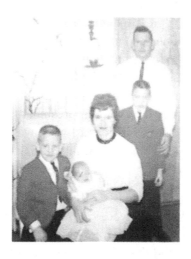

reserved to be with family - up in the morning to worship at the local baptist church, followed by homemade dinner, and usually some sort of evening activity together. It all seemed very normal to me, and in a sense, I guess it was. Yes, my dad was gone a lot working, but at the time it never sparked concern in my young mind. That was just how things were, it was *our* normal. Dad was just doing what he thought a father should do — provide for his family, even if that meant being away for 80+ hours a week. At that age, I wasn't able to recognize how this was affecting my mother, for she seemed to be solid and unwavered. She was steady, stable, and able to function just fine in the role that our life had created for her. Even while working two jobs and juggling the many responsibilities that came along with caring for her three young children, she stood strong and did a hell of a job.

It has only been in hindsight that I have realized just how much time my parents left me to fend for myself, and just how much turmoil was actually going on amongst my parents. It wasn't until a seventh grade basketball game left me with a broken arm in the middle of the court did I realized that not only was no one in the stands to support me, but that this was actually an indicator of a much larger problem. I sat by the front door of the gymnasium that night waiting for a ride home, and when my father finally arrived to get me some time later, instead of taking me to the hospital as most parents would do, he took me home so that he could get a shower and fix his hair first. I remember thinking that was odd - my arm was broken and crooked, a very serious and obvious fracture - yet my father was more concerned with his appearance than my health. After finally getting me to the hospital, my mom showed up, at which time my dad disappeared. It all seemed strange, but that was the first time I can remember having the thought that our family life wasn't as kosher as it looked from the outside. After my mom and I got home from the hospital that night, my dad wasn't there. He had gone out for the evening, presumably to the bars, and that wasn't in his normal character as far as I was aware of at the time. Unfortunately, this was only the beginning of many problems that would go on to surface, one by one, as the years went by.

Shortly after the accident at the basketball game, I was told we would be moving. I loved where we lived, so this made me angry. I was happy to be working on the farm, riding my horse, and spending time alone in the great outdoors. When I think back to how much of a role this played into the man I was becoming, I'm quite shocked. To this day, I still love my solitude in nature and largely credit that to these early formative years. So understandably so, I didn't want to move. The new house would be bigger, but I didn't see the need for bigger. My opinion was irrelevant, however, so away we went. The troubling thing is, I don't really recall my dad participating in any family activities once this occurred. It was like he didn't have time, consumed with work and whatever else he decided to indulge in, his family had become second fiddle.

I never directly witnessed any fighting between my mom and dad, but after our move into the new home, I did notice that things dramatically changed between them. We had much less time together as a family, we no longer attended church, and Sundays became just another day of the week. At just 15 years old, I had become the lone farm-hand, raising tobacco, hay, and tending to 50 head of cattle by myself, but again, I was happy to be doing this as my dad paid me well and I could spend more time outdoors. Dad named this new property, our new home, *My Leisure Farm.* He would explain this name to others with comments like, *"This land is what I do in my leisure time."* My immature mind thought, *Really, Dad? That's because I'm doing all the hard work!,* or at least that's what it felt like to me.

One evening after a long day of bailing hay, I was in the barn finishing up the last hay wagon, and I remember my mom calling my name from the house as it was time to come in for dinner. I'll never forget what she asked me when I walked in the door. *"Scott, do you think we could run this farm by ourselves, just you and I?"* I said yes immediately, since that was pretty much the way it had been for months on end. I had no clue at the time why she was asking me that question, but it would only be a few short years before I would think back to that conversation with great heartache.

For a 16-year-old kid, I felt that I was accumulating a lot of responsibilities. When I wasn't in school, I was working, now both on the family farm and for the family business, which my dad named *Weidle Corporation.* What originally started as a little side-gig with a backhoe, had evolved into a sand and gravel ready-mix concrete operation with full-scale excavation. It became a very successful company that took my dad from average Joe status to the CEO of a business with over 50 employees.

I must give my dad credit where credit is due, though. He is a self-made man who has exceeded his business and financial goals by a longshot. He was a hard worker - a man ahead of his time in business planning and marketing strategies. He developed all of this from his own concepts and ideas, too. There was no formal education to feed him this knowledge, and no internet or Google database to research how to build a successful business model or even create a payroll. He had a vision and he went out and created it.

Success often breeds change, and with that comes many benefits, but also many risks. Going from a simple country man to a man with power and wealth, changed my father. Dad was born with a facial deformity resulting from nerve damage sustained during the birthing process. This manifested in a one-sided facial droop that very much resembled the aftermath of a stroke. It is my suspicion that my dad struggled with confidence throughout his childhood and young adult life because of this, especially when it came to his interactions with women. Success changed that. He no longer had to worry about any particular flaw because he was successful. He was now powerful, wealthy, and was getting the attention that he had so desperately longed for. Success opened a door to the fast life, and Dad ate it up.

Chasing women and drinking alcohol became his mainstays. These became regular distractions for my dad's obligations and the source of his marital trouble. Over time, my dad would develop a severe problem with alcohol that he still struggles with to this very day. With my dad being on a path that not many could keep up with, our family inevitably began to suffer the consequences. This would ultimately lead to the breakup of our family, and my mother filing for divorce.

During the divorce proceedings, my mother became increasingly distraught. The woman I had never seen crack, who resembled a beacon of strength, hope, and stability, was beginning to crumble.

At this time, it was May of 1978 and I was 19 years old. The divorce was ongoing, and I had transitioned to full-time employment at Weidle Corporation after graduating from high school. I was out in one of the company trucks working one day when I passed our family home, which was only about a mile from our office. I noticed a police car in the driveway, lights flashing, and I immediately felt startled. I quickly pulled into the drive, got out of the car, and was headed towards the back porch when I was stopped abruptly by Lou, the German Township Police Chief. Lou put both of his hands on my shoulders and began pushing me backwards. As my football fullback training kicked in, he struggled to contain me. I vividly remember the moment Lou shouted, *"Scott! Stop! You cannot go in that way!"*

It was in that moment that I saw my mother, lying flat on the garage floor. Arms limp at her side, her body was lifeless.

My world stopped. I stared in disbelief, coming to terms with what this meant.

She had reached her breaking point and decided to end things on her own terms.

I was led in through the front door to our living room where my father was lying on the floor in the fetal position, sobbing uncontrollably. My father began shouting, *"Scott, I'm so sorry, please, please forgive me."* He repeated this over and over, and it still echoes in my mind like a broken record on repeat that you can't shut off. I turned away from him as I could not bring myself to console him in that moment.

I walked outside into the front yard to get my composure and process what was happening. Sweat dripped from my brow and my breaths were hard to come by. After a period of complete aloneness, I turned around and realized that the pastor of our church was standing right next to me. I hadn't even noticed his arrival. He spoke gently and attempted to console me, but I felt completely numb, completely in shock. I had just lost the one person with whom I had spent most of my time. Trying to process this was more than I was capable of. The pastor handed me the note that my mother had left for me, along with her wedding ring. I couldn't bring myself to read that letter until sometime much later. It was just too painful and the thought of reading her final words was the last thing in the world I wanted to do.

An ambulance eventually pulled into the driveway and away went my father to the local hospital. He had completely fallen apart, barely able to put one foot in front of the other. The way in which my mother had chosen to end her life, along with the planning that was involved in ensuring that my father would be the one to find her body, was too much for him to swallow. He had received her message loud and clear, but was unable to process it. He had emotionally and mentally checked out.

I'm not sure where my brother and sister were in these moments, and in fact, I didn't see them at all that day to my recollection. I don't recall much more regarding the events that transpired that day. Maybe I have repressed them; I *hope* I have repressed them. I do know, however, that I spent that night alone in our home. Alone, in the unfinished basement which I had taken over as my own personal apartment. Obviously nobody else wanted to be there, and I didn't blame them, but I didn't have anywhere else to go or anyone else to be with. My mother was my person, and she was gone.

I can see in hindsight that during my parent's divorce, my mother watched helplessly as everything she had always dreamed of, fell apart. When she realized that divorce meant the loss of her husband with whom she had stood beside through the birth of three children, through the creation of a family business, and through his infidelity, she lost all sense of happiness. Her world was shattered and she didn't know where to turn to for help. On the outside, my mom seemed so strong. She was devoted to family and had a very healthy relationship with God. I didn't know it at the time, but my mom was struggling with severe depression on top of everything else weighing on her shoulders. She had finally reached a breaking point, but even in the midst of these emotions, she still had her children at the forefront of her mind. In her letter to me, just hours before her death, she asked me to take care of my brother and sister. I know that she must have struggled with the decision to end her life, as it would leave her three children without a mother, but *that* is the power of the beast which is depression. It takes all sense of hope and joy from your life, and leaves you feeling as thought there is no way out. I did not understand these kinds of emotions as a 19-year-old boy, but I would come to learn years later just how devastating it can feel to lose the most important thing in your life: your marriage and family.

The next morning my brother and my maternal uncle came to the house. Together, we went to the funeral home to begin the arrangements. Still numb, it all seemed like a fake universe. I had never experienced a death in the family up until this point, let alone someone so close. It was something that I couldn't mentally make any sense of. I had never even contemplated the possibility that my mom would end her life, yet there we stood, forced to swallow the reality that death is permanent and sometimes life doesn't make sense.

My mother was so loved in our community. Hundreds of people showed their support for us during this time. The funeral service was standing room only at our local church. My brother and I proceeded alone in the car behind the hearse, driving our family's Mark VII Continental from the church to the cemetery. I could tell he was in deep pain. My brother and I were not very close at the time, which would be something that carried over throughout most of our lives, but I could always read him pretty well. This time, though, was different. It seemed as if he wasn't really comprehending our new reality, unable to process the shocking loss. His eyes were distant, void almost. We were both just trying to survive the new world we found ourselves sitting in.

Dad was absent the day of the funeral, still in the hospital with what we called at the time "a nervous breakdown," and he could in no way attend the services. In fact, it was several weeks before I would see him again. There was no family unity during this time, we were all just existing. My sister, only 14 years old at the time, clearly devastated and in shock, was staying with grandparents for the time being. I'm very grateful for this now, as I would have had no idea how to console and care for her during that time.

After the graveside services ended, the cemetery caretaker tracked me down and asked me to pay for the services they had provided. In that moment, I realized that as a 19-year-old boy, there was no more growing up to be done. The weight of this family was now falling on me. I couldn't mourn, I wasn't allowed to process the loss, I wasn't able to share in this grief with my siblings, and I didn't have a dad there to console me. This was my new life, and I hated everything about it.

To this day, no one places blame on the events that occurred with our mother. What good would that do? However, and rightfully so, my siblings and I carry around many painful emotions regarding that period in our lives. The loss of our mother would change the course of our family, forever.

Within three days, I was back at work. My mother was gone, my father was MIA, and I was the only Weidle at the family business. I continued to live in our family home alone, but I had never felt farther from home in my life. For the next two years, I would continue to run my dad's business in his place, while he was trying to put himself back together. I was learning the ropes as I went along... struggling, but surviving.

This wasn't the life I had envisioned for myself. I actually had dreams of one day becoming a pilot in the Navy. I had learned to fly as a hobby at the offering of my mom around the age of 16. She picked up on my fascination with aviation and wanted to see it through that I was able to explore this path. I soloed an airplane for the first time during my junior year in high school. It quickly became a passion that I seriously considered pursuing as a career. I was eventually accepted into flight school in the US Navy and discussed this possibility with my mom. She supported my goals and I was starting to think that this may actually happen; I could one day become a real life fighter pilot! I never intended to stay at Weidle Corporation, although I assumed that my dad wanted one of his sons to take over for him at some point. I later learned, the hard way, that this was *not* one of his goals.

From my perspective, my dad never fully returned to the business with any passion. From then on, it was sporadic and random involvement to put it generously. He never fully ran the company's day-to-day operations after my mom's death. He left it on auto-pilot, at least that's the way I saw it. I grabbed hold of the gear shifter as best I could, learning stuff the hard way, and just tried to keep things afloat. Many mistakes and obstacles later, by no formality, I became head of the family business and said goodbye to my dreams in the Navy.

In July of 1978, just a few months after we lost my mother, the house next door to my childhood home went up for auction. The couple who had owned the home passed away, and I knew the owner had a plethora of tools in his garage, so I decided to attend the auction to see if there was anything I could add to my collection. I made a few purchases, at which time the auctioneer began to auction the actual house. My grandfather, who attended the auction with me, suggested that I bid on the property. I hadn't even considered this at the time, but I think he knew, better than I, that a fresh start and place of my own would be good for me. Within minutes, I was the owner of my first home. At 19 years old, I walked over to the bank and secured a loan by myself. I now had a mortgage and a place to call my own, just like that. I quickly and excitedly moved into the house and was settled in by the following month. Shortly after leaving the old family home, my dad returned, and once again took up residence in the house where my mom, his wife, had died.

One of the first visitors to my new home was my father. I remember this day all too well. I was in the front yard doing various landscaping chores when my father pulled into my driveway on his motorcycle. I froze in place, not wanting to believe my eyes. On the back of Dad's Harley Davidson was another woman. I was stunned.

I remember hearing rumors about my dad's lifestyle, which presumably led to my parent's divorce, but this was the first time that I was face-to-face with this reality. Only a few months after burying my mother, here was my dad, already out publicly with another woman to come meet his son. I wasn't ready for this. On the inside, I was shaken to my core. I remained polite during the visit, but I'm honestly not sure how I had that kind of restraint as a 19-year-old boy, still grieving the loss of his mother. I didn't feel angry, just shocked, I guess.

My father, who had worked tirelessly to build a thriving business, support his family, and achieve such lofty goals, had become lost in his own success. He was a changed man, living a life that I would never have thought him capable of. He would go on to disappear for days at a time repeatedly throughout the next several years, slowly spiraling into a deep abyss.

I knew at this point in my life I needed security. I desperately needed and yearned for peace and stability, of which I had been robbed of for so many years. My new home afforded me a fresh start; a start that was away from my family home and the haunting memories that existed there. At the same time, I felt stuck at Weidle Corporation because I didn't have much confidence in the company's future given my dad's new way of living. I knew that if I didn't commit to the company though, there was no future there. So for the next eight years, I continued to work for, and informally lead, the family business. I collected a regular paycheck just like everyone else. I remember thinking to myself that although I was grateful for a paycheck, I needed more if I was going to be financially secure in my own right and make something of myself as my dad had done for himself. I didn't feel right assigning myself a higher wage just because I was a Weidle, and so I decided that I was going to pursue a few side ventures of my own to help establish and distinguish myself apart from the business. I wanted my own footing.

Despite what most people would have thought at the time, my dad never showed favoritism to me as his son. I was his employee, and that's it. I was fine with this because I hated the thought of undeserved privilege. The last thing I wanted was for anyone to think that I was born with a silver spoon in my mouth. I worked hard because it was in my nature to do so. I was taught from a very young age on the farm that you reap what you sow. I never asked for anything and I never got anything handed to me that I didn't work like hell to earn.

As the years went by and Weidle Corporation grew, we focused more on sand and gravel mining, and less on excavation. Because of this, much of our heavy equipment laid dormant behind our property. I remembered what my dad was able to accomplish with that original backhoe he purchased, and so I partnered up with a friend from high school and started a home-building business. I began utilizing that excavation equipment in the evenings after my day job at Weidle Corporation, and started to dig the basements for the new homes we were building. We ended up doing about one hundred houses over the course of the next ten years, and this turned into a nice profitable side business for me. Over the course of the following decade, I also became a developer and was able to purchase some commercial land in Germantown to turn into retail space. One venture led to the next, and I was slowly able to build a foundation that allowed me to be a little more independent of my father's impulsivity and control.

I would end up becoming very thankful for the proactive nature in which my dad instilled in me, because ironically, in 1986, my father sold the ready-mix portion of Weidle Corporation to a larger local concrete company, without any notice to me. I was devastated. I felt that all of my efforts to help my dad save and continue growing his company were thrown away at the drop of a hat, without the consideration that I may even have an opinion regarding this. It hurt, but I continued to move the remaining corporation forward with excavating contracts and gravel mining. There was enough left there that the company could still thrive, if done right.

In the early 1990s, I was continuing to develop both residential and commercial property on my own. I had come across a piece of commercial land that was perfect for a business that my mom had actually suggested to me years ago. It was something that she felt Germantown desperately needed: a car wash! I purchased the land and 15 years after my mom had suggested this to me, Germantown had its very own car wash, the first one in the area. Although she was never able to see this come to fruition, I know she was smiling down at me the day we broke ground. To this day, I still have an emotional connection to that little car wash, which still exists, because it was the product of something that my late mother had suggested. And for that, Mom, I thank you. This suggestion didn't result in just a little car wash, however. On that same piece of large rural land, I subdivided it several times and oversaw the development of Germantown's main business district, which acts as the town's central hub to this very day.

By the mid-1990s, my father was completely bored with the family business and wanted completely out. I very clearly remember him coming into my office one summer afternoon asking me how I would feel about him selling the entire company. Again, I was hurt, but I knew it was his company and I couldn't tell him what to do. It was his dream, his company. I told him I didn't like it, but that he had my blessing to do what he felt was best.

So, in 1996, my dad sold the sand and gravel portion of the company, and I relocated the remaining excavation portion to an office directly across the street, where it remains currently. During the sale of the sand

and gravel segment, I was forced into signing a non-compete with the new owners. For the subsequent decade, I was forced out of the sand and gravel business, but always knew that I would one day return to the industry as it was more of a passion to me relative to excavating. In 2008, I reopened the sand and gravel aspect of Weidle Corporation, and we're still digging deeper in that same little nook of land.

By the time 2008 rolled around, I had essentially brought the company full-circle, back to the business my dad started originally: sand and gravel, ready-mix, and excavation. Weidle Corporation was, and is, booming. Slowly, and with much turmoil, I had become a successful businessman within Weidle Corporation, within the realm of land development, and with my own local little car wash. Life was finally moving in a positive direction, despite the many heartaches brought on by my mother and father. Little did I know at the time, some of the rockiest roads and the biggest obstacles, were yet to come.

As I look back on my childhood, albeit unstable at times, I honestly wouldn't trade it for the world. As I could only come to understand later in life, as I have struggled to raise my own family and develop as an entrepreneur through trial and error, things aren't as easy as they seem. Life is hard and messy, and no man should be judged based on the decisions they make in the face of extreme adversity, as my father commonly has been. And so Dad, I thank you for the things you have taught me, and continue to teach me.

I love you, Dad.

Chapter 2

Rocky Roads and Overloads

"If you're going through Hell, keep going." - Winston Churchill

Working in the gravel industry, I always knew there would be many, quite literal, rocky roads in my future. Never did I imagine, however, the boulders I would soon face over the course of my 3rd, 4th, and 5th decades of life. My first twenty years had certainly been messy, but such is the case for many people at that age, and most seem to come out of it just fine. I dreamed of the same for myself - lofty visions of happiness, prosperity, and health. By the time I had settled myself into the new home I had purchased at the auction during the summer of '78, my next chapter of life was about to unfold.

In my free time as a 20-year-old single guy in the backwoods of Ohio, I would frequently visit a local restaurant; it was really the only spot in town to grab a decent bite to eat and have a drink. Little did I know at the time, but my life, on more than one occasion, would come to be drastically changed by the people I would happen upon in this little joint. Debbie and I met at this restaurant in 1979 and had an immediate connection. She was a local to Germantown, a 26-year-old single mother to a 6-year-old little boy, and taught special education at the local school district in the town where we lived. We dated for several months and very much enjoyed one another's company. It quickly became apparent that we were ready to take our dating relationship to the next step, and within a few short months, she and her son, Zac, moved into my house. The subsequent three years were great - trips to the lake, getting to know one another's families, and many discussions about the family we envisioned having together. In 1982, we had the traditional church wedding in downtown Germantown, and I officially became a stepfather to Zac. He was full of spunk and probably much more than I could handle, to be honest. Zac and I were never as close as I thought we should have been, but being in my early twenties and foreign to the idea of step-parenting, I didn't think much of it. I provided for him and welcomed him into our new family unit, but there always seemed to be a disconnect of some sort. I thought maybe this was normal, but having no comparison or reference, I never pushed it. It would be three years later, in April of 1985, when Debbie would give birth to our first son together, Daniel Allen. Our family was now a party of four.

Around this same time, we had decided to begin building what would become our family home for the next 15+ years. It was a beautiful house with plenty of space, situated on 15 acres of land just outside of Germantown proper. It was the picturesque home I had always dreamed of. The driveway lined with cherry trees, a fishing pond out back, and a swimming pool in the side yard. As if this wasn't enough, we warmly welcomed the birth of our second son, Wesley David, in February of 1991. Life was coming together and I couldn't have been happier. *This* was the stability I had longed for.

Throughout this period of my life, I was hopeful. I was hopeful that my past wasn't going to dictate my future, and I was hopeful that I would be able to nurture a family that wouldn't suffer from the same pitfalls in which I had come from. Unfortunately, it wasn't that easy. As our family developed and grew, I felt an overwhelming need and desire to provide a life worth living. I trace this back to the values that my father had instilled in me, but looking back, I can see where this went overboard at times. By the time Wes was born in 1991, I was away from home more than I was present, and Debbie was raising the boys without much help from me. Debbie had stopped teaching soon after Daniel was born to be at home with the boys full-time, but by the time Daniel was ready for preschool, she too decided it was time to go back to school, and took up teaching again.

By the time I was 30, I felt as though I was falling behind the curve as far as financial security was concerned. I let this fuel my work ethic and allowed it to motivate me to not only better provide for my family, but also to achieve enough financial independence as to protect us from the fact that my dad still technically had sole ownership of the company. It was also becoming increasingly more obvious that this family business was growing at rates that would likely outlive myself. I realized that if I stuck with this thing, I would potentially be able to leave my boys a business which they would have the opportunity to take over, if they saw fit. Right or wrong, I kept my head down and worked, and worked, and worked.

Life carried on and the years passed. Life was good, but with Debbie and I both working full-time and two young children running wild, things slowly began changing a bit between us. I really didn't know why and I still can't necessarily put a finger on it, but I could sense things weren't as good as they were in the beginning. Maybe it was because I was absent like my father had been, yielding to my compulsion to spend endless hours at work, or maybe it was just the normal monotony of life that many couples face after their honeymoon phase fades. Either way, I didn't like it and it scared me. I feared the stability wasn't going to last forever.

Drifting apart slowly turned into arguments, arguments turned into trust issues, and sooner than later, our marriage was in serious trouble. I was beginning to see warning signs that made me believe the foundation we had built our marriage on was cracked. I struggled to understand her, and she struggled to understand me. Her mood would go from high to low at a moment's notice and her actions began to raise grave suspicions within me. She was changing into a person that I didn't recognize, and having spent most of my time in the office, I'm honestly not really sure when or where these problems began for her. I knew something had to be contributing to the chaos, but was baffled as to how the two of us had so quickly gotten off course. As I sought out answers to explain the issues we were having in our marriage, I learned a great deal about an issue that would come to dominate my life through to the present time.

The disease of addiction.

At this point in the mid-90's, addiction wasn't an issue that was talked about frequently. You didn't turn on the news to see the latest overdose trends or the latest physician arrested for overprescribing. I certainly knew about the concept of addiction given my father's abuse of alcohol, but it seemed like everyone had the stereotypical dad, uncle, or grandpa that was an alcoholic, so what made mine any different? I had also heard numerous horror stories regarding Debbie's ex-husband, who had struggled with drug abuse for many years prior to his death, but the idea that addiction was a disease was a foreign concept to me.

It finally became clear to me that Debbie had become dependent on the use of prescription medications for pain and anxiety. At the time, the opioid crisis was basically unheard of, although it was largely already underway, especially under our roof. What started as a benign doctor's visit for help with migraine pain and anxiety, turned into an issue that she would severely struggle with for the remainder of the 1990's. Her intentions were never to become addicted to medications. She was simply taking the pills her primary care provider was recommending and prescribing. After being exposed to the euphoric effects of the medications, it was only natural to want more. Without any regulations in place at the time to prevent abuse, it was very easy to doctor shop and obtain as many prescriptions as one desired, and that's pretty much what happened.

It was only a matter of time before Debbie's addiction reach a level that we couldn't hide, and we both realized that she would need help to beat this. We sought out the stereotypical hospital-based treatment programs, but the disease had her in it's grips. This would become an ongoing pattern we would struggle to solve and became one of the more prominent issues that would ultimately tear us apart.

In full disclosure, I was not as understanding as I should have been. I didn't recognize the signs, nor did I understand the truth about the disease of addiction which Debbie was battling. I often thought that her hospital stays and doctor appointments were just another way to get the drugs she had become dependent upon. I thought this was just a lack of willpower on her part and not an actual disease that was out of her control to change. Boy, was I wrong. The communication between us was at an all-time low and I didn't know how to help her. In fact, my actions probably contributed to making things much worse for her, and for our family.

Because our children were still very young, they had no idea what was really happening and I never wanted them to. Nevertheless, they did witness far too many arguments between the two of us, and it wasn't long before I began seeing how much this impacted them. They knew their parents weren't happy, and in fact, were miserable. Debbie's substance issues began to dictate most aspects of our lives and I felt our family was spiraling out of control. The love in our relationship was all but gone. Debbie and I both built up walls around each other during this time, which only separated us further and didn't allow for the healing our relationship so desperately needed. I didn't know where to turn and ended up doing many things during this time period that I would come to regret; things that only fueled the fire.

Even as our relationship neared its end, I still loved her. She was the mother of my children and that was never going to change. However, our constant fighting wasn't good for the boys, and I think we both realized that they came first. In the back of my mind, I thought a separation might help Debbie realize that our family was at stake and this may motivate her to maintain consistent sobriety. She was always a good mother, even at the worst points in our relationship. Maybe it was naive on my part, but I never felt like the kids were at risk in her care. In 1997, I finally worked up the nerve to leave the house and begin taking the steps I felt were necessary to protect the boys and myself from the emotional trauma going on in the home. Our boys were caught in the crossfire, and our actions were very detrimental to them. I had to make that stop.

For the next year, Debbie and I's relationship was on-again, off-again. My goal when leaving was never to get divorced or to be permanently separated. I wanted things to be restored and I wanted my family back. After about a year of separation, we were both in agreement that we would try moving back in together and give it another shot. Things seemed to improve for the first couple of months, but ultimately to no avail. After about two months, things plummeted again. The arguments once again became unbearable and Debbie told me to leave, but this time, for good.

I was more than devastated. I was crushed.

I packed a suitcase in the middle of the night and went to the kitchen where I had one cabinet which served as my makeshift home office. In the cabinet was a shoe box filled with family photos and a few family videos. *These* were my prized possessions; more valuable to me than any of the material items that filled our home. I gathered my things and walked out of the house that I had so desperately tried to make a home.

As if this wasn't enough, I did make one last ditch effort about three weeks later to stop by our home during Super Bowl Sunday. I thought maybe this would spark some memories of past years in which we would watch the game together as a family, laugh at the commercials, and enjoy one another's company. Unfortunately, things didn't go as smoothly as I had dreamed, and within minutes of my visit, another confrontation was quickly escalating so I promptly left. After that, I never went back. I hated that we were heading for divorce, but I couldn't figure out a way to fix something that had become so badly damaged.

This broke me unlike anything I had ever been through to date. Even more so than losing my mother 20 years prior, and more so than having a business sold out from under my feet. For the first time, I understood the need and desire to stop the emotional pain which my mother had become consumed by. I was shattered and I remained that way for a couple of years. I fell into a deep, dark, depression; nothing like I had ever experienced before. I had no passion for work, I had no desire to get out of bed in the morning, and I certainly didn't care about the future.

For a month or so I lived at my office and then eventually moved in with my father at the house where my mother had died. I hated doing this, but I felt as though it would give me time to figure out my next move and may actually be good for my dad, too.

My first concern when leaving our home was the happiness and safety of my two boys. Daniel and I had a natural closeness, similar to the closeness that Wes and Debbie naturally shared. Not that either of us ever had favorites, it was just how the four of us panned out. Wes drifted towards his mother and Daniel drifted towards me. At the time of the separation, Daniel was about 14 years old and thus old enough to choose where he would spend the majority of his time. He chose to live with me, and Wes stayed with his mother. I'm not sure if Wes did this because of their closeness or out of some innate desire to protect her and not leave her alone. Wes has always been that way when it comes to his mother, and I'm glad that he was, and still is, that way.

Our divorce was hostile to put it lightly. Debbie got the family home, the furnishings, the car, and half my retirement fund. Court date after court date, the assets were divided and the children were being tugged from one house to the next. I remember the first few times that I was to get Wes for visitation on Wednesday nights, and it is a painful memory I wish I didn't have. He didn't want to come with me that night and I basically had to drag him out of the house. I hated to see this anguish in him, but what made it unbearable was knowing that we had caused it. Neither of them transitioned very smoothly. They felt stuck in the middle and I had no way to navigate this new dynamic. Eventually, I would build a new house several miles from our original home, and

34

both boys would come and go as they pleased. It wasn't easy at first, but as the time passed, we all learned our way around the new life we found ourselves living.

After the divorce was finalized, Debbie and I both went on with our lives. I never stopped worrying about her, but I did put as much distance between us as possible - both for my health, and hers. The only way to begin a new chapter in life is to finish and close the preceding one. Debbie would continue to struggle with sobriety intermittently throughout the duration of our divorce, but it does bring me great joy to say that she found sobriety around 2004 and has maintained control over the disease of addiction since that time. She since has also remarried and lives a happy, healthy life with her husband, Mike.

It has only been in recent years that I have gained a deeper understanding regarding the issue that Debbie faced - the disease of addiction. Perhaps if I had known what I know now, things could have turned out differently. Maybe we could have found her the help that she so desperately needed, or maybe I would have had the empathy to never leave her side. Just maybe, our family may still be together, but I cannot go through life with regrets or what-ifs. We live and we learn and we move forward.

You're probably wondering what ever happened to Zac, my stepson, throughout this whole mess. Zac was thirteen years older than Daniel and eighteen years older than Wes, so he was very much in a different season of life by the time things went south in Debbie and I's marriage. However, given the themes of this book, I think it would be an injustice if his story was glossed over.

Zac was a vibrant kid with an incredible sense of humor. He was naturally outgoing and loved to be the center of attention. Quite literally, he was the opposite of me in every sense of the word, but we all loved him for it. He kept us laughing and smiling through many of hard times, but he also kept us worried many of nights. Zac graduated from high school without any issues and seemed to be living a pretty normal life. He graduated from the local police academy and joined the police force in our hometown, which I think was partly driven by his desire to have the inside scoop, and partly by his desire to genuinely make the world a better place. Regardless, he thrived doing it. He continued in this role for several years, even meeting his fiance-to-be during a routine traffic stop. I recall one evening in particular driving home from work on State Route 4, when I passed a parked police cruiser in a known speed-trap, tucked in the corner of town. *"Shit!,"* I said to myself as the cruiser's lights and sirens promptly switched on. I pull over, rolled down my window, and up walks Officer Zac with that crooked grin from ear to ear.

Zac had always been a partier in high school, but never, to my knowledge, indulged in anything out of the ordinary. After Zac's friends went to college and developed lives of their own, Zac couldn't so easily stop. I think the genetics that he inherited largely played a role in his tendencies, given the substance problems of both his parents, but Zac also went through many hardships in life that I believe played a significant role. The divorce of his mom and dad, the death of his father, and probably the isolation I inadvertently made him feel in the family unit Debbie and I created, all of which set him up for failure.

As Zac went through his early twenties, drinking would periodically intensify and the abuse of pain pills and anxiety meds would wax and wane. Sooner than later, the weekend parties were no longer just on the weekends, but a mainstay in his everyday life. It wasn't long before this lifestyle wasn't conducive to policing the streets, and he was forced to resign from his position as a police officer, thus beginning the arduous process for Zac to get sober. Zac fought like hell for sobriety and was always willing to get help when he needed it. He put in the hard work and leaned on us when he felt weak. He went to multiple rehabs, sober living homes, and worked the programs. He just wanted to be normal, but addiction was too strong a demon to overcome.

On July 30, 2005, Zac lost his battle with the disease. We would come to find out that his overdose was largely a product of the opioid fentanyl, which at the time, not many people had heard of. Now, this seems to be a household name.

One of Zac's favorite people in the world was actually my brother, Ron. They had become very close throughout the years because of their mutual love for sports, keen senses of humor, and magnetic personalities. It brought me great comfort seeing their connection, as it fulfilled something that I didn't seem able to provide for Zac. Looking back on their lives now, it scares me to realize how many similarities and warning signs were present between the two of them.

Beginning in the early 1990's, my brother's life had also began to spiral out of control at the hands of opioid addiction and various other substances. Ron intermittently worked for our family business, but was never committed. He would get frustrated, quit, work elsewhere, and then come back. This process happened a good half-dozen times. Over the years, his substance abuse became so severe that he ended up on the street, and eventually had a lengthy stay in prison for charges secondary to his drug abuse. During this time, he was able to get sober, but upon release was sent straight to a methadone treatment clinic to prevent his relapse and treat his disease.

Ron stayed on this medication for the next twelve years. Although this kept him away from heroin and other street drugs, it required daily drives to downtown Dayton (about 30 minutes from our hometown) at 6:30 AM for his daily dose. Everyday, for twelve years, he did this. He sacrificed his ability to ever leave town for any extended amount of time, including for every family vacation, as this medication slowly took his freedom. Methadone slowly took control over every aspect of his life.

That is how powerful opioid addiction can become. It enslaves those in it's path to the point of total control.

On September 13th, 2018, after years of battling, my brother lost his fight against addiction to an overdose on heroin and fentanyl. I write further on the subject of my brother in Chapter 14.

Even in the midst of Ron's addiction, Debbie's addiction, and Zac's addiction, I still didn't get it. I didn't understand why these people, whom I loved dearly, were doing this to themselves. I couldn't fix them and I was getting ever so frustrated. It wasn't until the greatest loss of my life that I would fully understand the disease which plagued not only my family members, but countless families across the country and around the world.

Chapter 3

My Own Demons

"We all have a Monster within; the difference is in degree, not in kind." -
Douglas Preston

Although I would love to sit back and hide behind the demons of
my family, I know I would be doing a disservice to this book by doing
so. My own personal demons may look a little different than the ones
we've touched on thus far, but they're demons nonetheless and all too
common in this world we live in. We only hurt one another by
sweeping our own dirt under the rug. No one wins by hiding behind a
facade.

The individuals you've been introduced to so far - my brother, father,
stepson, and ex-wife, struggled not only with the disease of addiction,
but also with the stigma attached to such a diagnosis. It's typically not
just the disease that destroys a person, it's often the stigma associated
with it that puts the nail in the coffin. It's the stigma that commonly
leads to the hesitancy to ask for help, and causes, or exacerbates, issues
of depression and anxiety. Put all of those negative consequences
together in the presence of addiction, and you're asking for trouble.

I, too, battled demons caused by the stigma of labels.

I've been told that I'm one of the most introverted people on the planet.
Throughout most of my life I did not understand, nor did I care to
understand, what an introvert was. I had far too many other things on
my plate, and trying to figure this out didn't seem like a priority to me.
To be truthful, I thought being an introvert was more of a personality
disorder than anything. Whatever it was, it had a very negative
connotation in my mind. It wasn't necessarily that I thought being an
introvert was bad, but I knew the antisocial aspects of this trait were
commonly misinterpreted as being rude or haughty, and that obviously
isn't received well by most.

I've also always known that I struggle socially. I avoid social situations
at all cost, but if I'm forced to attend, I usually sit back and do my best
to avoid conversation. I've always hated small talk and probably
always will. I've always tried to keep to myself and interact just enough
to avoid being seen as disinterested. It's not that I don't like engaging
with other people, it's that I struggle to understand other people. In all

honesty, I tend to struggle with following conversations at all, let alone following along well enough to participate in much capacity. I'm usually three or four sentences behind, as it seems to take my brain a little more time to process words than most people. Even in small gatherings or dinner parties, I felt as though my brain was too distracted by the noise and other input it was receiving to have the capacity of comprehending a multi-sided conversation. I frequently found myself completely exhausted after even the slightest social engagement, requiring days of solitude to recharge myself mentally. This deficit in my personality rendered me "dysfunctional" by many. It wasn't until I was much older that I better understood the normal variants in personalities and the ways in which society has labeled these variants abnormal. I was labeled and misunderstood to be a rude and isolating human being, when in reality, I'm just an introvert. I don't find anything wrong with that, but society tells me otherwise. The stigma and accompanying judgement that has been cast on me for not being a happy-go-lucky social butterfly has been hurtful at times. I can handle the criticism, but it certainly hasn't done me any favors, and has cost me numerous relationships.

I still tend to struggle with finding a balance between social engagements and my own mental health and stability. I find each side of the coin necessary and beneficial, but finding that balance is more difficult than it may seem. I enjoy the occasional interaction or get-together, but the exhaustion I feel afterwards often drives me away from them completely. Socializing is so mentally taxing on my brain that my body naturally tries to avoid such scenarios. When I'm alone and have solitude, I feel recharged… energized, even. I strongly believe this is just the way I'm wired. If I don't get enough alone time to rest and recoop, I'm just not happy. It's that simple. I've battled this anomaly about myself for much of my life, but had no clue what to call it. Everyone seemed to have a label for it, except me. Was I antisocial? Was I just a loner? Or was I merely an asshole? I knew how I felt inside, but I didn't know what to make of it. I could sense what worked for me and what didn't, so why did I still feel the need to pretend? I forced myself to attend events that often made my family happy, but made me very uncomfortable, and something just didn't seem right about that.

I was 50 years of age before I started reading and understanding what introversion was. Through the book *Quiet*, by Susan Cain, I discovered that about ⅓ of the world's population is introverted, about ⅓ are extroverted, and the remaining ⅓ are somewhere in the middle. I read that it was normal for an introvert to obtain their energy and happiness in the quiet moments, and lose their energy in social interaction. This new way of looking at myself changed everything. I began to see myself as simply an introvert with a natural tendency away from social interaction. I began to see this as just a trait that I carried, as opposed to a flaw that defined me. Removing a stigmatized label and negative understanding of myself after fifty years was one of the most freeing moments of my life. It wasn't until I underwent the process of exploring the inner workings of what made someone an introvert, did I become able to be more comfortable with, and love, myself. It was only then that I no longer felt hurt by the judgement I sensed for just being my true self.

I'm also a workaholic, or so I've been told, driven by this subconscious pressure to fulfill a purpose and always be busy. I'm not really sure if this was something I was born with or if it developed at a particular moment, but I do recall a very brief conversation I had nearly 40 years ago that I'm sure played a large role. I remember sitting inside a small diner in Springboro, Ohio called Homers, about two years after my mother had passed away. It was the only dinner I can recall after that event where both my brother and my father were present. My father had just converted his 2500 square-foot basement into a huge social hub, complete with a full service bar, a dance floor with mirrors and disco lights, a pool table, and a lounge area with a TV. That might sound like a grand ole time to most, but to me, it sounded like my worst nightmare.

During that dinner, my dad shared with us that he was going to have a Christmas party in his new social headquarters. Then, he used a word that embarrassed every bone in my body. He said, *"I'm just going to invite the elite people in town."* My brother responded, *"...that sounds awesome, Dad! Can I come?"*

I sat in silence. I was mortified.

It's one thing to use the word "elite" when talking about it in third person, but to use it to describe yourself and your own social network was off-putting to me. I had no idea why I felt that way, but I did, and it followed me my entire life. I have never felt that way, but I do know that this conversation brought an awareness to me that I was sensitive about such a label. I hoped that I would never slip into that kind of pompous thinking. How could I ever bring myself to avoid inviting someone to my home because they weren't *elite* enough for me? Who even sets that criteria anyways? This felt like a form of discrimination, and to be honest, I still think that it is discriminatory. Discrimination and stigma very much work hand-in-hand. Those who carry a stigma are very often discriminated against. Whether it be individuals that are poor, addicted to drugs, members of the LGBT community, or single moms - if you have a stigmatized label for whatever reason, you're starting the game down by 15.

I think this encounter with my father helped set a certain tone for my life. Even from my earliest memories I never really desired to be anything more than a regular guy. I was determined to be successful without letting money or status become a priority. When I reached various goals I had set for myself, I simply viewed this as the result of hard work and God's blessings. I saw the negative impact that arrogance played in the role of good men who let it get the best of them, and I vowed to myself that I would never fall victim to my ego. This was in part due to that conversation at the diner, and in part due to another comment I would hear a few months later.

Clear as day, I can still remember one of my buddies saying to me, *"Scott, you were born with a silver spoon in your mouth. You're so lucky."* I was floored. I'm not easily offended, but in that moment, I was just that. How could someone think that about me? I worked my ass off. I baled hay, turned wrenches, operated jack hammers, and put in 12-hour days nearly everyday of the week. I didn't sit inside the air conditioned office all day; I was out there alongside all of the other employees of Weidle Corporation putting in the hours and getting my hands dirty. It would be small comments like this that drove my habitual work ethic to be something that allowed me much success, but also much pain and detriment. I promised myself that as tempting as it may have been, I would never ride the coattails of my father's success. I wanted to be successful for myself, by myself.

Throughout much of my twenties and thirties, I didn't necessarily recognize that my work ethic could be a bad thing. I didn't realize that I wasn't just driven to succeed and become independent, I was *consumed* by my efforts to succeed and become independent. I was a workaholic in every sense of the word. In the midst of it all, I lost sight of the big picture and lost the ability to enjoy the little moments, the things that really mattered to me. At the end of the day, it isn't the money that matters. It isn't the success or the accolades. It's the moments that we spend with the people we love, and I missed out on many of those moments because I was too consumed by my work and the drive to succeed. I placed success in front of being a father and a husband. Yes, I had a mission that I felt my family would benefit from, but that mission caused me to miss some very important moments in life that I can never get back, and the regret I now feel for missing those moments puts it all into perspective.

As my marriage unraveled and my family was torn apart, I began to experience feelings and pain that I had never even come close to feeling before. I had encountered my fair share of pain in the past… this wasn't my first loss or my first tragedy. Marching forward from those losses were very difficult, but nothing could have prepared me for the emotional turmoil that comes with divorce and the breakup of my family. The loss of loved ones that are still within reach was the most heartbreaking experience I had felt to date. I was a bruised and battered soul in the years following my divorce. I did not think that there could be any worse pain than what I had just lived through, but to my dismay, the worst was yet to come.

I remember lying in a field one night staring up at the stars thinking to myself that it would be easier to just give up, to just roll over and throw in the towel. I had given life a valiant effort, but still came up broken hearted and empty handed. Instead, I chose to stand up and fight the pain head-on. If I let my sons see me quit, what would stop them from doing the same? I not only wanted to be an example of resiliency for them, but I wanted to stop this vicious cycle of pain and turmoil which plagued both sides of their family bloodlines.

My own demons may look and present themselves a little bit differently in me than in my relatives, but I still recognize them as demons nonetheless and understand the need to overcome them. Depression,

42

thoughts of suicide, and self-doubt, are all powerful forces that can easily become all-consuming. They are common killers in today's society and they do not discriminate amongst who they choose to prey on. If I have come to understand anything, it is that mental illness is more common and more powerful than most of us realize. We can only make progress if we bring these issues to the surface and into the light.

So how did I survive this tortuous season of life? As a man who internalizes his feelings and prides himself on independence, how was this *not* a recipe for disaster?

My family.

As hard as I tried to be a self-sufficient person that didn't need to rely on anyone for any reason, I came to realize throughout the years that if I wanted to make it out of this thing alive, I would have to submit and lean on my inner circle. Although it seemed my inner circle was getting smaller and smaller by the minute, I thankfully wasn't left alone. There is no way I would have overcome the demons I faced without the support of my family. They have been stabilizing forces in my life and their stability was something that I largely underrated until I needed it the most.

The day that I had made the final attempt at salvaging my marriage with Debbie on Super Bowl Sunday was also the day that I would meet the woman who would go on to capture my heart and soul throughout the worst time in my life, and still has it in her hands today. After walking away from our home following the argument that Debbie and I had that day, I drove aimlessly looking for a way to occupy my mind and numb the pain. Ironically enough, I drove down to the only restaurant in town to have a drink. Yes, this is the same restaurant where Debbie and I met… did I mention that it's the only place in town?! :)

I went in and sat down at the bar. I thought that if I could just distract myself with the football game and have a beer, I may be able to tolerate the remainder of the day, and that was my only goal.

I never expected that the next chapter of my life was already about to unfold, and I never expected that there was a godsend on its way that would help keep my head above water - an angel in disguise.

A lovely young waitress walked over to take my order. *"Hi, Scott...,"* Carrie said, with a smile that felt like summer sunshine, *"...What can I get you?"* She took my order and promptly made sure I was taken care of. Carrie and I had actually met before, about six years prior after one of my company trucks had kicked up a rock and broken her windshield, but that was just a random interaction neither of us remembered much about. We only talked briefly that night at the bar, but it sparked an interest in me to know more about this stunning person. Little did I know at the time, but this was the beginning of something really great.

I began going to that restaurant more regularly and would sit and talk with her for hours after closing. There was a natural flow to our conversations. She said that she found my quiet nature appealing, but I was just being the typical introverted person that I am. It was refreshing to feel comfortable in my own skin for once. I didn't feel the need to act like someone I wasn't. I didn't feel pressure to fill the room with conversation when it wasn't organic. Soon thereafter, we began dating, and with time, I slowly let her into the chaotic life that I hid behind my quiet persona. I hesitated to bring her into a situation that I knew would be difficult for her to navigate. She was only in her mid twenties, I wasn't yet formally divorced from Debbie, I had two young children, and not to mention, I had an entire company that depended on me day-in and day-out. This wasn't the ideal situation I had envisioned, and I knew it wasn't the knight in shining armor scenario she had envisioned, either.

Regardless, it just felt good to have someone hear me out and offer constructive observations regarding the situations I had been dealing with all on my own. Carrie seemed to understand and her companionship was a much welcomed and needed refuge. She was focused on continuing her education in business and had a full-time job, but she would still make an effort for us to spend time together. She seemed to have a good head on her shoulders and had keen insights to offer, which really helped me turn a corner in my life.

Carrie had been born and raised in a neighboring community called Farmersville. She had a stable home life with her mother, father, and brother. Her father owned and operated a local John Deere store and her brother was studying to become a physician assistant. Carrie's home life was stable and quiet, much diffcrent from the home life I had grown up in, and this was a breath of fresh air to me. Our differences in life experiences were probably one of the key ways in which Carrie was able to bring healing and stability into my life, and into our relationship.

Daniel and Wes took to Carrie pretty quickly. They both loved their mother very much, but at the time, Carrie provided a sense of security that they were missing. This could not have been an easy thing for Carrie to remain steadfast through. She had no experience parenting and was now faced with an 8-year-old boy and a teenager who were both still very much struggling with the loss of their family unit. Combine this with a complicated and messy divorce between Debbie and I that would drag on for several years, and looking back on this now, I'm not really sure why Carrie didn't run for the hills.

Slowly, over the next decade, I would rebuild my life with Carrie by my side. About a year after meeting, we built a home together and would eventually marry ten years later, in 2009, in a small backyard ceremony with my two boys at my side.

I'm so very thankful that Carrie has remained with me through thick and thin. I know that I wouldn't have made it through the valleys, or out of the darkness, if she had not been by my side every step of the way. From the day she came into my life, she has been stable, consistent, supportive, and loving. I've longed for that person in my life since I was young, and I consider it a blessing from God to have found her.

Carrie is a wonderful stepmother to my children, a fantastic "Gigi" to our grandchildren, but most of all, she is my best friend and my companion for life. I tend to be a man of few words, so I want to take this opportunity to say just how deeply I love her and appreciate her. Thank you, Carrie. It is because of you that I'm able to fight my own demons, it is because of you that I got through the worst seasons of my life, and it is because of you that I am still alive today. I love you.

Chapter 4

Little Boy Diagnosed

"Some of us were born with different brains, but some of us have different brains because of the trauma and loss we've experienced. That's ok, too. It doesn't mean there is anything wrong with us. It's just a part of who we are now, and that part might just need a little extra love sometimes." - Wes Weidle, PA-C

Ok, enough about me. Let's get to the real reason this book was written: my firstborn son, Daniel. Daniel was my pride and joy. The epitome of what every guy imagines when thinking about bringing a life into this world. The thought of being a father scared me at times, but I always dreamed of raising a son. I looked forward to what it might feel like to have my own little boy on my lap while running a backhoe, and how meaningful it would be to teach him the ways of this world. When Daniel came into my world, he fulfilled every dream I had mustered up in my imagination. There was just something charismatic about the kid. His smile was priceless. His humor lit up the room, and his genuine demeanor was next to none. I know that it's easy for any father to say these things about their child regardless of who it is, but I've had countless people tell me that they, too, saw these qualities in Daniel and confirmed my biases. Daniel was born on April 22nd, 1985 when I was just 25 years young. We brought Daniel home from the hospital to our brand new home that we had just built in the Ohio countryside. It was the perfect place to call home and the perfect setting to raise a family.

Daniel was my little buddy when he was young. He was my shadow, following me around and mimicking my every move. We just had an organic connection that made him very easy to raise. He and I spent many of weekends working in the yard, fishing in the pond behind the house, and hiking to the creek that meandered through the woods near our house. We would eventually build an in-ground pool in the side yard as well, and I recall Daniel watching my every move as we struggled through that project. He rode with me on the backhoe and bulldozer every chance he could get. It was just as I had always dreamed of.

Daniel watched intensely as we dug holes and poured concrete; he was mesmerized by the whole process. Daniel also had a tendency to be a bit of a daredevil, too. I remember him sneaking around the corner when no one was looking to place his foot in the wet cement. I'm not sure if he did this because he wanted to leave his mark, or because he had seen concrete finishers do this to test the solidarity of their work, a common practice. Either way, Daniel came into the house a bit panicked with wet concrete on his feet and we couldn't help but laugh.

Daniel observed a lot of hard labor throughout the process of building our home. He observed me building, constructing, fixing, and creating. He jumped at the chance to help me out with various projects, and so on the weekends, our typical routine was to go to the local home improvement store to pick up our supplies for that weekend's projects. These trips were always just the two of us and we did them quite often. I would spend each weekend teaching him a different skill. Everything from using a screwdriver, all the way up through digging a pond and building a shed. He soaked up every lesson and was always eager for more.

Daniel developed a strong passion for the outdoors as a result of his childhood home, also. He learned how to fish on the pond back behind the house, a short 60-second walk from our back door. When I think back to this fishing pond, one specific memory comes to my mind. I was working in the garage one Saturday morning when I heard Daniel say, *"Dad! Come quick! Hurry!"* He was in the backyard and had went fishing without my knowledge. Up until that day, he had never gone fishing alone as far as I was aware. When I rounded the corner into the backyard, there stood Daniel with a large-mouth bass in hand and a smile so wide I could see his every tooth. I was so proud of him and he couldn't have been more proud of himself. I asked him to hold onto the fish for a few more seconds while I went to grab a camera to capture the moment. I'm really glad I did that.

Daniel was also a natural athlete and enjoyed playing football. We come from a town with a strong football tradition and he looked up to his older cousins, brother, and the older boys at school who played for our hometown team. Daniel dreamed of one day wearing that blue jersey, too. He was naturally competitive and loved challenges, so I knew he would end up on that field sooner or later. We plugged him into little-league ball as soon as he became old enough and I can still sense the excitement he had on his face the moment he got his first helmet. I don't think he took off his pads for a solid week after they were first distributed to him. He was so thrilled to get started and learn something new.

By the time Daniel had gotten a few months of practice under his belt, his coach saw some potential and pushed him towards the quarterback position. I'm not sure where he got his arm from, but he had a good one on him, and I was excited to see him excel and grow as he learned the art of football. I knew Daniel needed confidence and this would potentially be a great avenue for this to come to fruition. His coach was the drill sergeant type, an in-your-face military hardass who demanded perfection. This coach was clearly tough and intense, to say the least.

Typically, Daniel was up for any challenge. He liked to win and didn't shy away from a test, but his reaction to this hardened coach was something I'd never seen in him before. Daniel immediately pulled back and wanted to quit the team. At first, I wasn't sure if something was wrong or if this was simply a new experience that he would soon grow accustomed to. His response was more than to be expected, in my opinion, and it exposed an anxiety issue in him that I was not aware of before that time. Daniel managed to stick it out for the remainder of the season with this coach, but struggled. I could sense that Daniel dreaded practices and games, but it never dawned on me that this was a sign of anxiety. Daniel was clearly too young to adequately understand the emotions he was feeling, and this was supposed to be my job as his parent to recognize. In hindsight, I should have seen it earlier and been more in-tune with his emotional well-being. I should have sensed that my son was hurting, but I failed to do so. I didn't understand mental health and I did not yet understand my son.

People in our hometown are pretty cut and dry when it comes to expectations for young boys. Boys should be tough and strong, they shouldn't back down from threats, and they should certainly play football to express their aggression - *those* are the unsaid standards. If a young boy is scared, this isn't looked at as anxiety, it's looked at as fear and weakness. The proposed answer to the problem is to "just suck it up." I can't begin to count the number of conversations I've heard which can confirm this summary, and this pains me because those expectations are setting up our young people, boys in particular, for years of pain and suffering. We're setting them up for years of repressed emotions that will eventually reveal themselves in one form or another, and more times than not, this outcome isn't pretty.

Regardless, Daniel continued playing football through his freshman year of high school, but this never stopped causing him distress. In fact, I think it ended up making many things worse for his mental health. He felt obligated to play more than anything because the school in which he attended inadvertently labels the football players as the "elite" group of kids. I hated the fact that he felt obligated to participate in something that caused him further turmoil, but I was also trying to give him the freedom to make some of his own decisions as well as teach him the concepts of committing to things that he started. In the back of my mind, I still thought that maybe he could outgrow this with more experience and time. However, his performance anxiety was severe and he began resenting the pressure he felt on the football field. This would often reach a severity that resulted in him being physically ill before games because his anxiety was so crippling. Looking back now, I have no idea why I didn't feel a sense of urgency that this was a significant red flag and a concern which needed to be addressed professionally. I just let him continue on in agony. I had bought into the black and white assumptions that this was simply a fear he would, and could, grow out of. In reality, this wasn't a case for the "suck it up" mentality. In retrospect, I only now understand that fear and anxiety are not synonyms, and Daniel wasn't just scared. I had been raised and taught to believe that we should just "rub some dirt on it and everything will be ok," not knowing that this perspective isn't just ignorant, but actually harmful. The way I handled Daniel's anxiety in football is just one of the first mistakes I made as a parent.

Academically, Daniel did fairly well throughout elementary school. As he got older, though, his performance diminished greatly. I thought maybe this was just because his home life wasn't the greatest, as his mother and I were fighting frequently. We weren't exactly creating a conducive environment for him to come home to after school. We didn't monitor his homework or progress like we should have been, and I thought maybe we were to blame for his academic struggles. Either way, his attention span was minimal at best, and he was very much distractible, both at school and at home. We knew that even considering our home situation, his academic achievements were much lower than to be expected. Debbie, being a teacher, could also tell something was amiss. She had him tested for what was known at the time as Attention Deficit Disorder, or ADD, late in his elementary years, and the testing indicated enough evidence for a diagnosis. She took Daniel to his pediatrician following the test, and Ritalin was prescribed two times a day for treatment of ADD. Back then, I had no idea what that meant or how it could possibly affect Daniel, nor did I understand that Ritalin had a potential for abuse. It is a controlled substance, similar to Adderall. This medication did help Daniel in school for a short period of time, but it was taken with inconsistency given the chaos in our family unit. There was simply too much going on at the time for me to be able to say how much benefit Daniel really got out of this medication overall. What I *do* know, is that Daniel was displaying severe signs of anxiety at the time, and I'm sure that prescribing a stimulant medication in this context wasn't making the issue of anxiety any better. Any stimulating medication, such as Ritalin, has the potential to cause anxiety, and this is much more likely in an individual that already has untreated anxiety, according to numerous sources and medical professionals in the field of psychiatry. I suspect this was the case for Daniel. It is gut wrenching to see in retrospect that even when we were trying to better manage Daniel's mental health, we could have actually been making him worse because we didn't understand mental illness ourselves, and we didn't seek out the appropriate treatment providers.

Through the same testing process, Daniel was also diagnosed with a Learning Disability in reading and was assigned to a special class at school for students who required more specialized and individualized attention in their given subject of need. I knew that Daniel could benefit from this extra attention, but I also hated that he was being given a diagnosis that doubled as a stigmatized label. Being labeled "LD" didn't come with a positive connotation, nor did it do him any favors, in my opinion. However, Debbie was a special education teacher and I trusted her with this process. It was in this time, however, that she began battling her own demons, and I know this impacted the consistency of Daniel's treatment. I was in my own little world at work apparently and missed those crucial details that would go on to derail my family. I felt as though my world revolved around bettering my family, but in all reality, my commitment to work and drive to provide for my family had consumed me to the point that I was blind - a true backfire in every sense of the word. I could have, and should have, toned it down at work to be more present in the lives of my children and wife, but the only thing on my mind was financial security and opportunities for my family. So instead, I put on my blinders and practically lived in my office - a regret that haunts me everyday.

When Daniel was about 15, he began to have some physical health issues. He started to pass blood in his urine after any sort of physically demanding activity. This was greatly concerning to me and led to months of testing. We suspected a possible kidney problem and so his doctor ordered him to cease all physical activity until the source of the bleeding was determined, which never really happened. Daniel stopped all athletics and even most extracurricular activities at school because of this. This was a pivotal period in Daniel's life. *This* is when he stopped being the popular athletic kid and started hanging out with a different group of kids at school - a group of kids that were typically up to no good. Daniel's transformation from football stand-out to a young man battling anxiety, ADD, a learning disability, and now a physical health issue was not how we had envisioned his developmental years to play out. I do not blame this new friend group for the way in which his life turned out, but I'm sure it didn't bring many benefits his way, either. This was a crucial time frame that would greatly change the trajectory of his life and I did not recognize it early enough, nor handle it properly. Hindsight is always 20/20, but how could I have been so clueless in the midst of it all? I've come to learn that a child's developmental years are so incredibly impactful when it comes to the remainder of their life. Once the damage is done, it's done. We can learn to cope with the damage that occurs, but we cannot reverse it.

It was after Daniel made these changes in his school and social life that he also began smoking marijuana and drinking occasionally with his friends. It was easy to obtain and easy to conceal as he could still function pretty normally while under the influence of marijuana, and could restrict drinking to weekend parties. I didn't think much of it, honestly. I simply thought that he was being a typical teenager and it would end there. I've come to develop mixed feelings about marijuana, as I know that Daniel was using this to self-treat his anxiety, a known benefit for some, but I also know the role that it tends to play in the stepwise progression that is typically seen in the substance use of most teens. It's a "safe" go-between after the exhilaration surrounding alcohol quickly fades, but before more illicit drugs have yet to be considered. I think marijuana also provided Daniel with an emotional numbing that allowed him to tune out the tension and turmoil he felt between Debbie and I. It allowed him to just exist without the negative feelings I'm sure he was experiencing and didn't know how to deal with. Alcohol also has a known benefit in the case of social anxiety, as it decreases one's inhibitions and allows for more unfiltered social engagement. Daniel certainly leaned on this crutch, and used it often.

Daniel didn't handle Debbie and I's divorce well. I don't blame him for that, I blame us. We both exposed Daniel and Wes to things they cannot unsee or unhear. We put our own personal lives ahead of them for a period of time and allowed them to go unsupervised and feel unwanted. We put them in the middle and used them as pawns, even when it wasn't intentional. I know that Daniel had pain in his heart seeing his parents fight and his family fall apart. I'm sure he laid awake on more than a few occasions listening to Debbie and I argue through the walls of the home we had built together. Many kids witness the divorce of their parents and go on to lead normal lives, but many others aren't so lucky. Many others are emotionally and psychologically disabled because of the pain this can cause, particularly in messy, complicated separations such as the case between Debbie and I. Daniel wasn't one of the lucky ones. In my heart, I have asked Daniel to forgive me time and again for not understanding how this may have detrimentally affected his life and future when we were in the thick of it. I know now that it did, greatly. The emotional scars that can develop in children when their families fall apart are unseen, but are often more damaging than most physical ones. If I could visibly and physically see the emotional damage that our divorce, and the events witnessed throughout the divorce, caused our boys, they would be unrecognizable.

Although Daniel struggled with his emotions at times, he was still a great young man throughout this rough season in our life. Because he no longer had extracurricular activities at school, Daniel started working early in life, just as I had done. I had just built the car wash and quick-lube facility when Daniel was coming of age to begin working, and so this was a perfect fit for him. He loved cars and jumped at the opportunity to work on them and learn how they operated. He was a natural in his role there, which included changing oil, fixing tires, and other basic car repairs. I think he learned a great deal about work ethic and responsibility as an employee at the car wash, and I was happy to show him the ropes. It gave him structure, a new group of friends, and was conducive to his untreated ADD and anxiety. He could work with his hands and each new car that came in was a short, straight-forward project. He performed excellently in this environment, but now I can see that this allowed us to look past his underlying attention deficit because he could manage it a little better in settings such as this. If he could adapt his environment to his deficits, he could operate fairly well, but this wasn't always reasonable. He also wasn't around unfamiliar people in this role, so his anxiety was easier to conceal. Unfortunately for Daniel, this only delayed the treatment of real and significant problems that weren't just relevant in the workplace, but in his day to day life, too. The way these disorders impact our functioning outside of the work setting can actually be more damaging than inside.

As Daniel reached adulthood, his anxiety was in actuality becoming increasingly more significant and debilitating. Outside of work, it was almost palpable when I was around him, and he confided in me that this was in fact the case. Eventually, he shared with me that he was experiencing panic attacks that would occur at random, and this scared him greatly. He would become short of breath, his heart would race, he would tremble, and feel as though he was losing all sense of control. He also began avoiding any and all social events because of this. He seemed okay in small groups of friends that he was familiar with, but he avoided large gatherings at all costs. He had become quite paranoid that the people around him were judging him for any and every possible reason he could come up with in his mind, and I could tell that he was struggling with this. He didn't feel comfortable in his own skin and he didn't feel confident socially, although not many others could tell this was the case given his composure in most scenarios. He was also continuing to self-medicate with alcohol and marijuana throughout much of this time, which allowed himself to function on a minimal basis, really just enough to get by.

I saw a lot of myself in Daniel at this time, and that scared me. He wasn't merely an introvert like myself, though. In fact, I think I would consider him to be more like his mother in that regard, as they shared more socially extroverted personalities. However, his tendency to isolate as his anxiety increased was very much a product that I felt guilty for passing onto him.

Around the same time that his anxiety was peaking, Daniel began to complain of stomach pain, mostly near his right side. I actually noticed these pains even before he told me about them. He would hold onto his side while talking to me and others, and look as though he was almost holding in a breath as to not aggravate or increase the pain further. The next steps seemed pretty straightforward to me: take him to his primary care doc, get a diagnosis, treat the source, and move on. Physical ailments, as opposed to metal illness, seemed to be much more clear-cut to me, which aligns with how I naturally think about most things. Issues like anxiety seemed to be a different kind of problem. It was more subjective and there was no definitive test that could tell me this was just anxiety, or just a simple muscle cramp. So, we began down a path of trying to rule out every medical anomaly that could be causing these symptoms. It ended up being anything but straightforward as time would tell.

A visit to primary care turned into eventual referrals to a urologist, nephrologist, internist, gastroenterologist, and even a spine specialist. Five years of medical consults for side pain later, and we never got a diagnosis. We did, however, leave with a budding opioid addiction. What a great exchange.

As I would come to discover several years later, there could not have been a worse time in history to have an unexplained pain disorder than in the 1990's. It was in this same period of time that opioid prescribing increased by **_900%_** in the state of Ohio, according to former Ohio Attorney General Mike DeWine. Opioids were being dispensed freely, and Daniel was unfortunately one of the many victims of these dangerous prescription medications. He simply mentioned the word pain to his trusted medical provider, and was automatically given a prescription for Vicodin, a prescription opioid. He was still in his critical developmental years at the time - still a child in my eyes, really. I have strong beliefs that this played an enormous role in the way in which Daniel's brain would go on to develop for the remainder of his life, given the research that has since been performed and analyzed. We will dive deeper into this topic in later chapters.

Ohio's Opiate Epidemic

- In 1997, Ohio's per capita dosage averaged 7 pills. (Ohio State Board of Pharmacy)

- In 2010, Ohio's per capita dosage averaged 67 pills. (Ohio State Board Pharmacy)

- Increase over 900% in less than 15 years.

Daniel's side pain issues never worsened, and eventually went away before they could be properly diagnosed. He did suffer from recurrent kidney stones throughout his life, as have his mother and I, but I have never been told that there is a definitive link between the pain he was experiencing chronically and the kidney stones that were relatively easy to diagnose. I suspect that maybe the side pain he endured as a young adult, the bloody urine he experienced as a teen, and the gradual progression and anxiety and psychological stress throughout this same time frame, could actually all be related, however no medical provider has ever been able to tell me that with certainty. Regardless though, he complained less and less of pain as the years went by, but keep in mind his docs were also feeding him pain pills as a means to "treat" whatever was going on.

When Daniel was still a teen, it was easy for me to regulate his access to the opioid painkillers. He only asked for them when he really needed them, which wasn't daily, but it was still more often that I was comfortable with. I was starting to be concerned that he needed them psychologically more than anything, and as a consequence to that, his physical dependency grew stronger by the year - an unfortunate, yet common occurrence in today's society. Month after month, year after year, his medical providers kept writing him prescriptions for opioids as they couldn't find a specific source or disease to treat. I do not believe that during this time his prescribers were being malicious or neglectful by any means. His providers were simply being told by pharmaceutical companies that opioids were not addicting.

57

Pharmaceutical sales representatives for the medications, whom were motivated and compensated by commissioned-based pay, would come into their assigned doctor's office and explain that these magic pills didn't cause addiction, were safe, and effective for use in the primary care setting. And thus was the birthplace of the opioid crisis.

When Daniel took these medications, he noticed that not only did his pain lessen, but his anxiety also decreased. It was a result he hadn't expected, but one that he gladly welcomed and came to depend on. By his early twenties, Daniel began finding alternative ways to obtain pain medications. It wasn't necessarily that he was finding it harder to get them via prescription, but more so that he needed higher doses in order to produce the same effect that they had first produced in the beginning. Opioids are one of many medications that your body can grow accustomed to, so maintaining on the same dose over time will eventually result in diminished effectiveness. Therefore, if he wanted these little pills to remain effective, to decrease his pain and anxiety, he would need more, and more, and more. And thus the cycle began, long before anyone recognized it. Little did I know, we were well on our way to a problem larger than any of us could have imagined. This wasn't only devastating our family, but was also devastating hundreds of thousands of other normal American families who were also otherwise thriving.

Also during Daniel's early twenties, he worked for me at Weidle Corporation. He was a talented laborer and a very skilled heavy equipment operator, even more so than most of my seasoned vets in the field that I've employed for 20+ years. Daniel worked his tail off and had spent much of his life watching me on the bulldozer, so this all came naturally to him. Being Daniel's boss and father didn't always make for a smooth cocktail, though. Trying to be a caring and nurturing father while also being a neutral and fair boss that didn't let him take advantage of the situation was a very thin line to walk. I'll be the first to admit that I wasn't great at knowing where that boundary even was, let alone knowing how far back I should stay from it. There were times when I was more lenient with Daniel than I was with other employees, but I also knew the alternative - be too stern and risking our entire relationship. It's a position that I hated to be in at times, but in other moments, I loved playing this role. It brought me so much joy to watch Daniel grow and succeed with dreams of one day taking over the family business. I thought that if I could just have a little extra patience with him in the short term, it would pay off in the long run. I knew he was struggling some mentally and was on the verge of developing a pill problem, so I gave him the benefit of the doubt and probably let him get away with too much. If I could go back, I'm still not sure I would have done it any differently. I was emotionally tormented by this dynamic in our relationship. Especially as his addiction later worsened, there was an intense amount of tension and resentment between the two of us in the workplace. This was largely due to my lack of understanding as to why he was behaving the way he was. Again, at this time in our journey with addiction, I was clueless as to the gravity of the problem at hand, clueless as to how far it had progressed in him already, and clueless as to what addiction even was, despite being surrounded by it most of my life. However, I looked at Daniel differently than I looked at most other family members in my life. Maybe that is what they mean when people talk about the bond between a father and a son, or maybe I was just more heavily invested in him than I was with my brother, my ex-wife, and even my own dad. Either way, I was consumed by trying to be the fixer in Daniel's life. I can see now that this was really the way in which I coped with my own anxiety when it came to Daniel's safety and future. I thought that if I could control his situation, he would be in a better place, and therefore I would be more relaxed as well. Although he hated it, that's just how I operated.

I can recall one day in particular that Daniel and I were both in bulldozers on a job site. I had noticed that Daniel was developing a new habit which had become a tension point between the two of us. I hardly ever saw him without earbuds in his ears, and this drove me crazy. He was constantly listening to music, even while operating heavy equipment and even when riding in the car while there was music playing on the radio. I knew this was a safety concern while he was on construction sites at work, but I never won this battle with him. He insisted they stay in his ears. I finally got frank with him one day and told him to take them out. He looked back at me and barked, *"But Dad, it helps slow down my thoughts, I actually think more clearly with them in!"*

That was a lightbulb moment for me. After he made that statement, I knew his reported attention deficit was real and was still very much a perpetual problem. I should have never stopped his ADD treatment when he was younger. How could I have been so stubborn and ignorant? I realized that ADD isn't just an issue people deal with in school. It's a real world problem, too. When an adult has problems with their mind's ability to stay on task and control natural impulses, there are clear ramifications for what that means both professionally and personally. A missed opportunity that could still be addressed at this stage in his life, but one that we couldn't go back and get a second chance with. How would his life have turned out differently had he been appropriately treated for the deficits he dealt with? How much harder had it been for him to simply operate on a normal level without treatment compared to the rest of us? Realizing that Daniel had been struggling with this since he was a child was a hard pill for me to swallow, as I was the responsible party for his well-being at that time. I felt completely defeated as I grew to understand the impact this negligence had on my son for years. I had been distracted and consumed by my own struggles and issues, and in doing so, completely overlooked his. As I pondered deeply on how I had let this happen, I was, and still am, consumed by feelings of guilt and anger towards myself.

In 2005, it was clear to me that Daniel had made a decision and commitment to work at Weidle Corporation long-term and hopefully become the third generation owner to our company. It was then that I decided to help Daniel build a new home in one of the subdivisions I had developed. He was more than excited to have this opportunity and I

was more than happy to help motivate him by doing this project together. It was a great hands-on project that the both of us took on, side by side. We were both able to learn a thing or two and spend quality time together building a house from the ground up. Just the two of us.

By 2007, Daniel was 22 years old and was continuing to work full-time for our company as a commercial site excavating contractor. He was taking the appropriate steps within the company to progress in his role, and his personal life was finally taking shape. He was happy, and as a family, we were getting back on track. We spent holidays together, the boys were getting to know Carrie, and their mother had found sobriety. We would often go to Lake Cumberland in Kentucky for weekend getaways to our houseboat, a memory that I turn to often for happiness. We loved that place. Being a part of the gravel industry, it's only natural to have a love for water as freshwater lakes are commonly the secondary creation of gravel mining. So, it's only reasonable that our family had an innate passion for the lake. We loved water sports, boats, fishing - the whole nine yards. This became our family's way to spend time with one another doing something that we all enjoyed. When I

think back to this season in our life, I can almost audibly hear the laughter and physically feel the happiness that we experienced together on the lake. I don't have many moments in my life which can produce that sort of emotional recollection, but Lake Cumberland is certainly one of them. I yearn for memories when Daniel was his happiest - his most fulfilled - and this nearly always comes to my mind when I venture down memory lane.

Although Daniel's life was taking shape and showed signs of promise, it wasn't without flaw. He had a lot of budding potential both professionally and personally, as he had both a career and a developing family of his own, but he still liked to party on the weekends. To my knowledge, it wasn't out of control during his early twenties. He simply liked to have a good time when he wasn't bogged down by responsibilities and I didn't see much wrong with this, to be frank. He was surrounded by a group of friends that liked to drink and smoke weed, and so he followed suit. He was used to indulging in these substances in high school, and since most of his friends partook also, it was something that just followed him into his early adult life. Nevertheless, he was an adult, working full-time, maintaining a steady relationship, and I didn't feel as though it was my place to criticize his every move.

Daniel's firstborn son, Dylan Zachary, was born in February of 2007, and Daniel seamlessly transitioned into the dad role without hiccups. He loved it. Dylan brought him so much joy, and I really thought that this was going to be Daniel's turning point as far as taking on more responsibilities within the company and at home. This is usually the natural progression for most 20-somethings. Begin your career, meet your significant other, begin having kids, and the recreational partying naturally falls by the wayside. Unfortunately, Daniel didn't fit such a mold. From 2007 to 2008, I feel like Daniel's wheels were just spinning. I could see where he was trying to go, but it seemed as if he wasn't getting much traction. I grew frustrated with him at the time because I didn't understand why he wasn't making progress faster, but in hindsight it makes so much more sense now. An addiction to prescription opioids was beginning to consume his brain and control his decision making to a degree that I never thought possible.

In roughly August of 2008, I received a phone call from Daniel that opened up a new chapter in Daniel's story. Daniel was crying, and through a trembling voice he said, *"Dad, can you come to my house? I need your help."* I could feel the raw emotion in his voice as if he had been crying. I was startled, concerned, and confused. I dropped what I was doing and went directly to his house - a short, two minute drive from my office. He was lying on the couch sobbing. After a few minutes went by he was able to utter the words, *"Dad, I have a problem. A pill problem. I want it to stop... I need this to stop... but I have no idea how."*

I was shocked - speechless, really.

I had been working alongside Daniel on a daily basis. How could I have missed this? He was operating heavy equipment better than most experienced 40-year-old heavy equipment operators within the company. He was clean-cut, polite, had a baby boy, and a steady relationship. He showed up for work, and worked hard. Daniel couldn't have a pill problem, could he? Was *my* son addicted to pills? I didn't even really know what addiction meant at the time, but I had enough secondhand experience with it to know this wasn't good. I was dumbfounded that this had weaseled its way into my son's life, right under my own nose.

The fact of the matter is, yes, my son had a major, life-threatening problem that was beginning to take control of his life. He had a brain that was diseased, literally. We did not understand until many years later how the consumption of certain chemicals can often develop into a medical brain disease that, by definition, is chronic, progressive, and commonly fatal if left untreated. Not many people look at addiction for what it really is, a primary medical disease of the brain, and it had infected my son. But again, at the time, I didn't see it like that. I thought we just needed a 30-day detox, cut off the source, and everything would be ok. I had watched my brother and my ex-wife both go through the inpatient hospital system – neither with much success – but that was the only system I knew about. I prayed that wasn't still the case and hoped for better options. My game plan was to get him into treatment, whatever that looked like, as fast as possible and within 30-90 days, we could be done with this whole thing.

I didn't look at my son as someone with the disease of addiction because I didn't look at addiction as a disease. In my eyes, it was a problem of inner fortitude, and as long as I got him through the physical detox and controlled his environment for the subsequent months, we could get over this hump and this would quickly be a distant memory. This outlook was so incredibly damaging to Daniel. Addiction has since been formally classified as a disease by the

American Medical Association, a topic we will dive into throughout the remainder of the book. This classification is crucial to understand. Addiction being a disease means that it isn't a moral failing at all. It's a pathologic and biological process that changes the functioning of the brain in ways that are progressive and chronic. Through modern advancements in medicine, we have began to understand that addiction isn't merely a choice, it's a disease that no one in their right mind would ever choose to develop.

Daniel certainly did not want to develop the primary medical brain disease of addiction and it certainly wasn't as simple as insufficient willpower. No one had actually even told me that Daniel met criteria for opioid addiction until we were well into Daniel's treatment process. Throughout the early years, I was still very much under the naive perception that this was simply a "pill problem" that could be beat with a simple detox and removal of triggers. The word addiction wasn't even really crossing my mind. Nevertheless, a severe addiction to opioids is exactly what was going on. I have since come to the understanding that this transpired because of the accumulation of several combining factors. Although it would be easier for me to point fingers at this or that, I know a more accurate representation of what happened is very much multifactorial. It was the perfect storm of multiple components that when combined in the right person at the right time, can be catastrophic. I find it best to summarize this by four main variables. We have touched on each of these briefly thus far, but allow me to go into a little more depth as to explain each one so that we all have a better understanding of how this diagnosis can develop in susceptible individuals.

1. **Genetics** – Although no single gene has a causal factor when it comes to the development of addiction, many genes have been identified through genetic testing and research to have associations with, and contributions to, this disease. Some studies have even demonstrated heritability rates of 50% and higher. As if my family wasn't good enough evidence, I think it is more than plausible to say that Daniel had a clear genetic predisposition when it came to his baseline chances of developing addiction, given his family history. Genetics determine each and every bodily function and chemical reaction that occurs. Our genes determine our reactions to

medications and our reactions to stress. They determine our brain physiology and our brain structure. It is easy to see the numerous ways in which genetics can influence the likelihood for the development of addiction, or any disease, when we look at the many roles in which genetics are responsible for. Genes lay the groundwork for our every fiber.

2. **Environmental Stressors** – Stressors can come in many flavors, varieties, and intensities. Anything from the death of a loved one, to emotional abuse, to unexpected job loss can all qualify as stressors. What qualifies as a stressor to you, however, may not qualify as a stressor to me. What our body and mind does in response to a given stressor is largely variable given the individual. Without getting into too much detail, our reactions - both innate and conscious - are largely a result of the coping skills we've learned through life, in combination with our genetically-driven biological reactions. Witnessing a fatal car accident can leave one individual with PTSD, while another individual who witnesses the same crash can walk away emotionally unfazed. According to research, being exposed to stressors or trauma throughout life increases the chances that one develops the disease of addiction, and this is fairly common sense if you think about it. Everyone has to cope with stress in some fashion or another, and unfortunately, it is all too common in our society to reach for the bottle to help numb the emotions associated with stress. The more stress, the more likely you are to search for a coping mechanism that may or may not be in the form of a pill.

3. **Untreated comorbid psychiatric conditions** - Similarly, if someone is anxious, depressed, or has problems with controlling their emotions and impulses, they are naturally more likely to seek out ways to cope with these emotions. Some people are proactive in seeking out healthy treatment options and therapeutic techniques if they have access to care, but millions of other people aren't so lucky. Many other people reach for the downer to calm their anxiety, while others reach for the upper to feel normal or happy. *This* is why it would have been so important for Daniel to have gotten adequate psychiatric treatment that wasn't solely geared towards his addiction issues. It makes much more sense to first address his

underlying anxiety and attention deficit because I believe these were the primary reasons for why he used in the first place. Putting these disorders on the top of the priority list not only helps prevent millions of people from grabbing the bottle or the pill in the first place, but also significantly improves the relapse rates of those already caught in the throes of the disease.

4. **Exposure to opioids during the developmental period** - The human brain is actively growing and developing well into our 3rd decade of life, according to numerous different research studies. The earlier an individual's brain is exposed to an addictive substance, the more likely the brain is to develop abnormally. These negative impacts come in the form of decreased ability to regulate impulses and decreased ability to regulate the reward system within our brain. Whenever the brain in undergoing changes and an outside variable is introduced, such as an opioid, there is a risk of permanent change in the cascade of events that usually results in normal brain development. You don't need a brain scientist to bring that point to light, but I believe this was the case in Daniel's development. Opioids were introduced to his brain as a teen, and from that time on, he was never the same.

In order to better understand the impact of what opioids can do to the brain, we first must understand what opioids truly are. There are many misunderstandings that I feel should be addressed before we dive deeper into Daniel's disease process and treatment history. It's also worth noting, for clarity's sake, that opioids and opiates are not one in the same. An opioid is the general umbrella term used to detail both man-made and synthetically made byproducts of the poppy plant. Poppy plants produce an ingredient called opium, which can be directly extracted from the plant itself. An opiate refers to medications or substances that directly include opium in their ingredient list. This includes things like heroin, but also medications like morphine and codeine. Synthetic versions of opium are referred to as opioids, and include medications like fentanyl, oxycodone (Oxycontin), and hydrocodone (Vicodin). This is a confusing classification system, but you are safe to use the term opioid when referring to both natural and synthetic versions of the drug. Opioids are designated by the Drug Enforcement Agency (DEA) as Schedule II controlled substances, which is the most potentially dangerous substance class to be legally sold via prescription. Schedule I substances are not legally sold, which would include opiates like heroin. The DEA specifically states that schedule II medications are "dangerous" and have a high potential for abuse, with use potentially leading to severe psychological or physical dependence. These drugs act as depressants in our body, both in the brain, heart, and lungs. They diminish our pain response, but also depress other vital bodily functions such as our drive to breathe. They produce feelings of euphoria in our brain by rushing the reward system with a natural brain chemical called dopamine, which is responsible for feelings of happiness and motivation. Understanding these basic mechanisms of the medications helps us understand exactly how opioids have the capability of producing such enticing and controlling effects. We will dive into this in much greater detail in Chapter 9.

Now that we know the ways in which many individuals find themselves with a diagnosis of opioid addiction, or what is medically referred to as Opioid Use Disorder, and we know a little more about the chemical substances that are responsible for this, what can we do with this information? I would first hope this allows everyone to be better educated as to recognizing this behavior in our own lives, but also those around us. I hope this information allows us to see the ways in which many different factors can increase or decrease our chances of developing problems with addiction. And lastly, I would hope this changes our perspective about individuals who do struggle with this disease. No one wants to become addicted to drugs any more than someone would want to develop lung cancer. When a teenager picks up a cigarette for the first time, do they likely know that they could potentially develop cancer from this? Sure. When a teen, or adult, takes their first Vicodin, do they know the possibility of addiction? More than likely. So if both of these instances are initiated by concious choice, why are the outcomes looked at through such vastly different lenses? Lung cancer and addiction are both diseases, and they're both secondary to the exposure of legal substances, yet our societal response is wildly different. I can look back and analyze the parties responsible for Daniel's development of addiction until I'm blue in the face, but that doesn't provide me with much relief. There is no clear-cut answer and there isn't a single factor to blame, so our response to such a disease needs to just as broad. We need to attack it from multiple different angles, both proactive and reactive, which is what I tried to do with Daniel, albeit considerably insufficient as we will uncover throughout the remaining pages.

I have many regrets that you've read about throughout the course of this book so far and will continue to read. Regrets that I will likely never forgive myself for. I live with daily agony and remorse that I didn't see the signs earlier. I could have, and should have, done many things differently, and maybe, just maybe, things would have turned out differently. At the time, I was just doing the best that I knew how. I loved Daniel with all my being. He was the baby boy that I had dreamed of raising since I was young. I worked 24/7 in order to provide for he and our family, but at the end of the day, that just wasn't enough. I wasn't able to keep all of the balls in the air at the same time, and my pride and joy was the one that fell through the cracks. The only way I know how to move forward with this lump in my throat is to find purpose. I've dedicated my life to better understanding the diagnosis and disease of addiction so that other families may be able to recognize the causes and warning signs before it is too late. I'm driven by a desire to help others learn from my mistakes, and my hope is that this chapter has gotten you one step closer to doing that.

Chapter 5

Little Boy Fights

"Fighting for survival in a shattered world... truth is his only hope." -
Veronica Roth

In the fall of 2008 when I received the phone call from Daniel informing me that he had a problem and was in desperate need of lifesaving help, I simply asked him, *"Are you willing to go to a residential rehab for help?"* Without hesitation, he replied, *"I will do anything, Dad, I just need help."*

I spent the next 24 hours on the computer trying to educate myself. I had never looked into anything like this before, not even with my ex-wife, stepson, or my brother. I soon realized that picking a residential rehab felt like playing Russian Roulette with my son's well-being. I felt an extreme amount of pressure and concern that I would make the wrong choice in where to send him. I felt overwhelmed in every sense of the word. Often, I felt as though I had the weight of Daniel's life squarely on my shoulders, and those moments were some of the most excruciating times I can remember. It felt like we were on a race for survival and I was in the driver's seat. If I were to pick the wrong facility, it could cost my son his life. There was no room for error in this.

At the time, I knew of no one to reach out to for advice. Back in the 1990's, when I had last dealt with similar issues in my family, we just used mainstream hospitals that offered 30-day inpatient treatment programs which were usually within, or adjacent to, their psychiatric wards. I had witnessed this type of treatment in the past and so this was my only reference, however, those methods were all but gone or outdated by 2008. In all honesty, I really didn't want my son to be in that kind of setting anyway. It seemed ineffective, stigmatizing, and sterile. I felt that he needed someplace more individualized, warm, welcoming, and well-rounded.

After what seemed like a 1000+ Google searches and over 24 hours of searching, I eventually found a facility that I was reasonably comfortable with in Tennessee. I shared this option with Daniel and he responded, *"How soon can I go?"*

Two days later, Daniel and I were driving to the airport for a direct flight to Nashville, TN. It was 4:30 in the morning and the rain was coming down so hard we could barely see the road. I was a nervous wreck, my hands clenched the steering wheel until my knuckles turned white. I didn't want to let Daniel out of my sight, but I knew I had to follow one of my mottos - to let go, and let God. We were about to embark on a journey that would consume much of the next eight years.

During the 90's, most major hospital systems had a dedicated floor that was used to treat drug and alcohol withdrawal along with some other basic treatment modalities surrounding the issue of addiction. It was a fairly simple and straightforward system. Patients went into the hospital to detox, attend some group therapy sessions within their inpatient unit, and out the door they went. This made our options clear, but didn't always provide for the most nurturing or thorough approach to treatment.

Today, however, many mainstream medical hospitals no longer even address or treat the disease of addiction at all - unbelievable, yet true. Most treatment is now deferred or channeled to pseudo-medical clinics and/or residential rehabs. Generally speaking, this change in methodology is secondary to financial gains and losses, which in my eyes, is medical discrimination. I will reserve my discussion on that topic for a later chapter. The problem with this change is significant because the access to care has been greatly diminished. Available choices now are largely privatized, making them both insanely expensive and relatively unregulated - not a great combo when you would like quality of care to be at the top of the priority list, especially for a disease which carries such a grim prognosis.

Before diving into our journey with Daniel's treatment process, I would like to first share just a brief explanation of the options that exist regarding treatment facilities and medications. I will avoid detail as this may bore you, but please hang with me for a few short minutes so that I can share this basic language with you. You never know when it may come of use to you.

Basic options for the treatment of Opioid Use Disorder:

    1.   Inpatient hospital detox followed by partial hospitalization programs (PHP) and intensive outpatient programs (IOP)

2. Private residential rehabilitation (usually does not include medical detox or medication-assisted treatment, but some do)
3. Outpatient primary care or outpatient psychiatry
4. OBOT (Office-Based Opioid Treatment) Clinics
5. OTP (Opioid Treatment Program) Clinics
6. Outpatient therapy with individual therapists or group settings, such as AA and NA (Alcoholics Anonymous and Narcotics Anonymous, respectively)

Medication options (MAT - medication-assisted treatment) for Opioid Use Disorder

1. **Methadone** - This medication acts as an *opioid agonist*, meaning that it fills and stimulates the natural opioid receptors in our body, which in turn reduces cravings, prevents other opioids from producing euphoria, and reduces/eliminates withdrawal symptoms. It can be used acutely to taper off opioids such as heroin and Vicodin, or for long-term maintenance therapy. When given in controlled and monitored doses, it allows the recipients to function normally without being intoxicated, and also wards off withdrawal symptoms, a common reason many people remain stuck in the cycle of using. It requires daily visits to a designated clinic, referred to as an OTP, which is certified to administer the medication, and can only be prescribed by a limited number of providers who have a specialized certificate to dispense it. It is also a controlled substance because of the potential for abuse and dependence. Approximately 7% of Opioid Use Disorder patients are directed to methadone for their treatment.
2. **Buprenorphine** (when combined with naloxone, this is dispensed under the brand name Suboxone) - This medication acts as a *partial opioid agonist*, meaning that it acts similarly to methadone but does not bind to the receptor as tightly. The goal behind this mechanism is that there are lower risks and fewer side effects, theoretically. Similar to methadone, buprenorphine can only be prescribed by providers who have a specialized certificate, however this *can* be prescribed outside of specialty clinics, making it more accessible. It is also

commonly used for both the withdrawal phase of treatment, and long-term maintenance therapy. It requires daily dosing (however, long-acting formulations have recently been approved), and is also a controlled substance, just like methadone. Approximately **90%** of Opioid Use Disorder patients are directed to this option.

3. <u>**Naltrexone**</u> - This medication acts as an ***opioid <u>antagonist</u>,*** meaning that it <u>blocks</u> the opioid receptors in the brain, preventing the harmful and euphoric effects of prescription and illicit opioids. When taken consistently, it prevents the recipient from feeling the intoxicating effects from opioids, and also prevents overdose. It can be prescribed in the primary care setting without specialty certificates. Any medical provider with a license to prescribe can distribute it. However, it is only indicated for treatment in the maintenance phase, which begins after the individual has finished withdrawal and no longer has any opioid-based medication in their system, which can take up to a week or more of sustained abstinence. Given the fact that naltrexone acts as an antagonist on opioid receptors, it can precipitate withdrawal if given too prematurely. It can be administered in daily oral tablets, or in a once monthly long-acting injection (sold under the brand name Vivitrol), making adherence much more likely. Naltrexone is not addictive, is not a controlled substance, and also has a very low side effect profile. Only 3% of Opioid Use Disorder patients are directed to this option.

Not many people, including medical professionals, know much regarding the key differences between treatment options. As a father who was once desperate for answers when the time came, I feel it's a necessary component of this book to relay the knowledge I gained regarding the options that exist. Please stick with me as I share some highlights that I feel need to be brought to the light, and may help navigate those in need.

First, let's cover OBOT clinics. Generally speaking, OBOT refers to any outpatient opioid addiction treatment using opioid agonist medications outside of, or within, designated offices. In the context of this book, we will be referring to OBOT in terms of the physical clinics specialized for addiction treatment. They are licensed at the state level only, and are very minimally regulated. OBOT clinicians provide access to buprenorphine/Suboxone primarily, but only after first obtaining the specialized certificate which allows them to prescribe it. This is called a DATA 2000 waiver. OBOT offices operate with minimal guidelines, few rules, and typically offer a very limited scope of treatment. Physicians with any background can open an OBOT clinic, assuming they have received this waiver, which is done by simply completing an eight hour online training course, which isn't even pass/fail. The course provides instruction on the record keeping requirements of the DEA and some very basic addiction medicine training. In a quick search of OBOT clinics in my area, the first office that pops up is ran by a Gynecologist - not the ideal background if I'm searching for an addiction specialist, in my opinion.

OBOT providers commonly give patients a 30-day supply of Suboxone, an opioid-based schedule III controlled substance, with instructions on how to daily dose it themselves. This can be a potentially great medication to help avoid/reduce withdrawal symptoms and prevent overdose, but since it is an opioid agonist, it can still easily be abused. As a result, it has subsequently developed a high street value and results in continued dependence on opioids, just in a safer form. Relying on patients who have the brain disease of addiction to self-administer their potentially addictive medication without supervision via the honor code is a real concern in my eyes. The diversion of Suboxone is significant and I've personally witnessed numerous people abuse this medication and become physically dependent on it, as they were given 30+ day supplies at a time. In my unfortunate experience, most OBOT clinics and providers are demonstrating pretty low quality medical care as they are motivated by the large amount of money which can be racked in by prescribing Suboxone and churning out large group counseling sessions. When there are so few mandated requirements which set a standard for quality of care, providers can fill their schedules with as many patients as possible, therefore turning out higher profit. The theory behind OBOT was to increase access to care, but unfortunately, this has significant drawbacks. On top of prescribing Suboxone, they also commonly force patients into group-based intensive outpatient counseling classes. These classes are typically three times a week, three hours per session, for six weeks in a row. These classes are most commonly operated mainly as a profit center for the OBOT facility and rarely have a qualified staff member providing any beneficial education. They cram as many people into a crowded room as possible, and charge each one individually for the same time block. What average Joe can take off work three hours per day, three times a week, and still keep their job? None of them. Many of the Medicaid-dependent young adults in these settings learn how to get their free 30-day supply of bupe from clinics such as this, and then turn around to sell it for $600+ per box on the street. Many of them do this for months on end, all the while still stuck in the downward spiral of addiction. What a whack system.

When you put several individuals into the same room who are all either actively using or are freshly sober, it isn't uncommon for them to have a detrimental influence on each other during their smoke breaks or after meetings, and many of them link up to begin using together. This happened with Daniel several times. Daniel and I discussed this in detail in 2014. He said, *"Dad, I would go back on Suboxone as it does help me, but you know they will force me back into their IOP classes. You know that's where I've met all my connections who trip me up every single time. I can't keep doing that. I just need the medication."* In many cases, the IOP "therapy" classes required by these OBOT clinics actually result in detrimental harm. It all too common for those searching for sobriety to actually find the best dealers in town in these meetings, and it's where Daniel learned how and where to sell his Suboxone if he had wanted to. It's like watching two people with a virus infect the entire group because they haven't yet been treated. It can be a very dangerous and careless environment for someone that is genuinely trying to get help.

I don't think it's real outlandish to believe that the OBOT system needs drastic reform. If you can't tell, I'm not a fan.

In contrast, OTP clinics are licensed federally, are heavily regulated, and are required to offer much more thorough treatment. They require accreditation by the Substance Abuse and Mental Health Services Administration (SAMHSA) before they're allowed to operate, and have stricter standards regarding whom can direct such a facility. OTPs are much more comprehensive, as intensive personalized therapy and medical evaluations are required of every patient. Standards are clear, extensive, and regularly monitored. The result is a quality of care which produces real results, albeit produces less revenue. Consequently, OTP offices are very few and far between, and typically only pop up in the major metropolitan areas, which leaves the majority of the population without access to quality care.

Other outpatient options for treatment include stand-alone therapy and counseling. Two of the most common forms of this would be Alcoholics Anonymous (AA) and Narcotics Anonymous (NA). These are group-based, peer-lead, and free of charge. They are centered around the 12-steps of recovery, a series of principles and guidelines for participants to follow. Making amends with others, forgiving yourself, taking one day at a time, and commitment to change, are all parts of the program. Participants are encouraged to "work the program" by attending meetings daily for 60-90 minutes. One of the most impactful components of the program is the concept of sponsorship, which is the idea of having a mentor who is further along in their recovery, to act as a accountability partner and source of wisdom. This setting is largely effective for many people but can take months, if not years, to work through the material and find the right fit.

If the outpatient options as described above are not ideal options, as is the case when more acute care and monitoring is required, residential rehabilitation facilities could be a potentially good option. These are largely privatized facilities and vary widely as to the services provided. Some provide medical treatment and assessments, including detox, but most, in my experience, do not. Most are either religiously motivated or are proponents of more holistic treatment. They rely on the concepts of removing the patient from their physical settings for 30-, 60-, or 90-day periods in order to remove triggers and reset the brain. No cell phones, no social media, and limited access to family and friends. I believe each of these to be necessary steps in order to break old habits and introduce new lifestyle routines. The longer the patient sticks it out in this setting, the stronger their new coping mechanisms and skills will become. The downside, however, is that many patients don't stay long enough. They cannot be forced to engage, and because their brains are diseased, many will impulsively leave prematurely when the going gets rough. Secondly, private residential rehabs are extremely expensive, and the longer one stays, the higher the cost becomes. Insurance typically doesn't pick up a penny when it comes to residential private rehabs either, so unless someone has a family to fall back on, they aren't realistic. Not many individuals struggling with the disease of addiction have the resources to receive access to this type of care, unfortunately.

There is no "one size fits all" treatment. Just like there are many different treatment options for cancer and for high blood pressure, the chosen route for addiction depends on many factors that one must consider - some out of their control, and some in their control. It's just the reality of the world we live in.

The common goal in every treatment effort is to keep the patient alive and allow them to be a productive member of society. The route taken to achieve this depends on the different variables at play. In some cases, the cold turkey approach may be tolerable and even beneficial, but other times that isn't reasonable. Opioid withdrawal can last for weeks at a time. Not everyone has the time and capability to be laid up in bed writhing in pain from withdrawal for weeks on end. Sometimes it is in the best interest of the patient to remain as functional as possible, which is where methadone and buprenorphine come into play. These offer the patient a controlled, safe dose of opioids everyday so they remain functional, while not being intoxicated. The devil's advocate would say that the individual isn't sober if they are taking these medications, but if it allows them to function normally, I don't personally see anything wrong with this approach. For individuals who have a career, family, and other obligations, and cannot afford to go through withdrawal, it's a decent option. If these meds are taken as prescribed, which is the hard part, their risk of overdose and death are cut down drastically.

The ideal scenario would be that the opioid-based medications are used temporarily, only to transition the patient to an opioid-blocking medication like naltrexone for their maintenance treatment. This would not only protect the patient from overdosing, but would also remove the reliance on opioids. This transition can be a very tricky and meticulous process, though. You cannot go straight from an opioid agonist to an opioid antagonist as this carries a risk of throwing the patient into acute withdrawal, which can be physically debilitating and torturous. This gap between medications could last anywhere from 4 to 10 days, during which time the patient is vulnerable to overdose and death if they chose to go out and use, or relapse. I do acknowledge, however, that there are a few individuals who cannot make it through life without a daily opioid agonist treatment long-term, and sometimes for life. Their Opioid Use Disorder is just *that* overpowering and progressive. Taking either type of opioid agonist medication long-term can often decrease the quality of life, but many times, that's the only thing that can keep the person alive. My brother was one of these cases, and so I do recognize that not everyone fits the ideal protocol. We are complex beings, living in a complicated world, dealing with a disease that is largely unpredictable.

Either way, the end goal with MAT is to eventually get the patient to a place where their brain is able to reset and heal itself biochemically and psychologically. In order for this to happen, complete abstinence needs to be achieved and sustained. The longer sobriety is maintained, the more closely the brain realigns with its pre-addicted form. Clearly, individuals can take many different routes in order to get there - some more successful and more accessible than others – but the common denominator amongst them all is to achieve remission long enough to reclaim the brain.

When Daniel first told me that he wanted help, I was terrified and overwhelmed by the number of options that appeared to be available. My initial search revealed many newer slick for-profit centers. I knew that selecting the wrong residential rehab facility could potentially be a death sentence for my son, but if we didn't seek help, that could also be a death sentence. I can see how it would be easy for anyone to fall for the marketing tricks which many of these places took advantage of. The beach-side mansions looked like the perfect setting to heal and reset, but I tried to keep my blinders on when it came to stuff like that. I trusted my gut and tried to find out as much information about each facility as I could. I initially chose the facility in Tennessee because of how long it had been in operation, which was 20+ years, and because of the fact that it was a non-profit. Additionally, their website published their staff credentials, and more importantly, published the credentials of their facility board members. This place had all the signs of transparency and quality. It was in the boondocks of Tennessee and they cared for about 100 adults at any given time. Dorm style housing for sleeping and a private, isolated campus facility for daily education and recreational activities. The pedigree seemed authentic, which to me, was hard to come by.

As Daniel and I sat in the airport at 5:30 in the morning waiting for him to board his flight to Tennessee, I was sick to my stomach. I didn't know how I would be able to let Daniel out of my sight during this life-threatening crisis. I felt like a basket case and was hardly able to hold a conversation with him. We made our way over to a little coffee shop next to his gate and sat in silence; my eyes blood-red from crying. Daniel, on the other hand, showed no emotion. He was sober, but waited fearfully for withdrawal to hit him. He was anxious and scared for what was ahead of him, but he was ready. He desperately wanted the help and knew it was his only chance to overcome this. Daniel's desire to ask for help and his willingness to follow through was the affirmation that I so desperately needed. He was all in.

When they finally called his boarding group, my stomach was in knots and my heart raced. I was facing the moment I had been dreading for the past 12 hours – letting go. All I could do was hug him, tell him I loved him, and send him on his way. He walked off like a soldier on a mission. I was amazed at his ability to take this step by himself. He had never even been out of the state alone before, yet here he was, about to embark on this journey with so many unknowns, alone.

Daniel wrote home once or twice a week during his time in Tennessee. His letters and words gave us the reassurance and hope we were so desperately craving. He wrote about the facility, the 12-steps, and the future plans that he dreamed about achieving with his new found sobriety. The facility turned out to be top-notch. It was called Cumberland Heights and is still operating today. Daniel actually shared a room with a nationally known music celebrity while getting treatment here, and loved to brag about their friendship. This was commonly the first subject he touched on with each letter he sent home.

During his final week at Cumberland Heights, our family was invited to attend a three day session to partake in some counseling and training. The goal was to gain some insight into how to best support your family member when they come home, and to undergo some family therapy if there were issues that needed to be addressed. I went down alone for this weekend and it was a very good, much needed, step for the both of us. I learned so much during these short few days, but in the grand scheme of things, my understanding of addiction was still far from where it should have been. The stigma of this disease still had me in it's shadow, and a simple lack of willpower still seemed to be the foundation of the illness.

Daniel seemed ready to come home and was excited to get his life back on track. As Daniel and myself drove out of Cumberland Heights to head home, I was taken aback by the words on the arch of the exit driveway to the facility. Let go, and let God.

Once he returned home, he assured me that he felt safe and denied any desire to go back to his old ways. I felt an enormous sense of relief, almost as though I had been holding my breath the entire time he was gone. He went back to work and went back to raising Dylan, and I had hopes that I was getting my son back.

Several good months went by before I started to get worried that he was regressing. Warning signs started to pop up which made me suspicious that he wasn't doing as well as he said he was. Inevitably, he finally broke down and came clean. Relapse #1 was well underway. I was devastated, worried, and confused. How did I let this happen? He was still functioning and working, but nevertheless wasn't free from the power of opioids. Daniel's struggles typically came in cycles of short 2-3 day binges. He would be fine for a few weeks, get triggered by various events or people, and then he would break down and use for a couple of days, always to be followed by the inevitable crash and burn. He would subsequently lock himself in his room for a day or two, beat himself up emotionally, and come out fighting for stability and sobriety all over again.

By this time, we had learned of the more common treatment options, and wanted to avoid another rehab, so we turned to Suboxone. I took him to a local OBOT provider, and within a few minutes, he was given his first dose. Just like that, we were opening up the floodgates to something that scared me greatly, but also sounded promising. It was the quickest fix I could come up with and seemed to be the hot new item at the time.

Daniel was stable on this medication and functioned well. It allowed him to be a provider to his family, to keep working, and kept him away from the prescription opioids that he so desperately craved.

Daniel's second son, Landon Daniel, was born during this time as well, when Daniel was about 24. Daniel's boys were always his motivation to keep fighting. They seemed to fill a part of himself that he was missing, and they gave him a purpose to be alive. The addition of Landon to his family was an incredibly happy time for Daniel, and it thrilled me to see him be a father to two little boys, just like I had been. He was just a normal 24-year-old charismatic guy with a huge heart, and was doing his best to raise his family and stay afloat.

Daniel went through the next several years with consistently controlled sobriety for the most part, but the daily grind of life would eventually catch up with him again and pull him back into the throes of addiction. In reflection, this was aggravated by our lack of understanding about this disease being chronic and progressive, specifically. After what may have felt like remission to him, he stopped the twice per month visits to the OBOT clinic for his refills of Suboxone. Weeks later, he experienced exacerbations of his untreated anxiety, and it was only a matter of time before he was searching for something to calm his nerves. The slope was slippery regarding which issue caused him the most discomfort. The uncontrolled anxiety was easily tempered with just a small little prescription pill that was easy to purchase on the street, and that's exactly what he routinely did when he felt stressed.

In 2010, we decided it was time to reconsider the way in which we were approaching his addiction treatment. His short binge episodes were increasing in frequency and intensity, and it appeared that another rehab visit may be necessary. Yet again, I found myself glued to my computer researching our options, fishing through the marketing scams of every rehab from here to California. I actually reached out to a popular addiction specialist from the A&E show Intervention, and asked for recommendations and referrals. Not expecting a response, I continued to search for options. A few days later, I was contacted and developed a short dialogue with the lady that I had contacted from the show. She told me about a low-key facility that she trusted and suggested I consider it for Daniel. I did my due diligence and followed through with the referral, checking to see if it sounded legit. It was a 90-day program in San Rafael, California - a pretty big commitment. Daniel and I sat down to discuss what this would mean for he and his family, and ultimately decided to make it happen. I was scared shitless, but again, he was all in. Daniel was eager to get back into the fight, like a soldier ready to go back to war. It was this demeanor that Daniel demonstrated to me which not only impressed me back then, but still impresses me to this very day. We were not forcing this, Daniel was wanting it for himself. He was determined. The apple didn't seem to fall too far from the tree.

A few days later, I found myself having deja vu. Daniel and I were on our way to the airport at 4:30 in the morning with the same heartache and fear as before. On top of this, I had just learned of a local young man who had overdosed and lost his battle with addiction the night before. I wondered if Daniel knew him, and wondered if I should bring it up. After a silent 30-minute ride towards the airport, I finally mentioned it with hopes that maybe it would give Daniel a reminder of how serious and life-threatening this problem was. I could immediately tell Daniel knew this guy. It was his friend. The remaining car ride was quiet and somber. Neither of us said another word.

As hard as these situations were for the both of us, each time, I became more and more amazed at Daniel's desire and motivation to face them. He faced this disease head-on and believed wholeheartedly that he would overcome it. He didn't care what it took to do so, even if that meant putting his entire life on pause to try every method possible to reverse the damage that these little legal opioid prescription pills had done to his young life.

The facility in San Rafael was different. It did not operate like Cumberland Heights, or even any other rehab I had ever heard of. It was set up to function as six or so separate sober living homes with a central facility for daily activities. Daniel did well with this setting, calling home frequently to tell us of his progress. He even attended a couple of AA meetings with the late Robin Williams who lived nearby at the time, and roomed with the son of a well-known celebrity. Daniel once again found himself in a similar situation, able to call home to his little brother and brag that he was going to "make it big" because of his new found connections. Daniel felt a sense of affirmation being around these guys because he didn't feel alone or stigmatized. He realized that it wasn't just your stereotypical "junkies" that struggled with addiction. It was also the rich, the famous, and the successful. Addiction didn't discriminate, and this allowed him to lessen the blow of self-hatred that is so common with this disease.

Wes and his mother picked Daniel up from the airport when the 90 days had ended and I remember Wes telling me that he had never seen Daniel look so healthy, or smile so brightly. He had a glow and brightness to him that we hadn't seen in years. He was happy, hopeful, and determined to maintain his sobriety, and this made me beam with joy. I could breathe again.

I received a little coaching from Daniel's counselor in California over the phone that really hit home. He said, *"Scott, if when you leave for work in the morning and Daniel is lying on the couch, and he is still on the couch when you return home after a long day, be thankful. Don't become upset, as most parents would do."*

I replied, *"What!? Are you serious, man?!"*

He continued, *"...Just be happy he is there, alive and safe. He is fighting his battle the only way he knows how. When Daniel is ready to face the world, he will get up off the couch and go do so. Give him that space."*

Those words changed me. It gave me a perspective that I had lacked and was one that I would go on to reference time and time again. I'm not going to lie, it was really easy to get frustrated with Daniel and this disease. The disease didn't make sense to me and it was causing me so much pain and inner turmoil. So when things got ugly, I thought back to myself, *Stop. Be thankful Daniel is here, is alive, and is safe.*

Daniel continued to struggle after California. We were now two residential rehab stays into this thing, he had attended hundreds of hours worth of AA meetings, he even gave medication-assisted treatment a shot, and Daniel still found himself going back to the pills time and time again. I could tell he was battling these demons on a daily basis. It took every ounce of strength he had each day just to survive the daylight. But again, Daniel was a functioning young adult working and parenting on a daily basis. Very few people were aware that Daniel was battling this disease, but in reality, it controlled his every move.

Daniel and I frequently discussed all of the intensive outpatient training and counseling he had received, and jokingly said that he was now better trained than most of the people who lectured at his group meetings. We had come to realize that behavioral and environmental changes were simply not enough. We were both struggling to find a permanent "fix." I knew that he was dealing with depression, anxiety, and attention deficit issues, but was there more to this? Could he be bipolar? Could he have a personality disorder? As his father, I felt like it was my responsibility to save him and fix whatever was going rogue in his brain. Nearly every evening for five years I searched for answers. It didn't make any sense to me. For the life of me, I could not figure out why this kept happening. I was a problem solver, but this issue baffled me. Through this process, I became codependent. I couldn't be happy if Daniel wasn't stable, and I couldn't focus on anything else in my life unless Daniel was stable. I now recognize that this wasn't healthy for either of us, but in the moment, I was frantic to protect my son from a monster that neither of us could predict.

I remember early one evening when Daniel and I ventured out into the woods hunting for deer. It was early fall of 2013 and Daniel was in a pretty good place at the time. He was determined that this would be the evening he got his first buck of the season. I was just determined to drink coffee, relax, and enjoy the sounds of the woods. In the quiet, I sat silently and thought about all of the things I had done over the past couple of years trying to help Daniel in his fight against addiction. The sleepless nights scanning the Internet for answers. The countless phone calls to every treatment facility I could find a phone number for. The times where I felt like a deer hunter trying to figure out where Daniel was getting these little pills from. I had done a lot of crazy and dangerous things to keep Daniel safe, and very few people knew about this.

83

One night just a year previous, I sat quietly in my car on a run-down street in the neighboring town of Franklin. I was two hours in to what seemed like an entire night of waiting and watching. This had to be one of the worst areas of town I had ever been in. Trash littered the curbs and rusted out cars were parked on both sides of the narrow street. It was dark, damp, and cold. The clock on my truck's dashboard gave off the only light in my vehicle. It read 8:00 PM. A heavy fall wind would occasionally whip down the deserted street and shake a defaced stop sign just a few feet behind me, each time rattling my frayed nerves.

I had told Carrie I was working late at the office that night because I didn't want to worry her. If she knew what I was doing, she would have been out of her mind with fear.

Daniel wasn't your stereotypical drug user depicted in Hollywood films, yet his disease had led him to make some pretty unwise choices and associations. This night in Franklin confirmed that for me. I couldn't believe we had come to this.

I could see Daniel's truck parked about 200 feet from where I sat, the only truck on the street that looked drive-able. It was just getting dark as a set of dim headlights rounded the corner and slowly pulled in behind Daniel's truck. Daniel was sitting in the passenger seat and a tall, middle-aged man was behind the wheel.

Both got out of what looked like an old beat-up work van, and the two of them started walking towards one of the small wood-framed houses that lined the street. I jumped out of my truck and headed toward them. I called out to Daniel and he stopped dead in his tracks, clearly shocked to see me. No doubt was he embarrassed that I was there. He didn't say a word, just got into his truck and pulled off, driving right past me with no eye-contact.

As Daniel drove away, the middle-aged man he had been with continued on into his house and slammed the door behind him.

I wasn't going to just walk away. I had to do something, no matter how crazy and dangerous it might have seemed. Frankly, at the time, I wasn't even thinking about the risks. I was seeing red. I had to confront this man and let him know that his days of contact with my son were over. I walked up onto the porch, approached the door, and began pounding on it with my fist. I must have pounded for a good 2-3 minutes non-stop. Finally, a scruffy face peered through the window beside the door.

"Get the f**k away from my door!," he yelled through the glass.

"Not until you hear me out," I replied without backing down. *"I'm Daniel's dad!"*

I began pounding again and attempted to kick the door down. Finally, the man slung open the door and stepped out onto the porch.

"What the hell do you want, man?," he said.

I stared him down and replied, *"I know you've sold pills to my son, and it stops now!"*

He looked me square in the face and said, *"Man, you're crazy, I don't have no pills."*

I took one step closer and put my finger right in his face. I was operating on full adrenaline.

"You listen to me, you son of a bitch. I know who you are and where you live, and if I ever find out that you have any more contact with my son, I won't stop until I see you in jail," I said in a fit of rage.

"Whatever man, I don't want nothing to do with any of this shit," he snarled. And with that, he turned, walked into his house, and slammed the door.

It wasn't until after I was back in my truck that it really hit me. The danger of what I had just done soared past anything I had gotten myself into before, but I really didn't care. I would do anything to save Daniel, and I certainly wasn't going to let this pill peddler take down my son.

I started driving back home that night after the confrontation in Franklin. I knew where Daniel would be heading. Every time he got upset or flustered, he went to the woods. This is where he found solace. I drove to his usual spot and sure enough, there was his truck. I parked and sat for a couple minutes debating with myself. *Do I go and find him, or do I just go home and give him space?* Daniel was a master at navigating these woods, especially at night, and I doubted that I'd even be able to find him out there. I felt it might be best to let him think this one out for himself, so I decided to head home. The next morning when I got to my office, there was a note on my desk.

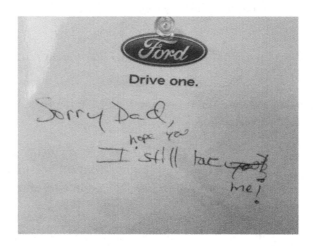

Daniel and I never mentioned this again.

When Daniel went through lapses in his sobriety, I would covertly start watching his every move. I didn't like doing this, but I would do anything to protect him. If that meant that I had to track him to see where he was getting his pills from, that's exactly what I was going to do. I knew Daniel was probably getting these killer pills from multiple people, and it wouldn't be hard to put an end to it if I knew where they were coming from. Daniel liked to tell others, *"I swear, my dad must have a GPS implanted in my ass because he knows my every move. I can work my ass off for nine hours, but as soon as I take a much needed break to sit down, guess what? My dad shows up! Every single time!"* He told this story often because it made everyone laugh, and it still makes me chuckle to this day.

I had discovered the identity of someone else who was one of my local hometown suspects by doing a reverse phone number search on Daniel's company phone. A number and name had popped up a few times, but Daniel had never mentioned this person to me before. I recognized the name though, and knew exactly why he was talking to my son. This guy had been an old buddy of my brothers, and Ron had told me in the past that this guy routinely sold his prescription morphine pills on the street as a side hustle because his preferred substance was heroin. This dude simply took the med supply that he got from his primary care doc, and sold it for profit, infecting the very neighborhood I had grown up in. Once I put this together, I went directly to the guys house and began knocking on the front door. This time, the house was on a suburban street in Germantown, an area with very little crime and white picket fences. The yards were well kept and the houses manicured.

As I stood there on the porch knocking, I got no response. A dog was barking from inside the window, staring at me through the screen as if he could sense my aggression. Faintly, I could hear someone inside the house trying to quiet the dog, and I felt in my mind these actions already made him guilty. So I beat harder, and harder, and harder. After some time, I went back to my vehicle to calm myself down, but it didn't work. I only got angrier, so I went back to the door and pounded some more. I pounded as hard as my heart was beating.

He finally came to the door and I said a few choice words, similar to the scenario in Franklin.

"You have any future contact with Daniel again, and I will do everything in my power to put you in prison," I said.

I later found out that this guy was an active supplier of all types of opioids to several people in our hometown, likely feeding his own Substance Use Disorder, of which I had no compassion for. I turned him in to the local police, but shockingly, nothing was done about it.

My hope in sharing our experiences with the supply chain for prescription opioids is that people would come to realize that the disease of addiction is eveywhere. It's in white-collar towns, in blue-collar towns, and everywhere in between. It strikes poor people, rich people, stupid people, and smart people. We all buy into stereotypes to some degree, but in our experience, we didn't fit that prototype. Daniel's addiction didn't begin with street drugs or back alleys, although sometimes it ended up there. It began with the overprescribing of prescription opioids, which wormed their way into our family and left a path of destruction in their wake.

Daniel was fighting a battle for his life and it was almost as if he had these little gnats surrounding him everywhere he went, reinfecting him every time he seemed to make progress. It took everything I had in me not to hunt down every last person whom I knew had been involved in contributing to my son's addiction. I'm not a vigilante type, but when your child is in harm's way, you will go to the depths of the earth to save them, and I was willing to do just that.

Around the end of 2013, I was beginning to feel desperate and started seeking alternative options for Daniel to try. It didn't seem like the mainstream options were giving us much success, but I knew this couldn't be the only choice we had. I discovered an article on the Internet regarding the use of a medication called Baclofen for the treatment of Opioid Use Disorder. It's actually a muscle relaxer that had already been found to have some success in the treatment of Alcohol Use Disorder, off-label. I read all I could find about it and it seemed to be pretty promising. There were many stories that I could relate to regarding failed attempts at rehab and therapy, only to find success with off-label options, like this. The problem with any off-label (meaning not approved by the FDA for this indication) or unconventional treatment was finding a doctor who was willing to risk their license to give it a chance. Most medical practitioners will not offer medical care for addiction at all, let alone use medications that aren't FDA approved for it, so I knew it was going to be a long shot to find such a provider. Nevertheless, I was grasping at straws and knew that we had nothing to lose and everything to gain.

I was concerned that I had progressed to this level, but I also didn't know if I really had a choice. I found a provider in Chicago who had began utilizing Baclofen for Opioid Use Disorder, but I suspected traveling two states away for a controlled medication was an incredibly risky move. Baclofen is a controlled substance, as it has a potential for abuse and dependence, but to a much lesser degree than opioids, according to the scheduling class established by the DEA. Regardless, the risk didn't matter to me. I had to do something. If it meant that I had to cross the ocean to get it, then that's what I'd do. Daniel was a human being and deserved to have access to quality health care, just like everyone else. He proved to me that he wanted the help and he was willing to work hard for it, so I continued to put in the effort on my part.

After much consideration, we decided to pull the trigger. Daniel, Carrie, and I made the trip to downtown Chicago to meet with this physician and begin treatment with Baclofen. Sadly, after a few months, there was no positive result for Daniel; another disappointment in our search for a permanent solution.

Daniel's third residential rehab admission was clearly on the horizon. Again, it was different from the ones we had already tried. We didn't want to keep trying the exact same approach if it had proven unsuccessful in the past, so we always sought out something different, even if it was another residential rehab.

This time it was in a large mansion-style home in Cincinnati, called The Ridge. It only housed 15 men at a time, so it was much smaller than the facility in Tennessee. His roommates this time included a medical doctor, a college professor, a school teacher, and some blue-collar folks like Daniel, all suffering from the same disease of addiction.

They invited the family down every Wednesday evening to attend their counseling and educational classes right alongside the patient. They believed that in order for the patient to have a chance in the real world, the entire family unit needed to be on the same page regarding the problem at hand and how it exactly worked. Carrie and I went to every class, a 70-minute drive each way, and Wes drove down from college to attend most of the sessions with us as well.

The lectures that were given at these Wednesday night meetings changed the course of my life. They were intensely powerful and strongly grounded in science and research. I would be a lost soul today if we hadn't been a part of this group.

This is when the switch flipped in my brain. This is when I began to realize that addiction was an actual brain disease. Until this happened, I was still unknowingly passing judgement upon Daniel. Judgement that

I didn't see or realize, but that was obviously felt in his heart. I was guilty of judging my own child and was likely perpetuating his problem because of it.

During our first class at The Ridge, a physician appeared at the front of the room. He had developed a six-class curriculum titled The Primary Medical Brain Disease of Addiction, which was written in dry-erase marker on the board behind him.

I had never heard this terminology before. Previously, when I had heard people allude to addiction as a disease, I thought it was a cop-out. I thought it was just their way of removing responsibility from the person struggling with substance abuse as to place blame on anything but the person. I thought I could see through this philosophy because logically, it didn't make sense to me.

I have been surrounded by addiction my entire life - my son, my father, my brother, my ex-wife, my stepson, nephews, employees - and up until this point, I had resisted thinking addiction was anything other than a lack of willpower to change behavior. Again, I'm a black and white thinker.

This doctor gave me the information I needed. In sixty minutes, he had convinced me that I was dead wrong in my understanding of the issue. An understanding that dated back three decades. An understanding that hurt countless people along the way, all because I just didn't get it. I was grossly uninformed, and I admit that.

Daniel completed his third attempt at rehab and returned home. Once again, he claimed to be a "new man" and felt confident that this was it. I remember him telling me, *"Dad, I feel great. I got this, don't worry."*

Daniel remained stable for a few months following the completion of The Ridge program, at which time he was blessed with his 3rd and final baby boy. Gavin Cruz was born on May 31st, 2014. Daniel had yet another jolt of motivation, happiness, and pride, that I knew he could only get from his three boys. With each addition, his children encouraged him to remain stable and sober, as he so desperately wanted to be involved in their life and upbringing. Although I knew he was struggling to provide for them financially, I honestly didn't even discourage him from continuing to have kids because I knew there was no stronger driving force for sobriety than to live for his kids. I was feeling that for myself. Daniel was maturing and he felt a strong motivation to continue his fight against this disease because of his three boys. He wanted desperately to be a provider and father to them. This motivated Daniel in a significant way that nothing else could have done.

After several months of stability, inevitably, another rough patch was brewing. Daniel was already looking for his next pathway to recovery when he found the medication naltrexone (Vivitrol). Vivitrol is a once monthly injection which lasts for 30 days and blocks the effects of opioids, as mentioned previously. He wanted to give this a try and affirmed that he had been sober from all opioids for a period of about 10 days, so he would be eligible to start right away.

After a few days of searching, Daniel found a Vivitrol provider about 45 minutes from home and within a week, he received his first injection. Around this same time, we also decided to begin treating his anxiety and attention deficit problems, as to be more well-rounded with our approach on this go-around. We saw his primary care doc who prescribed Daniel Adderall XR for ADHD and Ativan for anxiety. I was skeptic about this medication combination because I knew these medications could also be addictive, but I also knew the potential pay-off. If he was less anxious and less impulsive, he would be significantly less likely to return to opioids. Combine this with an opioid blocker that prevents him from overdosing all-together, and I thought we may have finally found the perfect combo.

Two weeks after his first injection of Vivitrol, Daniel said to me, *"Dad, for the first time in a long time, I don't have cravings to use."* I was so happy because I knew Vivitrol was giving us hope. It was working. It wasn't just keeping him safe, but was also beginning to heal his brain as there were no longer opioid-based medications in his system. I could finally sleep at night knowing that I wasn't going to wake up to the dreaded phone call, and Daniel could actually start looking into the future because he knew he was safeguarded from relapse for at least 30 more days. That played a major role in his stability. All his previous rehab training was the "one day at a time" mentality, but not this one.

Finally, I thought. We had found a medication that worked and Daniel was sober and happy. The following eight months were the most stable and consistent Daniel had been dating back over eight years. I had almost forgot what hope felt like, but during those initial few months on Vivitrol, it started to come back to me.

The physician who was providing Daniel with Vivitrol operated out of an OBOT clinic. I went with him to this facility towards the beginning of his treatment, and immediately saw some red flags. The first order of business from their standpoint was money. They required $250 cash or check for the office visit up front, even though Daniel was on Medicaid. No further discussion was to be had until they had this in their hand. When I accompanied Daniel to the first appointment and sat in the room with he and the doc, the conversation was random and nonspecific. At one point, the doctor began talking about a fee increase if Daniel was really set on Vivitrol as opposed to Suboxone. Once I heard this, I suspect he observed that I was about to commit a felony, and he reversed course. The reason I was with my adult son for a private medical consultation in the first place was for this exact reason - to protect him from quacks like this! My hunch on this so called "clinician" proved to be correct. This provider was eventually arrested and the state medical board pulled his license - all public knowledge I easily found on the Internet.

Even though my gut told me something was off with this clinic, all I really desired was for Daniel to have access to this simple and non-scheduled, non-controlled medication that any provider had the ability to prescribe. To say we were desperate is an understatement. There were very few, if any, other options.

Throughout the spring, summer, and fall of 2015, Daniel did great and that was my number one priority. He was routinely getting injections of Vivitrol from this clinic, and was addressing some of the underlying problem areas such as his anxiety and ADHD with his primary care doc. I began to witness a stability in Daniel's life and behavior over the course of 2015 that I had prayed many sleepless nights for him to find.

One week before Daniel was scheduled to have his ninth Vivitrol injection, the clinic called and said that the doctor was going to be out of the office for a few days and instructed us to call back to reschedule. Daniel did that twice, and was not able to get a new appointment. We were given numerous run-arounds, but ultimately, no solutions.

"We don't know when the doctor will return to work," the office manager informed Daniel. The clinic never followed through after they cancelled his appointment and absolutely no hand-off was made to assure that Daniel's treatment was accounted for. After numerous attempts to contact this clinic for his 9th Vivitrol injection, and endless searches for another medical practitioner to take over Daniel's treatment, we appeared to be at a dead end.

How could an OBOT clinic just all of a sudden stop functioning with no follow through? Was that even legal? I was beginning to panic. We had fought so hard and had finally found a promising safety net. It took so much work to find the only medication that worked for Daniel, and I feared that the world was about to crumble around us, yet again.

As the medication passed it's 30-day limit, I grew increasingly scared that we were at risk.

Vulnerable and susceptible to a relapse, or even worse, death.

Chapter 6

Little Boy Lost

"Blackbird singing in the dead of night, take these broken wings and learn to fly" - Paul McCartney

Throughout this book I have made mention of my desire to teach my sons how to be best prepared for life. The fact is, both my sons have taught me much more than I have taught them. Looking back throughout Daniel's struggles with addiction, I'm astounded by the ways in which he remained steadfast and sought out ways to channel his inner struggles. It feels as though with each day that passes by, I am taught yet another lesson in which Daniel is responsible for. Each day that goes by, I also gain strength and wisdom from Wes. It's a humbling experience, yet without a doubt, is the most incredibly rewarding aspect of being a parent. It's mind boggling to me at times that these two beautiful souls came from my DNA.

About four years ago, Daniel began teaching me the process of finding inner peace. He had come to embrace the quiet solitude of nature in order to quiet his own mind, and so I, too, have gradually come to appreciate this. Daniel discovered this sanctuary for himself as he learned the art of hunting small game and fish, his number one hobby. I believe it to be true that this passion was accelerated not only because of the land Daniel grew up on, but also because our family business has always maintained large parcels of land, some heavily wooded, some with open pasture, and some with lakes.

In 2000, I purchased a 200-acre parcel of undeveloped land, which adjoined a 7000-acre local metro park. This parcel also hosted a lovely old home that is registered on the state of Ohio's historical places of significance list. The majority of it's restoration work had already been completed, but there was also an adjacent wooden bank barn, which was constructed in 1853, and needed extensive repairs.

I purchased this land and property thinking about the potential it had for residential development. However, Daniel quickly was able to see the value in the land and property untouched. He had a knack for seeing things like this, which I commonly missed. It was exciting for me to see Daniel enthusiastic about things such as this, as the land was like a playground for him. I had no timetable in mind for developing the property, I just knew it would be there when I got around to it. In the meantime, a friend of mine by the name of Dave was an experienced hunter, and he took Daniel under his wing to teach him how to hunt deer in the woods that filled this parcel of land.

For those of you who aren't so savvy when it comes to deer hunting, it's a late-fall, early-winter sport. Deer are more active at sunrise and at sunset, so hunters will go out early in the morning while it's still dark and cold. Often, hunters are situated up high in their deer stands before the sun even rises, or well into the dusk of the evening. You must get yourself embedded into the deer's environment, then sit and wait quietly for the deer to happen upon you. It takes patience, a lot of patience. Daniel spent many mornings and evenings, over and over,

Daniel Weidle

October 31 · 🌐

Beautiful morning for some hunting!

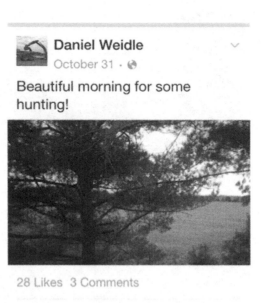

28 Likes 3 Comments

👍 Like   💬 Comment   ↗ Share

hoping that a deer would walk past his stand. I mention this because Daniel did not usually have much patience. In fact, he practically had none when it came to most other areas of his life. Take him to the woods, however, and he was a different person. He found peace, he found stillness, and he felt his mind become calm. He could remain there for hours at a time and it was quite miraculous to watch having known how he operated at home and at work. I can't think of any other place or activity that gave Daniel this sort of solitude.

Daniel and Dave soon setup several deer stands on this land, and it became a bit of a playful turf war over the years to come. Daniel would often invite me to join him, but the workaholic demon in me declined more often than not. This is yet another one of my many regrets that I still hold onto.

I did join him on several occasions, though. Early in the darkness of morning, 25 degrees outside, we would venture out into the woods. Daniel was in his element and always guided me along. He would help get me all set up, soaking in every second of this role reversal so that he could be the boss and tell me what to do. He would get me situated on the ground with my back up against a tree, while the professionals were staked out in their favorite deer stand up in the best tree. Once setup, I was able to experience an environment that most never get to encounter. The stillness of the world seemed so surreal. No human raucous, just the rustling of the leaves and the sounds of the wildlife. You could almost feel a rhythm as the various species of animals communicated amongst themselves. Your own senses become heightened to the very subtle noises of a branch being stepped on, or leaves rustling - by what, you didn't know. It was then that I realized why Daniel spent so much of his free time out there. It was a feeling I had also longed for.

Thanksgiving weekend of 2015, Daniel came to my house dressed in full hunting gear. He walked in with his typical "the one that got away" hunting story. He said that he had just shot a huge buck and had tracked it for two hours, only to come up empty handed. He said he wasn't done searching, just taking a break for some water and food. That was my cue. I put on my gear, and out the door we went. I had never tracked anything in my life, but I knew Daniel would appreciate the company and support.

We arrived at the spot where Daniel believed the deer would bleed out and met up with another of his regular hunting friends, Nathan. I became the 3rd wheel, watching them follow a blood trail for miles. They showed me signs that I would have never otherwise noticed, and I was thoroughly impressed with their skill and determination to find this deer.

We never found that particular buck, but I enjoyed that day, even more than Daniel did I'm sure. I reflect on it often, reliving it over and over. I would go to the ends of the earth to have moments like this back again.

During the off-season for deer and turkey hunting, Daniel was still the most frequent visitor to these woods. He would frequently spend his time fishing and hiking through the grounds, and often came back to tell me about his discoveries. He could always find something to get himself into up there. It was his way of keeping his mind, body, and soul occupied and in-check.

Daniel and I discussed the idea of turning this uninhabited property and land into a sort of addiction treatment center. Daniel knew that he needed to fill his time with constructive work, something that would give him purpose. So he proposed that we try to develop this area into a sober living type of facility, even maybe with a working-recovery farm. We both felt the land had the potential to provide this type of environment for residential treatment to those going through similar issues as Daniel. Daniel often told me that although he was still struggling with addiction, he was being given the knowledge and tools through treatment to be a substantial peer-support counselor. Daniel felt this calling even through his own relapses. He always had a heart for helping others and knew it would also help his own sobriety to be given a calling - to have a reason to keep fighting. He was at the height of awareness regarding his disease, and by 2015, had over 1,000 hours of addiction education under his belt. We both began to learn from each other and I knew he had the capability in him to help others who were in his shoes. He was pleased that I was understanding his disease, finally, and I was pleased to see him fight the hard fight. He knew it was going to take a lot of proactive steps to stay sober, but he was willing to go the extra mile.

Daniel was naturally drawn towards the outcast and towards the less fortunate. He was filled with compassion, more than anyone else I know, really. He had no boundaries or preconceived notions regarding the folks he wanted to surround himself with, and I really think this was secondary to the fact that he knew what it was like to be stigmatized and marginalized himself. I think it speaks volumes that he wanted to consume his spare time helping those whom were struggling. He didn't just want this because he knew it would help his own sobriety, but more so because he knew someone else would be in a better place because of his experiences and past tribulations.

Daniel's other preferred method of finding purpose was to volunteer for different local ministries. He spent many Sunday mornings at Southbrook Christian Church as a greeter because it allowed him to put a smile on the face of a stranger and utilize that great, big, loving personality of his. He also volunteered on a food truck for several months, whose mission was to feed the homeless. It combined two of his greatest hobbies: helping others and eating! He loved this organization and their mission so much that he even washed dishes in the back room of their storefront eatery for months on end. He had a heart that was just bursting to give, to love, and to be sober. As strong and powerful as these desires were, they were equally matched by the intense cravings to use.

Daniel had shown me many times just how strong he was, both by how he fought to find hobbies that were conducive to his recovery, and by his ability to ask for help if he needed it. When he would realize the need to go into rehab, he would simply tell me. He craved sobriety as much as his mind craved the drugs. He desperately wanted to break the chains - to break the cycle. I'll admit though, it wasn't always easy to maintain a level head as I tried to help him along this journey. It wasn't always easy to look at Daniel as this perfect person with a heart of gold because his addiction made him do some crazy things at times. When it got bad, this disease turned him into someone that I didn't even recognize, and I hated that for than anything. To watch someone that you love and care for with every fiber of your being morph into a person that you don't recognize is painful beyond belief. There is no possible way for me to compare this to anything else I've ever come across.

When an individual with the disease of addiction gets sober, but then returns to drug use, they usually feel terrible, remorseful, and even depressed. The typical family reaction is usually to shun the person as a means to motivate them back into sobriety. Many people think that hitting "rock bottom" will teach the person a lesson, as if the individual with addiction isn't able to understand the consequences of their drug use until they experience them firsthand. I don't know about you, but I think that logic is horseshit. You're meaning to tell me that you're just going to just let your loved one destroy their life because their brain is diseased, and hope they just learn their lesson? If you're someone that tends to gravitate towards this type of thinking, do me a favor and ask some people who have personally tried out this philosophy, and see how it worked out for them. I can guarantee you it doesn't end well, it isn't effective, and it actually causes more damage. I have heard thousands of stories over the past several years, from countless families just like mine, all of which have allowed me to better understand the consequences of this mindset. Please, learn from my mistakes, I'm begging you.

Over the years of working with Daniel, he told me many times how simple affirmation made him feel so good. That's all he wanted - to simply be praised every now and again - instead of being constantly criticized for every move he made. So just remember, if you're trying to help someone through this horrible disease, affirmation and support work best. Stigma, shame, and judgment will do far more harm to the both of you. It's simple. Love them unconditionally, through it all.

If you happen to have any biblical christian faith, ask yourself, *what did Jesus do?* He was attracted to those whom society had mistreated and stigmatized. His passion clearly centered around extending a helping hand to people that needed it. His entire mission revolved around loving the less fortunate. Let's do the same. Whether you believe in the Bible or not, let's try to be more like him. It is a philosophy that will only bring goodness into the world, and who doesn't want that?

Jesus didn't shame people that were hurting or diseased. In our society, however, we are all guilty of doing this when it comes to those impaled by addiction. The depression that commonly is accompanied by the guilt of relapse pulls this population down to the depths of the earth, and rarely do these battered souls ever see a hand reaching down to pull them up. This can, and should be, a change we are all striving to make.

People battling depression walk around every day in a theoretical egg shell, fighting like hell to keep everything intact. They, better than anyone else, know how fragile their egg shell is. Some are even walking around knowing that they have small hairline cracks in their shell and it's just a matter of time before the entire thing shatters. This is how Daniel lived his life.

Every. Single. Day.

What good will come out of hurling insults, judgments, and shame towards them? Consider what happens to the yoke once it comes out of the egg shell. Once it breaks, you can never put it back together. The damage is done.

Daniel tried so damn hard to overcome the negative perceptions that others had about his disease, but often felt as though this was like climbing an insurmountable mountain. It seemed like everywhere he turned for affirmation and acceptance, he found a dead end. It would always inevitably blow up in his face when the person that he turned to found out that he struggled with addiction. It's unfortunate that many battling this disease feel more comfortable on a bar stool than a church pew.

Why?

If a person battling the disease of addiction has any outward appearance of it, what is the standard reaction by the typical christian if this person were to be sitting in the back pews of a church service? I would bet money they get ignored. Even if it is obvious this person is struggling and needs help, most christians would turn a blind eye and hope that someone else deals with it. Even if no contact is made, the person with addiction commonly feels and senses the judgmental thoughts that are inevitably being cast in their direction. Daniel told me frequently that when he was struggling, it wasn't hard for him to read the body language of the people he sat next to at church. They may have had their hands up in worship, but in every aspect of their actions, they were making him feel like the scum of the earth.

Take this same person with addiction out of the church pew and sit them on a bar stool. I can almost guarantee there won't be any judgmental looks coming from the other patrons of the bar. They will be acknowledged often and conversations will come easily. People with addiction often feel the most accepted and welcomed in this environment, so why not go back? I don't blame them, I would too.

This discrimination towards the disease of addiction is rooted not just in our medical system, but in our churches, our criminal justice system, our government, and our society as a whole. No wonder we have the most significant man-made epidemic in the history of mankind.

Giving people with addiction the love, support, and affirmation they so desperately crave, is crucial to their survival. It's what Jesus would do. People with addiction are hurting and desperate. Shaming and shunning this population only perpetuates the problem.

Often, I was told that I enabled Daniel in his addiction because I was too loving and too supportive. Maybe to a degree, at times, I did enable him, but do not confuse love, support, and affirmation with enabling. There is a fine line between enabling someone that has this disease and loving them *through* their disease, and this line changes depending on the situation and the context. I'll be the first to admit that I frequently toed this line, but I was always trying to be cognizant of where it was at.

Through the love I had for Daniel, I made sure that despite the consequences of his disease, he always had his basic needs met, but I tried diligently not to go much beyond that. I did my best to make sure he always felt loved and accepted, always had a roof over his head, and food in his belly. If I were to consistently go above and beyond that, such as providing him with cars and cash, I would consider that enabling. It's almost never acceptable to give someone that is actively using, access to their own transportation, and certainly not appropriate to give them cash. If their brain is diseased, you simply cannot trust them to make logical decisions with that freedom. It's not a punishment, it's simply a safeguard. You can love and support people with addiction without enabling them, but I can't tell you exactly how to walk this line. Every case is different and every case requires different considerations.

After Daniel learned the ropes of addiction treatment, he would often tell me, *"Dad, you worry about your side of the street, and I'll worry about mine."* He had a good point. Brooding over someone else can often be detrimental, but observation is a must. It's a nonnegotiable if you truly love them. You can't control other people, so stop trying. However, if you saw someone actively hurting themselves, and you knew it wasn't entirely under their conscious control, wouldn't you want to intervene, too?

Daniel and I would often butt heads because of the role I played in his life. I often felt so conflicted in how to develop our relationship without interfering with his happiness. He wanted his freedom, and I also

103

wanted him to be independent, but in the safest way possible. Sometimes having unfiltered freedom just wasn't always in his best interest, and as his parent, I still felt it was my responsibility to make sure he wasn't going to self-destruct. Carrie often remained a neutral person in Daniel's life, and I greatly appreciated the fact that she could often operate as a buffer between the two of us when things were particularly difficult. Daniel respected her, was always kind to her, and felt comfortable sharing things with her that might have been bothering him. She did her best to help him sort things out in his head, both the rational and irrational. Often, Daniel got stuck in the past and blamed others for his struggles. While some of that was legitimate, he couldn't undo the past or the things others had done, and he needed to move forward. Carrie was one of the only people that was able to help Daniel do that because it was a different perspective. Daniel struggled at times taking advice from myself because there were still hard feelings regarding his childhood, his independence as an adult, and his status as my employee, but I was able to rely on Carrie to help facilitate this relationship and keep it moving forward. I forever owe a debt to Carrie because of this.

I also believe that Daniel was so sensitive to the pains of life that he didn't want anyone else to feel what he did, so he made it his mission to make everyone else feel happy. The laughter never stopped when he was around. He frequently had us in stitches with his stories and I truly believe this was one of the best medications he ever received. Laughter and love. This is why he spent so much of his time surrounding himself with family and friends. When he felt positive energy from others, he did well. When he felt accepted and loved, he did well. When he felt like he was bringing good into the world, he did well.

Daniel once told me that he didn't use opioids to get high, he used them to simply feel normal. He said that one of his biggest struggles with addiction was that we (his family) hated when he was under the influence at family gatherings, but this was actually the only time in which he felt comfortable and normal in his own skin. This conversation almost brought me to my knees. As I realized the agony he was battling, my heart ached. He wasn't this stereotypical junkie that was addicted to the high, he was just trying to be like everyone else - to simply function without feeling miserable. After seeing this perspective, my understanding for his disease and mental health grew exponentially. The way I went about my interactions with him changed.

The way I reacted to his relapses changed. And the way in which I came alongside him to fight changed.

Daniel was a lost soul, eagerly craving to find himself. He yearned to establish his footing in a messy, complicated world that always seemed to knock him down. At the end of the day, all he wanted was to find and feel peace and happiness, just like you and me.

Chapter 7

Text On the Beach

The sun was just beginning to rise over the gulf. It was already hot, even by Florida standards for late December. The water was relatively calm, and I was sitting alongside my wife on the beach listening to the gentle sound of the small waves breaking against the shore. This is what people work all their lives for - retirement on a resort in southern Florida. It all seemed surreal. *What am I doing here?*, I thought. Inside, I felt so out of place. My body was here, my wife was here, my dog and Harley Davidson were here, but my heart and mind were 1,000 miles away, back home in Ohio.

It was December 2015, and the snowbirds from the north were all firmly nestled into their winter homes. Was I now one of them? I felt like a square peg in a round hole, but I looked the part. My 40-year workaholic lifestyle had gotten me all of the toys I had ever wanted. I had more than achieved my business goals, and now here I sat, sipping coffee on the beach, pretending to be retired. When I pulled my RV out of my driveway on December 7th 2015 to make my first migratory flight south to assume this role, I already felt fake.

It took me several years of internal dialogue to get me to this point. Most of that dialogue was implanted by Daniel and I can still hear him now. *"Dad, you need to stop working so much. Take some time off to relax. I can run this place."* I knew he was right. The same types of words were also coming from my wife, Carrie, too. Everyone in my life knew I was running myself dry, but I still didn't really have an organic desire to stop and slow down. Although, I did have some sense of relief in realizing that I was finally crossing the finish line of my long and arduous career, one that had been complicated by many hardships and unforeseen circumstances. I had checked the boxes and I had no desire to acquire any more material things. In fact, I wanted to simplify the things I had already accumulated. I knew that I only needed to hang on for a little while longer, maintain the status quo, and Daniel would soon be ready to take over the reigns of the business that had been so heavily weighing on my shoulders since the age of 18.

I had been burning the candle at both ends for too long, and deep down, I was afraid it would eventually catch up with me. If I didn't make this relaxation and retirement thing a priority, I knew it wasn't going to end well. I was also disappointed with myself for not knowing how to stop and smell the roses. It was so incredibly hard for me, and still is, to enjoy moments that everyone else easily gets pleasure from. On occasion, I would tell Carrie that I wished desperately to have a week or two without having any overwhelming responsibilities weighing me down. I had felt this heaviness constantly for many years, and sometimes my only desire was to have a second of relief.

I felt compounded by the never-ending, self-imposed pressure to prove myself as independent of my father and worthy of my own success. The comment from years prior that someone had hurled at me, *"Scott, you were born with a silver spoon in your mouth,"* never stopped influencing me. In the pursuit of proving myself, I also realized the opportunity that I had to build our family company into something that would survive me and provide a bright future for both of my boys. I wanted Daniel and Wes to have the same, if not better, opportunities than I did. I wanted them to learn the value of hard work, to learn that it isn't just about a paycheck, and to learn the importance of working towards, and for, something that they're proud of.

I wanted more than anything for Daniel to become the 3rd generation manager/owner of our sand and gravel operation. Daniel had always shown an innate interest in this field of work, and being the older son, I had always envisioned him taking over my role at Weidle Corporation. Wes was six years younger than Daniel and so he was still years away from discovering where his interests would lie, but I always made an effort to keep them in the same boat as far as their opportunities at the company were involved. Daniel had shown me early on that he wanted to be involved at Weidle Corporation and so I tried to do my part by giving him those opportunities. If he proved to me that he was committed and capable, I planned to let him saddle up.

He often chastised me for holding too tightly onto my responsibilities within the company, when he was capable of handling most of them. I didn't do so because I was trying to control him or the company, but rather out of a desire for him to mature a bit more. I didn't want him to get in over his head before he was ready to take on such a daunting challenge. In hindsight, this was probably how I made sense of the ways in which the disease of addiction had been preventing my son from performing at the level I knew he was capable of.

It has only been in recent years that I have come to realize how my hardwired drive to work, provide for my family, and prove myself, was actually extremely detrimental to both myself and those around me. This interfered, and at times completely disabled, my ability to be present in the moments I spent with my sons and with myself. Everything that I had done up until this point in my life was for the betterment of my children and family – from building our home on 15 acres of land, to a pond for us to fish on, a pool to swim in, and even a dirt bike track for Daniel in the backyard. Once I realized that none of this was enough, and that my first marriage was still going to fall apart, I didn't stop to reevaluate. Instead, I decided that maybe buying a houseboat on Lake Cumberland in Kentucky would help us become a stable family again. In my early childhood, trips to Lake Cumberland provided so much happiness and joy to my siblings and I, so why wouldn't that help my family situation, too?

Unfortunately, I was missing the most important points of all. I had done all of these things in good faith, but in doing so, was unable to see the big picture. I could see the trees, but not the forest. What really mattered at the end of the day? As only time would tell, my real craving is simply to just be with my family. To spend quality time together and simply enjoy being in one another's presence. When it's all said and done, it doesn't matter what material things we have or where we take vacations, for all I really desire is to be with the people I love. People and love are forever, things and experiences are temporary. Yet, here I sat on the beach in the winter of 2015, realizing that it's impossible to go back and have a second shot. It was during this trip that I started coming to terms with the fact that I had wasted many of years being too tense and hyper-focused on work, and it was time to turn this ship around - but how?

During a prior winter beach vacation a few years back, I had noticed someone on the beach each day that mesmerized me. Everyday, I would see this same person, seemingly so relaxed and without a care in the world. He had a perfect tan and always had a smile on his face. He caught everyone's eye, young and old, and it wasn't long before I realized this guy had something I wanted.

This person had taken a three-wheel bicycle, installed a giant freezer and umbrella on it, and walked the beach with it everyday, selling ice cream to the people he met along the way. To most people, that probably doesn't sound like anything of interest. But to me, it really was, and here is why... This guy seemed very content as he pushed his

cart, stopping every 20 to 30 yards to hand out his ice cream. I put myself in his shoes, and felt incredibly jealous of this simplicity. I could hardly fathom how great it must feel to be faced with only one decision each day, which was when to turn around and return to wherever he started from.

Believe it or not, being the workaholic that I am, I actually called the Fort Myers Beach town hall and asked what it would take to get a permit to do that. They said this type of permit was no longer available and the person I was referring to had been grandfathered-in with a permit exception. I share this in humor of myself, as I wasn't serious about getting this permit, but wanted to dream for a brief second. What exactly would it feel like to live a life where I only had one simple decision to make each day, and that decision wouldn't really impact anyone else? What would it be like to live that relaxing, simple life? Something in theory, I craved, but in practice, drove me crazy.

If I attempted this retirement route, I knew the only place I could try this would be in Fort Myers Beach, Florida. I had walked this beach almost every winter for at least two weeks during our business off-season for many years. I did this with my boys each morning when we were there, and the majority of those walks were just one-on-one time - time that I tried like hell to soak in. I started to consider purchasing a motorhome when talks of semi-retirement began because I thought it would give me the freedom I needed. I could come and go as I pleased, starting off with 4-week trips at a time. I didn't want to commit to anything drastic as far as lifestyle changes, but rather just play it by the seat of my pants. This gave me the flexibility to remain accessible to my company, and more importantly, to my boys.

It took me a year or so to find the type of motorhome I wanted, but eventually I came across the right one, and made the purchase in December of 2014. It was too late to figure out the logistics of an extended stay for that particular winter, so the goal was to give semi-retirement a shot next winter, for the first time. We decided that in a years time, we would take the motorhome down to Fort Myers Beach, stick our toes in the water, and see how it felt. If we liked it, we'd stay, and if not, we'd come up with plan B.

I had become accustomed to a lifestyle of constant work for 40 years, and I knew it would not be easy for me to slow down. I was still hands-on managing several businesses at the same time that I was also trying to plan an entire winter 1,000 miles away from home. Who was I kidding? Certainly not myself or my wife. I don't even think my dog bought into the role I was trying to play. Regardless, we made it happen, and I blindly dove into this thing head first. By mid-December 2015, I found myself baking in the southern heat with only the noise of the waves crashing in the distance.

One of the problems with self-imposed retirement is the mental backlog that can come rushing over you like an avalanche you've spent your entire life running from. Even though my body wasn't moving, my mind was still working overtime. Because I'm a processor and analyzer by nature, I typically have to go through some type of mental download before I'm able to clear my mind. When I found myself trying to unwind in preparation for an entire new season of life, I felt bum-rushed. I was reliving my entire life inside my head in those first few moments of solitude on the beach. I began with my childhood in a stereotypical midwestern country town; my parent's turbulent relationship and divorce proceedings; the untimely death of my mother; the breakdown my father experienced; the disastrous relationship with my first wife; watching my brother become homeless and then go to prison; the challenges of being a father; the joys of finding my soulmate; the years spent chasing and grasping the brass rings; the loss of my stepson; and ultimately the heartache of watching a brain disease whittle away at my firstborn son. The latter would prove to be the biggest challenge of my life, without a doubt. Little did I know in those first few moments of semi-retirement that my biggest challenge to-date was still on the horizon.

As I sat there on the beach in those days, I was first and foremost making an attempt to get myself back into a good headspace. Diving into memories on the beach when my family was whole seemed to be an easy place to start. There was only one other Christmas I could remember not being with at least one of my sons, and that was during the ugly divorce years. The boys and I had spent several Christmas mornings at Fort Myers Beach, the first being around 1987 when Daniel was only about two or three years old. On that Christmas day in particular, I remember being on the beach with our toes in the water and the warm breeze hitting our skin, watching our 2-year-old play in the sand. You could hear Jingle Bells in the distance, followed by a

jolly, *"Ho, Ho, Ho, Merry Christmas!"* It was Santa walking down the beach with full red suit and white beard in the hot Florida sun. Daniel was mesmerized, but probably with equal parts fear and excitement. I thought about that memory frequently as I sat there in that same spot 28 years later, trying endlessly to get that same feeling back.

My typical mental protocol during my annual vacation was to rewind only the past one to two years in my mind to specifically focus on any regrets that I may have struggled to come to terms with. About a decade prior, I learned that taking potential regrets into consideration when I made decisions often helped me deal with the outcomes, good or bad. My typical thought process when faced with significant decisions, business or personal, was to develop three different possible solutions to resolve any given issue at hand. Then, I would begin the process of forecasting the ramifications of each of the three potential solutions. If any one of the choices had the chance of causing personal regrets, even at a remote level, this became a very good reason in my mind to avoid it at all cost.

While I continued to let my mind unload and process, it was only a matter of time before I began to apply this mental protocol to the past couple years of my life, just as I had done in the past. This time was different, though. I wasn't concerned in the slightest with my business decisions or work regrets. I was all-consumed by my thoughts of Daniel's addiction. I sensed that he was in a critical period and I was in full-blown panic mode because of it. I felt like I was in a unique position to have significant influence with Daniel, as I understood him like no other, and along with that, felt the pressure to be the point man for his safety. I was his father, and although he was a grown man, I never stopped being his guardian. In all honesty, I think that's how parenting should be, not just in the case of addiction. When you bring a life into this world, you should never really stop being responsible for that life. I will stand by that belief until the day I die.

Over the course of the following several days, I tried to unravel all of the events surrounding Daniel's battle with addiction up until that point. Since I learned best by analyzing my regrets and mistakes, my goal was to dice through each and every one of them to figure out how I could do a better job going forward. Until I went through this process in my mind, I couldn't totally relax or live in the moment, as the ice cream man did.

I thought back to the many detours and obstacles we had encountered. When you're naturally a pretty self-critical guy, it's pretty easy to start rattling off the many turns I shouldn't have made. I recalled the many ways that I hadn't looked out for Daniel's best interest. I regretted stopping his Ritalin when he was young and yelled at myself for misinterpreting his anxiety. I regretted the fact that I put so much pressure on Daniel to achieve, which was all just a subconscious consequence of my own workaholic nature. I regretted the years in which I failed to understand his opioid addiction as a primary medical brain disease. And I regretted the many moments I let slip by without telling him how much he meant to me. I kept coming back to this fear that he didn't know how much I loved him.

So on Christmas morning, while I sat in my beachside recliner, I got out my phone and sent him a text, which read,

"Love you Daniel, Merry Christmas. Please find a way to forgive me for my shortcomings. I'm sorry. I love you. -Dad"

He replied, *"You are my dad, my hero, makes me proud when people say... 'is your dad Scott Weidle?' Lately I have matured and grown a lot. I am struggling so bad because of the life I have lived."*

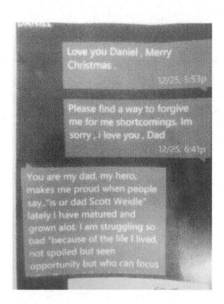

That response brought me comfort and peace, but I was still fear-stricken. I knew all too well that the anxiety and tension I felt were just a part of who I was, but deep down, I knew there must be a way to shut that off. I was consumed by the worry that Daniel was at risk and this controlled my every thought.

I have tried mightily for years to find things that could lessen the stress which seems to always hover over me. If anything in this world can calm me, it's usually the sound of water, hence why I've spent so much of my "free time" at the lake and near the beach. I told myself to embrace this new season of my life; to retire my thoughts as well as my body; to just be *in* the moment as Daniel had urged me to do; and to enjoy a destination where I had been bringing my family on winter vacations for over two decades. I had created many wonderful memories walking this beach and collecting shells with my boys, and I've kept every one of them stored inside my heart. Now, I could be in this happy place for an extended period of time, so why not just be content?

I took a deep breath on Christmas morning 2015 as I let the warm air, tainted with salt water, flow over me. *Maybe I could get used to this retirement thing,* I thought in that moment. In a way, it gave me an out - a way of putting my toes in the water while not having to commit to this whole "golden years" thing. I spent that morning practicing this new way of thinking. It wasn't easy, but I was willing to give it a shot if that meant I could finally find some inner peace and relaxation. Somewhere along the beaten path I had lost my way, but I was bound and determined to get back on track.

The day after Christmas, Carrie and I decided to grab some breakfast at our favorite place in Fort Myers, overlooking the beach and ocean. During the meal, I mentioned to Carrie that it was odd I hadn't heard from Daniel yet that day. We were already in our beach attire, and after breakfast we stepped out onto the hot, white, sandy beach for some much needed sun and peace. I hated that I was spending the holiday season away from my boys, but I was with Carrie and I enjoyed that we had this time to ourselves very much. She is one of the only people on this earth that has been able to keep me grounded and provide me with consistent, unwavering support. I was giving it my best effort to just relax in the moment and be present with her.

Then it happened. The phone... and not even a call, but a one line text message.

"I'm so sorry, Daniel was my best friend."

"Was!?," I said aloud. At that very moment, everything in my world stopped. Everything I had worked for, everything I wanted for my future - from passing the family business to the next generation to the faux retirement - all of it, gone in a split second.

With a simple text message, my heart sank. It felt as though every ounce of air had been pushed out of my lungs and I was the only person in existence. The beautiful white sand suddenly felt like quicksand and I was sinking faster than I could think. I could hardly move.

Carrie got up and began running to the RV which was about 100 yards away on the other side of the street. Carrie was actually running, while I had difficulty putting one foot in front of the other. I felt like I was frozen in time.

In these moments, which felt like hours, I replayed Daniel's entire life in my head. The regrets began to overwhelm my mind immediately. Why had I left Ohio? I should have been there. I could have saved him. I had done it numerous times over the past 10 years since Daniel's addiction was first triggered by using prescription opioids to treat an illness at the age of 16. Now, hundreds of miles away, I had been absent when he needed me the most. I had failed him and myself, and he had to pay the ultimate price.

Once I made it to the RV, I had no confidence I would ever make it home. Why would I even want to go back? We were in total shock, neither of us even saying a word to each other. We were throwing things into the RV left and right. Things that needed disassembled, we didn't bother to deal with and just threw them in. We loaded the Harley on the back, started the engine, and braced ourselves.

This was the day after Christmas, typically the busiest day of the year for incoming travelers at a beachside RV park. The sandy road leading in and out of the pseudo-resort was only one lane, big enough for just one RV at a time. There was a line of incoming RVs patiently waiting their turn, but we needed to go the opposite way, and fast. I pulled into this single lane and immediately caused chaos. It didn't take long before we were the recipients of angry glares and beeping horns. The park managers headed our way with their hands in the air, cueing us to put it in reverse. The guy came up to my window and said, *"Sir, you can't leave right now, you should have told us prior and we could have helped you."* I was still unable to formulate words, so I just stared back blankly, unable to even explain our situation. Carrie quickly jumped out and told him what was happening - that we had just learned of our son's passing.

It was automatically like a biblical event unfolded before our eyes. The RVs coming at us parted like the Red Sea did for Moses. We didn't have to wait for each one to tell the next, they all just moved.

Once we got on the public roadway, the dreaded 24-hour drive home began. I had still not talked to anyone from home, just that awful one sentence text. No one would return my calls. I guess nobody really knew what to say to me, and I get that. Finally, I was able to reach Wes. He was in Columbus, where he resided, when he had gotten a call from Daniel's stepdad that he and Debbie had found Daniel unconscious and the ambulance was on its way. Wes knew what this meant, so he raced home in a panic, fearing the worst. Wes was en route to Daniel's house when I got ahold of him, and when he answered, he could barely speak.

Through trembling, broken words, he said to me, *"Dad, I just got the call. Medics couldn't save him. He's… he's gone."*

Wes was broken. I'd lost a son, and he'd lost a brother for the second time. In the moment, I was so focused on my own pain that it was hard for me to think about what he must have been going through. Just three months prior, he had also buried his childhood best friend and cousin, Andy, to an overdose on opioids. His pain had to have been crushing.

Wes arrived at Daniel's house just as the coroner pulled up to remove his body. The house was filled with family members and first responders, but all Wes wanted to do was crawl in a hole and hide from the world. He entered the house, tears streaming down his face, unsure of what he was about to witness. The coroner asked Wes if he'd like a moment to say goodbye in private. He took him up on that offer, but was surrounded by police officers whom were unwilling to give him space and privacy. He clenched onto Daniel's body, which lay clad inside of a black body bag which only revealed Daniel's face. His tears dropped onto Daniel's cheeks as he hugged and kissed his big brother one final time. My entire soul crumbles when I think about what this must have been like for him, and again, I was absent, unable to be there for my boy.

The drive home seemed like an eternity. I was driving the RV as fast as I could, but it felt like I was moving in slow motion. I had made this drive dozens of times, many with Daniel, but I realized during this trip, that would never happen again. I played those memories over and over in my mind like a record on repeat. At every stop along the way I stared at the text message which shattered my world. I kept repeating to myself aloud, *"I could have done something!"* Why did I think it was ok to be so far away from home when I had a son who was battling a potentially fatal disease?

Nothing could have prepared me for this pain. Daniel had relapsed before, but I had always been there to help him pick up the pieces and get him back on track. Not this time, not when it counted.

Carrie tried to comfort me even though she was equally lost in the pain. The long stretches of silence would be momentarily interrupted by crying, questioning, and praying. Carrie handled the incoming calls from home as I was in no condition to talk. We were already being expected to make decisions regarding which funeral home to use, where to hold the services at, and even when to schedule them. These were decisions I never, ever, thought I would be forced to make, let alone while in complete and utter shock. I trusted Wes and his mom to make most of these decisions, and I'm thankful they were able to take some of this off my shoulders to allow my body to simply survive, because I wasn't capable of much else.

As I passed one billboard along the roadside, I read the words, *"Merry Christmas, Travelers!"* I scoffed and was immediately overcome with emotion. Christmas was the last thing on my mind and there would never be another merry one as far as I was concerned. I had lost my baby boy and now that would be forever connected to this holiday season.

The drive home was practically unbearable. It was a straight shot, 24-hour trip, and I was fighting to stay alert. My entire body just wanted to collapse behind the wheel. I remember stopping at every rest stop on the tail end of the drive, getting out, and running several laps around the vehicle to get my adrenaline pumping just enough to make it to the next stop. As the RV got closer and closer to our home in Ohio, so did the realization that I was about to face the most agonizing days of my life. I had never felt so lost before. I wanted to be home and yet I wanted to be anywhere but home at the same time. During those moments, I honestly felt like a man without a home.

By the time we arrived back in Germantown, I was a shell of a man. Barely functioning, I was hardly able to comprehend how to open up the garage door. As I turned off the motorhome and the noise of the diesel engine stopped, I just sat there. I didn't even want to get out of my seat, let alone face the inevitable. The tears started to roll down my cheeks. It's strange the things you focus on when your mind is numb. A bird in a large pine tree on the property next to mine was chirping. Several small animal tracks crossed the yard. It reminded me of times I spent with Daniel in the woods. Times we would never share together again.

Details began rolling in as the hours passed regarding what had happened to Daniel. I learned that Daniel's mother and her husband had found Daniel in his bedroom. I hated this. This was her second tragic loss of a child to an overdose. First Zac, and now Daniel. No parent should ever have to bury their own child, let alone two. She was shattered.

I began calling some of the family members who were at Daniel's house in the moments after he passed, trying to gather details and information to help my mind process the timeline of events. While driving back in the RV, I had already called one family member in particular because I could trust him, and gave him one request. *"Find Daniel's phone and keep it for me,"* I instructed him. I knew it would be the next morning before I would finally arrive home, but I was determined to eventually get to the bottom of what had happened. Someone was going to pay for this. Even within the first 24 hours, I was already experiencing the whole gamut of grief emotions. Sadness, shock, and anger seemed to be predominant. Where had Daniel gotten the drugs? What had triggered his use? I thought maybe his phone would give me information that I could use to answer some of these questions and find justice.

Once I got home, I called this relative back, and he informed me that he had been unable to retrieve Daniel's cell phone. The Germantown Police had already confiscated the phone and wouldn't give it back. I'm sure they had similar thoughts... to check and see who Daniel had contacted the day of his death and begin tracking down leads. It would be another six months before I was given access to my own son's phone again.

I knew I had to do something. It was already eating me alive to think that someone, somewhere out there, had contributed to my son's death and they were likely roaming free like nothing ever happened. I could not wait for the police to act. I wasn't a "wait" kind of person. I was used to stepping in and taking charge.

I sat down and tried to recall every detail of the last few conversations we had with Daniel. I remembered how Daniel had just called the night before to check in on us. He had spoken to Carrie and made small talk about what we were doing. It was a wonderful conversation, in fact. He asked if we had eaten at one of his favorite spots, Strawberry Corner. Daniel loved that place because it had been our family dinner spot in Fort Myers for years. About 20 minutes into the call, his mother beeped in, and he said he needed to go. Little did we know that would be the last time we would hear Daniel's sweet voice.

Sometime later, when I had the chance to talk with Daniel's mother, she said that she, too, had a warm conversation with Daniel that night. They had even made plans to go to church together the next morning. When Daniel didn't show up the following day, Debbie and her husband, Mike, went over to Daniel's house to see if everything was ok. Daniel's vehicle was sitting in his drive, but the lights were off and he didn't answer the front door. They proceeded to go around the back side of the house to see if another door would be unlocked. Seconds later, they discovered Daniel. It was clear that he had been gone for several hours, there was no going back.

I cringed as I forced myself to think through those details, but I knew it would be the only way to solve my inner yearning for resolution, for truth, and for answers. Randomly, it dawned on me that Daniel's work computer was in his office and might hold some answers, so I sped over to the plant to begin investigating. Daniel never shut down his work computer and never signed out of his Facebook page, which was fortunate because none of us had his passwords. I was praying this would still be the case.

When I got to the office, I sat down behind Daniel's computer. I began to sob uncontrollably as I looked at the pictures of his children sitting all around. He kept some of his devotionals posted up on sticky notes and scrap paper, pinned to the wall. I read the words, *"Ask God to empower you and trust in him moment by moment. God can do anything you can ever imagine or dream of."*

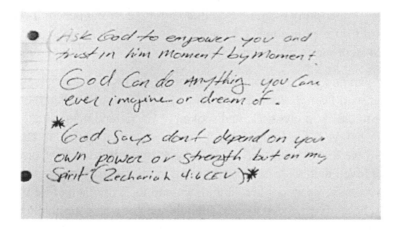

Were these just words? Where was God now? I couldn't answer that, nor did I really care to. I had too many questions that kept running through my head. Were there any clues on Daniel's Facebook account? Was I about to find out who was responsible for killing my son?

I went into his private messages on Facebook and there it was. A message from a woman Daniel went to high school with and had kept very infrequent contact with via social media. The day Daniel had taken his final dose of illicit opioids, she had responded to one of his recent posts, which read:

"I'm a broken person. I wasn't even allowed to see my kids on Christmas!"

She replied by saying that she knew what he was feeling and was interested in meeting if he wanted to talk. Daniel replied to her and said that he only used every now and then, and I quote, *"Vivitrol was the shit and really helped, but they make it so damn hard to get."*

The next response from the girl sent chills up and down my spine. It was a photo of some heroin, followed by the sentence, *"This is all I have left, but I'm going to get some more, would you like me to get you some?"*

I was stunned. Infuriated. Rage engulfed my entire being as I read that sentence. In all actuality, I really wanted to stop reading right then and there to begin an immediate manhunt for this woman, but I kept reading.

Initially, Daniel replied that he was trying to stay away from it, but as the conversation continued, his demeanor changed. You could tell Daniel was becoming weakened by the temptation and urge, weakened by the disease, and eventually they set up a time to get together. The conversation ended there.

I took this information to the sheriff's office the next day. They launched an investigation followed by a sting operation. Search warrants were issued and her house was put under surveillance. Because she did not know that any of this was happening, she actually showed up at Daniel's funeral. I knew this was happening and it was almost more than I could bear, but I remained as calm as I possibly could. I clearly had a lot going through my head that day, but the fact that this girl was walking around acting all innocent and polite ate at me like a necrotic cancer. I wanted to blow up, literally and figuratively.

There were undercover officers at Daniel's funeral service, and after the funeral, they follow her to a local bar, and then home. The police made a raid later that evening at her residence. She was taken into custody but she denied meeting up with Daniel that day. Unfortunately, there was not enough evidence seized in the raid to hold her, and she was subsequently released. They couldn't prove the two of them met up.

Whether or not she provided Daniel with the heroin that ultimately killed him that night may never be known, but I can tell you one thing with certainty. She is guilty in my book. The photo she sent him and the conversation they had most definitely triggered something in Daniel that caused him to secure heroin that evening and use one more time… his final time.

His final public post on Facebook, just twelve hours before his death, said everything that needed to be said:

"I usually never post especially about personal struggles. But I don't care anymore. Christmas alone with not 1 of my 3 children is torture, not 1. It's hell on earth. I really am a good person, but the disease of addiction is a bitch and sometimes it's the only thing that gets you through the day. It only prolongs the process and makes it worse. Just venting y'all. That's it."

As the events of December 2015 unfolded, I can now clearly see just how defeated and tired Daniel felt. Throughout Daniel's final 30 days on earth, he felt an incredible amount of emotional turmoil. He experienced feelings of abandonment and shame, he felt misunderstood and stigmatized, he felt unloved, and he felt depressed. He was bombarded with trigger after trigger. He was not able to see his children on Christmas. He had someone on Facebook offering him heroin. He was left alone every night during the holidays, a time when most people are surrounded by loved ones 24/7. And he had recently been denied medical treatment that would have saved his life. Naturally, he felt an overwhelming hopelessness.

Just one month prior, he was the most stable I had ever seen him. We had finally, after years of trying, found the only medication to hold promise. Then, for no reason, he was denied access not just by one doctor, but by five different medical facilities, all of which completely failed him. As a result, I was about to bury my own flesh and blood.

Bob Dylan once said, *"When you cease to exist, then who will you blame?"* Two people ceased to exist on December 26, 2015 - both Daniel and myself, but I was still alive enough to blame myself.

Chapter 8

Shattered

"Grief is a lonely walk. Others can be there, and listen, but you will walk alone down your own path, at your own pace, with your sheared-off pain, your raw wounds, your denial, anger, and bitter loss. You'll come to your own peace, hopefully... but it will be on your own, in your own time." - Cathy Lamb

The noise and duties of the funeral services were over, and I was now alone, very alone. Alone time had never bothered me before, and in fact, I preferred it. But this was different. This was a deep, dark void that I was so incredibly uncomfortable with. Helping Daniel fight this battle was over, and Daniel had lost the fight. I, too, had lost. I was numb and angry at the same time. In my mind, I was convinced I would not survive this. It was just a matter of time, I thought. The pain was too great. I beat myself up over every decision. I replayed each event of Daniel's young life in my mind. I thought about all of the things he would never be a part of - his children growing up without him, holidays and family gatherings without his humor and funny antics, and our family vacations to the lake - never to be had again.

At the moment I received the text message about Daniel, I knew immediately that my own life was at risk. I anticipated a grief that would likely result in my demise.

I shouldn't have gone to Florida. I knew it before I even pulled out of the driveway in the RV with Carrie. I knew it when I was in Florida, and I certainly know it now. On numerous occasions, I was very close to hopping on the next flight home and calling it quits on semi-retirement so that I could help Daniel. I would never forgive myself for choosing to stay in the sand. Never. A regret that will follow me the rest of my life.

I started praying and asking God to take me out of this life so that I wouldn't have to do it myself. I had lost my firstborn son, my best friend, the person that was going to take over the family business and outlive me. I had lost my purpose for living. I was falling deeper and deeper into depression, and nothing could stop me from plummeting into this darkness. I was mad at God, I was mad at myself, I was mad at the doctors, at the legislators, and the pastors. I was a combination of every wicked emotion I had ever feared.

I was living and sleeping on the recliner in the great room of our house. Carrie wasn't sure how to help me understand or cope with these emotions, but she remained by my side everyday. I certainly didn't know how to deal with myself either. I would just sit in the recliner and stare at the ceiling, day after day. Life had no meaning, and I was now in the midst of every nightmare I had every conjured. I had survived the death of my mother, the choices of my father, the loss of my marriage with Debbie, the death of my stepson Zac, and numerous battles alongside Daniel, but this wasn't like any of that. I was breathing, but more dead than alive. My past turmoils paled in comparison.

I failed Daniel at a critical time in his life. I knew that much. I had spent years learning his triggers, his signs, and I had spent countless hours trying to track down the root cause of the problem. I had confronted his suppliers both in private and in public. I had beaten on their doors, blocked their cars, threatened them with legal action, and reminded them I had evidence to put them away. I had put myself in harm's way by doing so, but I didn't care. Yes, doing those things often caused Daniel to become angry with me, but I also heard Daniel say several times to others, *"If it wasn't for my dad, I would not be here today."*

It was nearly impossible for me to swallow the truth that despite all I had done to save Daniel, it all went to shit in one night. That reality continues to gnaw away at my being, and probably always will. How do I move forward knowing that I could have done something? I didn't see a way out of this.

Only to appease Carrie, I went through the typical pathways that everyone wants you to utilize to get help.

I went to counseling only to become more distraught.

I saw a psychiatrist only to be prescribed meds that would keep me sedated for days on end.

I attended a christian men's group.

I tried EMDR (Eye Movement Desensitization and Reprocessing) therapy.

Nothing even came close to easing the complicated grief and heartache that consumed me from every angle.

For months, I avoided any public area that risked an encounter with someone I knew. I was not capable of having any conversations with anyone who might attempt to console me or shower me with the stereotypical sayings that grieving people often hear. I cringed at comments like,

"Daniel is in a better place now… his pain is over."

"Hang in there, time heals all wounds."

Or my personal favorite… *"God will never give you more pain than you can handle."*

Really!?! Daniel had just lost his battle, at least in part because he had so much internal pain that it was unbearable at times. My mother also had so much emotional pain that she took her own life, and she was a devout Christian! Where was God then? I know these people mean well, but they made me so damn angry. Numerous of my own friends, some of my own family members, church-goers, strangers, and even medical professionals made comments to me in those first few months that inflicted more pain than comfort. It was often those careless, judgmental opinions that often felt like more of a relentless twisting knife than the actual grief itself. I know it wasn't usually intentional, but either way, it drove me further and further away from human interaction, and deeper and deeper into the abyss.

I recall one cold winter day in early 2016 when Carrie dragged me out of the house to go see a movie in a neighboring town. I don't even remember what we saw, but afterwards we went next door to a little pizza shop. I sat down as Carrie went to the counter and ordered for the both of us. As I was sitting there, I looked around and saw nothing but happy families, most with small children. I was immediately triggered. It became more than I could handle as I realized that I will never again get to enjoy those precious moments that I was witnessing other families partake in. I sat there by myself, breaking down into uncontrollable tears and heartache. I put on my sunglasses to hide my eyes, but the tears ran down both cheeks as we sat there in silence, forcing ourselves to eat pizza and appear normal.

To this day, I still become distraught when I'm near a beach and see families play in the water as Daniel and I once did.

To this day, I have not been able to enter the main sanctuary of SouthBrook Christian Church as this is where Daniel and myself sat many of weeks, waging war against the demons of addiction. If and when I go, I sit in the lobby and listen to the message on the loudspeaker.

I doubt that I will ever be able to return to Fort Myers Beach or Lake Cumberland because of the extreme pain I feel in my heart when I even think about going back.

I have not yet been able to reconcile with myself the many reasons why, and how, Daniel's life turned out the way it did. I may never reach that point, and that's ok, but for now, I'm putting one foot in front of the next because that is my only option.

During one of my men's group meetings, which I attended periodically on Thursday mornings, we dove into a book called *Breathing Underwater*, which is exactly how I felt and still feel like on some days. This book, by Richard Rohr, is about spirituality and working the 12-steps into your life. Not much different than the Alcoholics/Narcotics Anonymous 12-step programs for recovery. Working the 12-steps in either arena is not a task to be accomplished because you read a book about it, or because you simply went to a meeting. It's about working on different aspects of yourself. You must do so in a methodical way, and you can't move on to the next step until the one at hand is done. It took Daniel close to a year to work through his issues with this process. But even once you do, one must stay diligent in the practice or it is easy to slide back down the slippery slope and end up at square one. I found myself coming to the realization with how applicable this was to my own recovery in grief. I had to be incredibly intentional in processing everything that happened and everything that I felt, or else I'd never breathe above water again.

When I attended these men's group meetings, I rarely shared much vocally because the heartache and grief was still so raw. I could barely speak without cracking. I did, however, find comfort in simply listening to other men talk amongst themselves. The topic didn't matter, I just needed to listen to some conversation in order to stop my own mind from the constant, awful noise.

I did receive some simple, powerful advice at these meetings that I will never forget. Charlie once said to me, *"Scott, sometimes the most important thing you can do every day is to simply get up and put the keys in your hand and walk out the door."* He was right. Some days, that is all I have the power to do. To simply get out of bed and leave the house. And that's okay, as long as I'm making the effort and I'm not giving up. No matter how easy it may seem to you, at times, this is my only daily goal. To simply survive.

Also in this men's group, I met a guy named Victor. I had learned before that Victor also lost his son tragically a few years prior. The fact that someone else could somewhat understand what I was feeling ended up being the driving force behind why I showed up week after week. Each Thursday, Victor would share a few of the experiences he had gone through while his son was with him and after his son left this world. He openly talked about how significant the pain feels for people who lose a child. At one point, I finally worked up the courage to ask him, *"Victor, does the pain ever stop?"*

There was a long pause while he thought about how best to answer that question. He replied, *"No, it doesn't, but you will learn how to carry that pain. It may take years, but you'll eventually learn how to live your life with this new part of you."*

I felt doomed. *Years?!* At times, I didn't think it was possible to carry this pain around for another day, let alone for years to come.

I processed those words over and over during the course of the following few days. I came away with a great sense of respect for just how brutally honest Victor had been with me. He didn't give me the lame condolence talks that many folks do. I continued with these Thursday morning meetings off and on because I needed to hear more brutally honest words from Victor. After awhile, though, I began to feel as if I was adding too much heartache and sorrow to this group of Christian men. During the first year, I couldn't even talk out loud in the group without breaking down. It wasn't long before I felt so very far out of place. Everyone else seemed so well put together, while I felt like a crumbling mess of a man.

I kept going, however, and with time, I was able to be more vocal. I began to advocate for the misunderstood disease that took my son from me to this group of me that I had come to know and respect. I started to share things with the group that I had learned about addiction and the opioid epidemic in an effort to raise awareness within the church community. I wasn't overbearing, to my knowledge, but simply wanted to share how and why addiction had been documented in medical journals to be a disease, and not just a disorder. One member of the group was active in the church AA meetings, and was actually the weekly lead speaker. After I had finished sharing, I asked him what his opinion was. He said he wasn't able to process addiction as a medical disease. It was his position that addiction was a thinking problem, not much different than someone with a porn or sex addiction. That bothered me a great deal, to watch a church organization perpetuate the stigma associated with this medical disease. How could someone so close to the problem not see it for what it really was?

I would go on to have many similar conversations with people all over my hometown and it felt exhausting. I was simply trying to show people the truth about addiction and opioids, yet everyone seemed to be stuck in this old school mindset, which was really making the problem worse. I felt dumbfounded and alone as I began to realize just how uninformed our society had become, and people like Daniel had suffered because of it. It drove me to further isolate myself because I didn't feel like I was getting anywhere with anyone. In my mind, I had discovered an earth shattering truth that shook me to my core, yet not many seemed to care. Was the only reason I had this kind of reaction because it took my pride and joy away from me forever? I guess that isn't uncommon for advocates of any issue, really – it's usually the grieving people left behind that do the most work because they're the ones who realize the gravity of reality and pain associated with waiting until it's too late. How was I going to get people to step into my shoes?

I spent countless days and nights by myself out in the field on the land where Daniel used to hunt. I felt close to him there, and still do. I would just lay down and look up at the sky, wondering if he was out there; wondering if he could hear my thoughts and understand my regret. I craved ever so desperately to talk with him and feel his embrace. I worked through much of my inner feelings and pain out in these woods by myself. I reflected on the past and wrestled with my soul as if we were in a cage match that would never end.

I thought back to the ways in which I could have done better. I analyzed my regrets and began being brutally honest with my feelings. At the time, it was very easy for me to see my own flaws given the fact that I was so depressed, and it almost felt natural to tear myself apart in the search for answers. It became clear to me that my overachieving personality had put pressure on Daniel to live up to my standards. In attempts to simply teach Daniel how to have a strong work ethic, I was actually causing him more harm by setting unrealistic expectations on his shoulders, which in turn, increased and heightened his anxiety and stress.

Was I also the Sergeant Carter-type person that Daniel encountered in his pee-wee football days? If so, Daniel had no way of quitting the team to get away from me. I had in essence trapped him in this environment.

Was I a part of the problem?

Hell, was I the root cause?

The first step in recovery is to admit you have a problem. I had no problem with this step.

Through the effort of this book I have spent yet another year ripping off my bandages to share my wounds with you. I suspect when reflecting back over the years of 2016, 2017, and 2018, I have been working through my own 12-step program without even realizing it. It isn't uncommon for people who are working the 12-step programs to find and discover aspects of themselves that they never even knew existed. I have not attempted to do this program in any formal fashion, but I can absolutely see how this would be possible in the light of grief, given my basic knowledge of the curriculum.

The following bullet points illuminate the 12-step methodology. I have read these points over and over again. I know Daniel was extremely proud of the fact that he had worked so diligently on implementing these steps into his own life, which was a several year process. It seems as though I have spent nearly three years on #5 alone.

1. We have admitted that we were powerless over our addiction, and that our lives have become unmanageable because of it.
2. We have come to believe a Power greater than ourselves can restore us to sanity.
3. We have made a decision to turn our will and our lives over to the care of God as we understand God.
4. We have made a searching and fearless moral inventory of ourselves.
5. *We have admitted to God, to ourselves, and to another human being the exact nature of our wrongs.*
6. We are entirely ready to have God remove all these defects of character.
7. We humbly asked God to remove our shortcomings.
8. We have made a list of all persons we have harmed and become willing to make amends to them all.
9. We have made direct amends to such people wherever possible, except when doing so would injure them or others.
10. We have continued to take personal inventory and when we were wrong, promptly admitted it.
11. We have sought through prayer and meditation to improve our conscious contact with God as we understood God, praying only for the knowledge of God's will for us and the power to carry that out.
12. Having had a spiritual awakening as the result of these steps, we tried to carry this message to other addicts, *and to practice these principles in all our affairs*

I encourage everyone to utilize these key steps, whether you happen to be spiritual or not, and whether or not you've ever had a substance problem. This material can be applicable to any area of your life that brings you struggle. These steps have helped me in ways I never imagined, and I believe they can probably help you, too.

As I've mentioned before, one of the flaws that I've struggled with the most about myself is that I've never been able to live in the moment - to soak up the *now*. I hear people use this terminology often, and it irks me every time because I've struggled with that most of my life. I'm getting better, but I went years without feeling much enjoyment at all, out of anything. I was all about tomorrow, next week, next month, next year. Goals, goals, goals. In December of 2015, before Daniel passed, I just wanted the world to stop for a few days so that I could see what it felt like to be *in* the moment. Even changing my environment didn't allow me the ability to stop and just exist without being consumed by something to stress about, worry about, or work through. In retrospect, I now understand why and how Daniel was trying adamantly to help me stop and enjoy the day - to stop working and just enjoy the nature all around us, as he did. But obviously at the time, I wasn't planning on my world stopping so suddenly, and now since his passing, this has been one of the most difficult aspects to wrestle with. If I had learned this skill earlier, maybe I wouldn't have so many regrets, maybe I wouldn't have missed so many moments with my son that I can now never get back, and maybe, just maybe, I wouldn't be the shattered, broken man I have come to see in the mirror.

Daniel's body ceased to exist the day his spiritual body went to heaven. Myself, on the other hand, was shattered into dozens of pieces, left to pick up the wreckage and attempt to salvage what was left. As I am writing this, it has been about 40 months since that day, and each day that passes, I try to pick up another one of those pieces of myself, however many pieces no longer fit like they used to. I'm slowly becoming whole again, but in a very different, misshapen form. There will forever be a void in my soul that no one but Daniel can fill, and I'm slowly coming to terms with that. I refuse to *move on*, but I am learning how to *move forward*. I'm learning how to keep my head above water and stay afloat. I'm learning how to channel my regrets into change. I'm learning how to utilize the painful emotions I feel as fuel and motivation to advocate for people like Daniel. And most importantly, I'm learning how to be a better husband to my wife and a better father to Wes, because they are still here and they love me dearly.

I have a long road ahead of me, but I'm making progress because people don't give up on me and I don't give up on myself. There is life to be lived and goodness to be brought into the world. If the world has taught me nothing less, it's that nothing changes if nothing changes. If there is something you don't like in the world, or within yourself, you must go out and change it because no one is going to do it for you. I've come to recognize so many injustices within our society throughout this entire process, and it has become my mission, the thing that keeps me alive, to facilitate that positive change. This book is just another step on that journey.

Through my new pursuit of purpose, I'm picking up the pieces.

I also wanted to take a moment here to say thank you to some of the individuals whom have helped keep my head above water during this deep, dark season of my life.

Victor - Thank you for your honesty and for sharing with me your pain and survival story after the loss of your son.

Dave and Charlie - Thank you for reaching out and pulling me into your circle, and trying to understand the complicated grief of losing a child.

Carrie - Thank you for your never-ending love and loyalty to me. You have stood by my side throughout the depths of the valley, and not once wavered. I would not be here today if it wasn't for you.

Chapter 9

The Disease

"Addiction is a brain disease. This is not a moral failing. This is not about bad people who are choosing to continue to use drugs because they lack willpower." - Michael Botticelli, Former Director of the White House Office of National Drug Control Policy.

One of the top goals that I hope to achieve by writing this book is to raise awareness for the disease that has so heavily devastated my family. I believe this can be done in numerous different ways, but education should always be the foundation upon which we build. If you don't first understand the issue at hand, nothing else matters. Having an accurate and fundamental understanding of the disease of addiction is a crucial knowledge point that I have come to realize most Americans are missing. I hear it in daily conversations with strangers, I hear it in random comments made in passing, I see it on TV, and I experienced it within myself for many years. Some people look at this as a topic of debate, however, if you really look at the facts, it's not up for debate at all. Addiction is a disease, point blank. In fact, this isn't even a new idea. The American Medical Association has backed this idea formally since 1981, when they released a statement detailing the amount of scientific evidence which proves addiction to be a pathological process, as opposed to a choice.

I mentioned previously that I first learned how addiction was a primary medical brain disease while I was attending the patient/family educational classes at the rehab facility Daniel was attending in Cincinnati, called The Ridge. Shortly after, Dr. Todd Carren, MD, released a six-video lecture series detailing the exact information he had relayed to us in those Wednesday night meetings. You can find these clips on YouTube, and they have helped me immensely in furthering my understanding of addiction. I have summarized his key points in this chapter, and my son, Wes, has also supplemented that information throughout this chapter to help us all come to a simple and basic understanding of what addiction really is. Whether or not you personally know someone that is struggling with addiction or not, I believe this information will serve you well. Individuals struggling with addiction are all around us, and you never know when it might be your son, your daughter, your brother, or your friend that finds themselves on the receiving end of this devastating disease. I encouraged you to do your due diligence and be prepared ahead of time, unlike I was.

When we throw the word *disease* around, what are we even talking about, technically? Many things can be called a disease, some of which are accurate, but others, not so much. According to Dr. Carren, the defining factors that must be met in order for a given problem to be formally classified as a disease are:

1. It is detrimental to human life
2. It has a known set of signs and symptoms
3. It can be proven with a medical test that when given, is always abnormal

Let's look at hypertension, or high blood pressure, for example. Untreated hypertension can be detrimental when we understand the damaging impact it can secondarily have on eyesight, kidney function, and increasing the incidence of strokes. It has a known set of signs and symptoms, which can include headaches, blindness, and fatigue, just to name a few. And lastly, it can be objectively proven and tested with consistency by measuring your blood pressure, a simple noninvasive test that everyone has inevitably experienced at one time or another.

Now, let us look more specifically at how this same criteria can apply to the disease of addiction. Addiction is detrimental to human life. Accidental overdose on opioids is the number one killer among the 18-25 age group in the United States. Furthermore, drug overdoses claimed the lives of over 70,000 Americans in 2017 alone. That is roughly 190 people just like Daniel every single day. Stats like that can't be argued, it is clearly detrimental and devastating. Secondly, addiction has a known set of signs and symptoms. Enough people have suffered from this same excruciating experience that we are now able to trend and map the different behavioral consequences and outcomes. There are incredibly too many to list, however some of the more common and obvious include irrational and impulsive behavior, dehydration, tolerance, and cravings. Lastly, addiction can be consistently and objectively identified through brain scan imaging. These are rarely done in clinical practice because of their price tag, but scientific research has made vast advancements in the ability to utilize this tool to interpret severe and significant differences in the brains of people who suffer from the disease of addiction. This is where we'll camp out for the majority of this chapter.

When a functional brain scan is done, it looks at the ways in which our brain cells use glucose, their primary source of fuel, as well as the utilization of oxygen by the blood vessels in our brain. Glucose consumption will light up on the scan, and this indicates to us what areas of the brain are being more or less active. The brighter and darker the illumination, the more active that particular brain region is assumed to be. Similarly, oxygen can be tracked throughout our blood stream, and the more oxygen a given brain region demands, the more active it is presumed to be. Comparing a neurotypical brain with the brain of someone who has the disease of addiction reveals stark contrasts.

Two main brain regions are implicated in this particular disease: the frontal lobe and the nucleus accumbens. When you break down their basic functions in combination with the ways in which various chemicals and drugs impact them, the resulting behavior that we see in individuals with addiction is much easier to comprehend. I struggled for years to understand why the people in my life whom I loved so much, made decisions that were so obviously dangerous and damaging. It wasn't until I understood the basic brain deficits that were going on under the surface, that I was able to have some compassion for the victims of addiction.

First, let's inspect the frontal lobes of our brain. This is where we store all of our information about socially acceptable behaviors and receive the ability to control our impulses. This is the area that we rely on when we need to make a choice about what is wrong versus right, and safe versus unsafe (socially learned behavior). The frontal lobe is typically the most dominant and active part of our brain at all times, as we are constantly interacting with people and making decisions about how to navigate the world around us. We rely on impulse control not only when we go out to the bar and need to resist drinking too much, but also in everyday activities like conversations and driving. When people refer to someone as having "no filter," they really mean that they have poor impulse control, which is a hallmark feature of the frontal lobe in our brain. In the brain scan of every individual with the disease of addiction, the frontal lobes become extremely inactive. The repeated use of addictive substances essentially turns off our brain's ability to decide between safe versus unsafe, and right versus wrong. It significantly reduces our ability to control our impulses and urges, which not only has detrimental consequences when it comes to the urge to use different substances, but in each moment of the day that we depend on restraint. It's no wonder why individuals who have this disease aren't making choices that make any sense to the rest of the world. The brain region responsible for this function simply isn't working.

Next, let's explore the inner workings of the nucleus accumbens. This is simply a clump of brain cells closer to the base of our brain that is commonly referred to as the *reward center*. It is responsible for promoting and encouraging the survival of our individual bodies and our species as a whole. It does so by stimulating our brain with different neurochemicals, particularly dopamine, which is responsible for feelings of happiness and motivation. Naturally, when we participate in activities that our body requires for survival, such as drinking water, eating food, sleeping, and even having sex (because it results in procreation, and thus the survival of our species), our reward center is stimulated by dopamine and thus we feel happy and motivated to repeat the behavior.

It may be helpful to look at this as a survival hierarchy, which our brain innately has stored in its reward center so it knows how to prioritize our basic needs. The more crucial the given behavior is to our survival, the more intensely the reward center is stimulated, and thus more dopamine is released. It seems like a foolproof way to promote our well-being, that is until something hijacks it, and addiction does just that. Most addictive substances act directly, or indirectly, on the nucleus accumbens as well, however, they stimulate this group of brain cells to a much greater intensity and for a greater length of time compared to any of the naturally salient factors, such as water or food. Because of this, the reward center is tricked into viewing the drug as the number one priority on its survival hierarchy ranking list. The more dopamine that stimulates the reward center, the more motivated we become to repeat the behavior that was responsible for it, and thus the reward center becomes tricked into seeking out the given substance before any of our basic survival needs. On functional MRI scans of the brain, the reward center is significantly more active than in the neurotypical brain, which confirms this theory.

137

The compounding impact of an inactive frontal lobe with a hyperactive reward center makes for a lethal combination. It provides so much clarity and explanation as to the behavior that we see portrayed among individuals with addiction. It clearly isn't a choice, but rather, has been scientifically proven to be a dysfunction in brain chemistry and function.

The other aspect of the disease of addiction that is paramount to our basic understanding, is the fact that it is a progressive and chronic disease. This means that it tends to get worse with time, and has the capacity to become a lifelong struggle. At the foundation of this truth, is the concept of tolerance. Most people have a good idea of how this works, but when we zoom in to see how tolerance actually develops chemically, it allows us to see why addiction is not just a disease, but is a progressive and chronic one, which is the key to acknowledging its power and ability to cause the destruction that we have seen in my family, and many others.

Tolerance is why we are able to become addicted to various substances, like prescription opioids, but we don't get addicted to water and sleep, the natural triggers on our primitive reward center. Both of these stimulate the same reward center, but the unique ability of addictive substances to produce tolerance separates the two. Tolerance means that with each use of an addictive substance, the same effect will not occur, and therefore requires the user to increase the dose with each use if they still desire to feel the same result. This occurs because most addictive substances can trick the brain cells into becoming hyper-excitable, which simply means that our brain cells misinterpret the signal, and produce a stronger reaction than is proportionate to the amount of stimulus, or substance, given. This results in our brain cells developing an inaccurate new threshold required for future stimulation, and thus explains the concept behind why our brain would need more and more of a drug to produce the original effect experienced. This is a very basic overview of this phenomenon, but without diving into too much unnecessary detail, gives us the basic information required to have a good foundation.

Throughout the course of writing this book, I discovered something called the opponent-process theory, which I believe can help us reinforce this concept from another angle. It matches up almost perfectly with what Daniel, and many other people in my family, experienced. The opponent-process theory is a well known model for understanding addictive behaviors and motivation, which was first conceptualized back in the 1800's, but has been thoroughly expanded on since. It essentially states that when someone is repeatedly exposed to something that positively impacts their emotional state, this will eventually be matched by the antagonistic, or opposing, emotion. This dichotomy usually results in the original emotion becoming less with repeated use, but the opposing emotion becoming stronger. In the case of addiction, when someone indulges in a potentially addictive substance, they reach a level of pleasure that will inevitably resolve, not just because the substance wears off, but also because the opposing emotion is acting on it, resulting in worsened emotions. The next time they use, they need a little bit more of the substance to reach the same level of pleasure, and again, their mood inevitably will decrease as they are met with an even stronger opposing emotion, but this time even farther below baseline because they used more of the substance and subsequently got a stronger opposing reaction. This pattern escalates until the individual is simply using in order to return to baseline - to simply feel normal - as opposed to getting high. It explains both the concept of tolerance from a psychological standpoint, but also illuminates the opposing forces at work, which explains why individuals are so strongly drawn back to using over and over again even when they experience negative consequences.

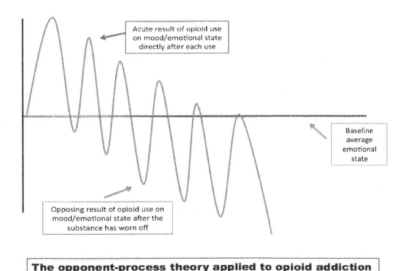

Acute result of opioid use on mood/emotional state directly after each use

Baseline average emotional state

Opposing result of opioid use on mood/emotional state after the substance has worn off

The opponent-process theory applied to opioid addiction

*graph created by Wes Weidle, PA-C

Putting together this information about how substance use is capable of impacting and impairing the most detailed and minute aspects of our brain, allows us to better understand just how easily this disease can overtake one's body. In a matter of days to weeks of repeated use, our brain can begin to display changes, and this occurs at an even quicker rate for individuals exposed during adolescence and young adulthood. The brain isn't finished developing until most individuals are well into their twenties, and up until brain development is finished, it is fairly easy to change how our brains function. This explains why people that are exposed to opioids, alcohol, and various other addictive substances during their formative years are much more easily hooked than adults who have completed brain development.

This also explains why it is so difficult to treat addiction once is has started. By the time most people are seeking treatment and attempting to defeat this disease, their brain development has reached maturity. Reversing years of physiologic changes to the mature brain is incredibly difficult to do, but this *is* actually possible. Research has shown that the brain does in fact have the capability to reverse and return to baseline functioning, as long as sobriety is maintained for about 1-5 years, in most cases. Knowing this gives us great hope that pursuing long-term addiction treatment is absolutely worth every penny and inconvenience. If we know it is possible to reclaim the brain, we must not give up on these vulnerable and innocent people.

I believe that the American Society of Addiction Medicine hit the nail on the head regarding the role of the brain in addiction. They take it a step further, and state that addiction has significantly more to do with the brain, than it even has to do with the drugs themselves. *"It is not the substances a person uses that makes them an addict; it is not even the quantity or frequency of use. Addiction is about what happens in a person's brain when they are exposed to rewarding substances or rewarding behaviors, and it is more about reward circuitry in the brain and related brain structures than it is about the external chemicals or behavior that "turn on" that reward circuitry."* (ASAM, 2011).

I share the above quote with hesitation because it has the potential to be misinterpreted to say that any potentially addictive behavior, such as pornography, eating, gambling, or sex, are equal in severity to opioid addiction. I strongly believe that not to be the case. One of my biggest pet peeves is when I hear people compare these two issues as if they're on the same level. Although there may be some truth to the fact that these behavioral addictions can be strong, powerful, and have the capability of significantly derailing one's life, I strongly feel as though there are key differences that put these issues in very different boats. If they were equal in regards to what was going on in the brain, why has opioid addiction been the only one to produce such staggering statistics? People are dying left and right from this powerful disease, at rates higher than anything we have ever seen in this country to date, and yet I still hear people compare their addiction to pornography to my son's opioid addiction as if they were one in the same. In my eyes, that is like comparing brain cancer to the common cold.

How come our society is so far behind the eight ball when it comes to understanding these basic scientific facts regarding addiction? Is it simply that the brain abnormalities are unseen, therefore out of sight out of mind? If that were the case, why don't most other brain diseases carry the same stigma and misunderstanding that addiction carries?

When someone has dementia, their brain function is impaired to the point that their behavior can become odd, irrational, and confusing, yet we don't look down on this population as being immoral and selfish. Many times dementia is actually caused by things that we do to ourselves throughout the years, whether this be the consequence of different medications, uncontrolled blood pressure, or even uncontrolled diabetes. However, we don't typically fault the person for what happens to their behavior as a result of the brain changes that have occurred. Yet when someone takes prescription opioids, as recommended by their trusted doctor, and they subsequently develop addiction, the resulting behavior is demonized and fault is squarely placed on the shoulders of the victim, the individual who now suffers from the brain disease of addiction.

As with all psychological and mental illnesses, people only see the behavior. What can't be seen are the internal changes happening at the chemical level. It's not simply a behavioral problem. Behavior is always a product of brain function. Compare neurology and psychology, for example. These are both studies of brain function, however, neurology specializes in the brain's ability to control the body, whereas psychology specializes in the brain's ability to control behavior. Now compare the way in which our society views these two medical specialties. Neurology has virtually no stigma or negative connotations. Psychology and psychiatry, on the other hand, carry an immense amount of judgement and negative assumptions. Think about the first thing that comes to your mind when someone says, *"I'm going to see my neurologist today,"* versus when someone says, *"I'm going to see my psychiatrist today."* I would bet the automatic thought was very different. *That* is what I'm aiming to change with this book, and *that* is what I believe will change as our scientific understanding of addiction deepens.

Through the advancements in modern medicine and research, we can confidently come to the conclusion that addiction is in fact a disease. It is not a choice. It is not a moral failing. It is not insufficient willpower. It is a deeper, more complex problem than most people understand, even within the medical community. Scientists and researchers have documented the science behind addiction in detail over and over again. I hope that I am able to help bridge this gap and facilitate a more thorough understanding of this disease to the general public so that we can have more empathy, understanding, and patience for those whom it effects. I know that if I would have had this information years ago, my life, and the lives of those around me, could have potentially turned out much different. I can't go back in time and fix that, but I can move forward and help change the people it will affect in the future. My mission is to spread this knowledge far and wide so that people like my son don't feel so misunderstood, stigmatized, and isolated. If we want to help, we must first understand.

"Alcoholism and addiction have touched millions of people in this country. If you don't suffer from it, you know someone who does. We are your wives, your mothers, your daughters, your sisters. We are your children, your colleagues, your employees, your friends. We are Emmy award winning journalists, Grammy award-winning singers, and Oscar winning actors. We are diplomats and doormen, presidents and accountants, housewives, and handymen. In the face of this disease we are all equal, the playing field leveled. If we are truly fortunate, we have employers who did not abandon us, family who stood by us, and perhaps someone who helped us find our way back, who never forgot that beneath all the appalling behavior there was a human being."
- Elizabeth Vargas

Chapter 10

Little Pill, Big Problem

"Never before have we prescribed so much medication for non-lethal conditions that have killed so many." - Tom Frieden, former CDC Director

Like so many other people who have developed an opioid addiction because of these deadly opioid prescription pills, Daniel worked hard, played hard, and lived his life without any indication that there was a huge problem brewing just under the surface. You would have never looked at Daniel and thought there was anything wrong. Little did we know just how much of his life was actually controlled by a simple, little pill. After Daniel admitted his problem to me, I began to learn as much as I could in order to help him. Again, I didn't see the magnitude of the problem at the time, even though this wasn't my first rodeo with the disease of addiction. I began doing extensive research to figure when, why, and how this had victimized my son. I had considered myself to be such an involved father, so how was it that he had been prescribed an extremely addictive and dangerous medication right under my nose, and it so quickly took his life up in flames? How did my little boy end up in the grave at only 30 years young?

I thought back to moments where I had been clueless as to what was going on before my very own eyes. I remember one Friday evening in particular that haunts me. After arriving home following a normal workday, I wanted nothing more than to sit down on the sofa, relax, unwind, and watch a little TV. Carrie was away visiting family, and Daniel and I were going to have the house to our selves. It had only been a couple years since my divorce from Debbie had been final, but life seemed more at peace than it had for quite some time.

Daniel came bouncing through the front door with all the tact of a SWAT team, which wasn't unusual. He liked making an entrance. It was part of his fun-loving nature to utilize the element of surprise and provoke laughter.

This night especially, he was in one of those moods and started telling me a couple of jokes he had heard earlier that day from some of the guys at work. He slung off his coat and tossed it onto a nearby chair in the corner of the room. After literally having me laughing until my stomach ached, he said, *"Get on the phone, Dad, and order us up an extra-large pizza. I'm starving and a comedian can't work for free!"* I chuckled as he went off to his room to change clothes.

I got up off the couch to call the local pizza joint, when I noticed a small little pill lying on the floor next to the jacket Daniel had just been wearing. I picked it up and laid it on the coffee table, and proceeded to order our food. I didn't think much of it at the time, honestly. It appeared to be a little prescription pill and I just didn't want the dog to eat it. Having known what I know now, this should have been a huge red flag to me. At the time, though, I had no clue about the secret demon Daniel was battling. It didn't even cross my mind he was taking a prescription pill of any kind, for any reason.

I sat back down and started watching TV again. Daniel came into the living room and we proceeded to eat our pizza and watch movies together. Apparently, he noticed the pill on the table, and at some point, when I wasn't paying any attention he picked it up. I didn't even think about it again until the next morning when I was cleaning up from our movie night, when I realized it was no longer on the table where I had put it. Even then, I naively thought maybe Daniel could have just knocked it off the table accidentally or it had gotten thrown away with the trash. Little did I know that he had a pocket full of what I later found to be Oxycontin, which he had easily gotten his hands on through a guy he met at the car wash, where I had encouraged him to work. To this day, I still see that little pill lying on the floor, and it haunts me. Had I known then what I know now, that night would have turned out very differently.

Several years later, I also learned of numerous other sources Daniel had utilized, which contributed to his exposure to opioids. An all too common story as I've learned - kids inadvertently finding the jackpot in their grandparent's medicine cabinets, which frequently act as a mini-pharmacy to whomever is home. Daniel would often spend time with my dad, or Grandpa Ron, as he would call him. Daniel loved to hear his grandfather brag about his car racing days back in high school, and my dad loves to have people around who will listen to him reminisce about his good ole days. Those two had a lot in common when it came to their love for cars. They would spend hours together, just shooting the shit and cracking each other up. They often watched NASCAR together out at my dad's pool house, which came fully equipped with a water slide, big screen TV, and lounge area. Daniel looked up to his grandpa very much, probably even worshipped him at times, and my dad often lived vicariously through Daniel's young adult life.

If you remember, my dad has a reputation for being a big flirt with the ladies. He loved to go dancing in his prime, and he loves a woman's attention, even to this day. He was a big binge drinker, however, and had many embarrassing moments because of his love for booze. Daniel didn't care, though. He thought of my dad as a hard-nosed rebel, and I suspect Daniel was drawn to that in some way; drawn to the fast cars and hot women.

One Sunday afternoon in particular, Daniel was hanging out at my dad's pool house, and they decided to have a couple of beers together while they watched the Indy 500. At some point that afternoon, Daniel let himself into dad's house to use the restroom. A few minutes later, he came back and resumed the race, and grabbed another beer. It wasn't long until my dad noticed Daniel acting a little "off." Nothing real obvious, but his demeanor was a bit different than before he had left the pool house to use the restroom. Dad didn't think too much of this at the time, but later, when Daniel's disease became family knowledge, he realized what had happened. My dad later told me that he had nearly a full bottle of painkillers in the medicine cabinet of his bathroom. It was a rather large bottle that a doctor had prescribed to him a few years prior after a mild back injury, but my dad had held onto the remaining script in case of future pain. Dad didn't realize what had happened until sometime later, when he was cleaning out the cabinet and discovered that the nearly full bottle was almost gone. He put two and two together, and instantly felt an enormous amount of guilt for allowing that to transpire.

At one point later down the road, Daniel admitted to taking the pills from his grandpa's bathroom, and even admitted that this occurred on several different occasions. He said he felt terrible doing it, but he knew his grandpa probably wouldn't notice, and his craving for the drug was simply too strong to resist.

This same story has played out time and time again in the lives of people with this disease all throughout our country. It doesn't always begin with a script written directly to the patient, but rather is commonly introduced as a result of excessive amounts being written to seemingly "safe" people. How many millions of these little killers are sitting in medicine cabinets across the country right now, just waiting to be misused? And more importantly, how do we stop this flood of pills from continuing to pour out into our streets, into our homes, and into our children?

After Daniel passed, I tried to absorb as much information as my brain was capable of handling on the issue, and I was shocked at what I was learning. It almost seemed too obvious to me. Once I got a good handle on the facts, on what was actually happening in our medical system and in our government, I was enraged.

As a reminder, opioids are classified amongst the most dangerous substances permitted to be sold legally with a prescription. They're controlled and scheduled for a reason – because they're dangerous! Not only do they have extreme potential to ignite addiction, both psychological and physical, but they also decrease heart rate, decrease the drive to breathe, and subsequently can cause death. For these reasons, opioids are supposed to be used only in cases where they are absolutely necessary, and even so, with extreme caution.

Regardless of this danger, we saw a 9-fold increase in the dispensing of opioids in Ohio between the years of 1997 and 2010. A 900% increase of a controlled, scheduled medication that had warning labels all over it; how does something of that magnitude just *happen*?

I thought that maybe medical providers in the 90's just didn't know about addiction, but I came to find out that's simply not true. It was actually relatively common knowledge in the medical community that there was a strong potential for abuse, addiction, and dependence with opioids specifically, yet these pills were, and still are, given out so freely. As I've come to understand, although the issue is complex, the answer is actually much more obvious than one might think.

Back in 2000, Ohio ranked #12 in the nation for all-source opioid overdose deaths with 250 total in that year. Come 2014, Ohio climbed the ranks to the #1 spot in opioid overdose deaths with 1,630. If that type of increase wasn't mind-boggling enough, wait until you hear the stats for 2017. Not only did Ohio still top that list, but also the number of deaths rose 260%, claiming 4,293 lives in that year.

In each year from 2014 to 2017, more people have died from opioids in Ohio than any other state in the union. More than California, which includes about 27 million more people than Ohio. More than Texas, which includes about 16 million more people than Ohio. More than Alaska, the biggest geographical state in the United States, and so on...

Ohio has also topped the charts specifically in the number of synthetic opioid deaths during this same time period, 2014 to 2017. Synthetic opioids would include medications like tramadol and fentanyl, among others. In 2013, synthetic opioids claimed 167 lives in Ohio. Just four years later, synthetic opioids claimed 3,523 lives in Ohio. That is an increase in over 3,000 deaths in only four years! The runner-up to Ohio in that year, New York, wasn't even close to the #1 spot, either. They had more than 1,200 fewer deaths compared to Ohio. Clearly, something different is happening in my tiny home state of Ohio, and it is only getting worse. Do you think it's a coincidence that the dispensing rate increased by 900% during the same time at which these death rates were skyrocketing?

That was a rhetorical question.

At the current time, this epidemic is claiming on average five lives every hour in the United States. That is five more human beings just like my son, every single hour, of every single day. By the time you finish reading this chapter, the opioid epidemic has likely claimed another life. As I sat in my living room scrolling through this data, I could feel my heart rate increasing and my blood pressure rising. How had my little boy become just another statistic? Why is no one else seeing this? How do facts like these not spur on more action that we are currently seeing?

How. Is. This. Happening.

Renowned physician David Kessler, former head of the FDA, doesn't hold back when talking about the disastrous impact that these deathly opioid pills have had on our society. Dr. Kessler stated, *"This* (opioids) *has been one of the greatest mistakes of modern medicine... The FDA has a responsibility, the pharmaceutical companies have a responsibility, and physicians have a responsibility. We didn't see these drugs for what they truly are."*

Furthermore, former Ohio Attorney General Mike DeWine, who is now the governor of Ohio, stated that about 75% of current heroin users actually started with prescription opioids. *75%!*

3 in 4 people hooked on heroin started with a prescription medication.

At first, that blew my mind. Originally, I never really linked the two issues. I thought heroin was the fault of Mexican cartels and drug lords, not our own stateside medical providers. I had this preconceived notion that heroin users were so much different than people with prescription pill addictions. I didn't see the correlation at all, but after I stepped back and looked at the numbers, as well as the way in which everything transpired in Daniel's life, it all made sense to me. Daniel started with prescription opioids and then turned to heroin because they're extremely similar chemically. When people can no longer acquire or afford their prescribed opioids, they often turn to illegal sources to achieve the effect in which their body so strongly craves. This is especially the case when the provider who started the medication cuts them off abruptly, and doesn't offer any follow through regarding treatment or transition of care. Not only is heroin usually cheaper, but it can also be bought right off the street, allowing the user to bypass the entire medical system. We have essentially created a system where we are channeling patients straight to illicit, unregulated drugs because we have exposed them to a legal, regulated medication and participated in the development of a brain disease, which we then refuse to treat. More on that later...

In my pursuit of answers, I blindly stumbled upon a graph from the Center for Disease Control (CDC) that changed my perception of this issue, entirely. This same graph, seen below, highlighted the fact that prescription opioids have killed **more** citizens than heroin in every year from 2000 to 2014... thousands of more people, in fact. It was in the

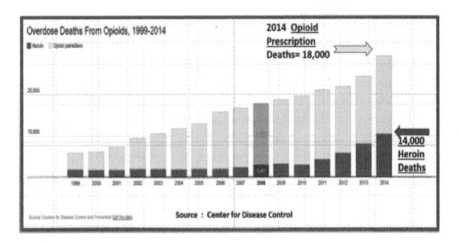

interpretation of this, that I understood this epidemic really was fueled by prescription opioids and not illicit street drugs. After I comprehended this graph, I sat in disbelief. Couldn't we control prescriptions? How are there not laws and regulations to prevent stuff like this from happening? It never even crossed my mind that this aspect of medicine was so excessively unregulated.

Dr. Joe Gay, a prominent doctor of psychology from Ohio, did a lot of the early research regarding the problem of opioid dispensing. Dr. Gay has been treating addiction from a psychological standpoint for several decades and noticed the increase in Opioid Use Disorder around our nation's hot spot, southeastern Ohio. He discovered, through extensive research and data analysis, that there was not only a significant increase in the dispensing of prescription opioids, but also that there was a **significant** correlation between the increase in prescribing of opioids and overdose deaths. This research directly analyzed and confirmed the trends that I had began seeing in the raw numbers of deaths and opioid scripts.

Dr. Gay uncovered a nearly one-to-one correlation between these two factors - a correlation of 0.979, which is essentially unheard of in statistical analysis when it comes to stuff like this. The closer the correlation is to 1, the more confidence one has in linking the two variables. In essence, this shines a spotlight directly on the medical community as the responsible party for the opioid epidemic that we find ourselves to be in.

When Dr. Gay shared his findings with Orman Hall, who at the time was the director of Ohio's Department of Drug and Addiction Services, Mr. Hall reviewed the data and confirmed the analysis to be legitimate. Mr. Hall was shocked. He has been quoted as saying, *"I have never, in all of my years in data analytics, seen a correlation of that magnitude."*

Mr. Hall has also used the following graph in various presentations to illustrate and highlight the intensity at which prescription opioids have contributed to overdose rates in Ohio, compared to other substances. When heroin and crack cocaine were introduced to Ohioans back in the 70's, 80's, and 90's, there was not a staggering elevation in the number of overdoses. Once we began to see the spike in dispensing of opioid

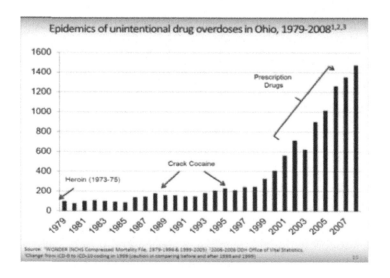

prescriptions, however, the number goes through the roof. These deadly little legal killers are clearly in another category when it comes to their potential to destroy and devastate.

I believe that the issue of overprescribing is rooted and sparked by several different forces which all come together to create the firestorm that we are currently experiencing. Most prominently, the power and influence exerted by pharmaceutical companies, the fact that our medical system is driven by profit and founded on consumerism, lack of quality education, and the absence of adequate regulations on our primary care medical providers. Put all of those variables together, and you're asking for a death sentence.

Before we dive too deep into this, I feel it necessary to have a bit of a disclaimer. Not all docs are an issue. Many physicians are just as appalled as I am by the state of our current opioid epidemic, and they understand the need for reform. Many of them exercise a great deal of restraint when it comes to prescribing these dangerous drugs. Many of them are well versed on the scientific data surrounding these medications, and many of them have a great amount of compassion for their patients. I have met countless medical providers who are truly doing everything they can to combat this problem. I also want to be clear when it comes to my opinion of prescription opioids. Although they are obviously dangerous and have significant drawbacks, I do think that they have their place in medicine. The medical community does need this class of medications as a tool in the treatment of pain, and I acknowledge that. However, the evidence is clear that this should be limited to very specific scenarios involving severe acute pain, some surgeries, cancer victims, and end-of-life comfort care. Going outside of these limits has resulted in the destruction of families and lives all over the United States, mine included. The premature jump to an opioid script for every toothache, bump, bruise, and backache, has got to stop. It is killing our own people at rates that will likely take years to recover from. Dispensing opioids in this fashion, at the magnitude at which we have seen for the past decade, has almost single handedly caused this man-made epidemic.

As I blindly made my way through the treatment journey with Daniel, I became all too familiar with our healthcare system and medical industry. I've always known that the system we have in the United States is broken, but it wasn't until it failed *my* son that I thoroughly understood just how backwards it really was. I learned through various news and journal articles about the concept of medical consumerism, which I now believe to be the driving force behind our inept medical system as a whole. The medical community has fallen into the trap of medical consumerism, much like retail consumerism. Most outpatient offices, including primary care, operate on a for-profit basis. Profit is only achieved when the providers in the office are seeing a certain number of patients per hour. Depending on the operating expenses of the office, this can vary, but on average, primary care providers are required to see a new patient every 10-15 minutes. Hour after hour, day after day, each facility sees a steady stream of patients in order to maintain this profitability and pay their employees. The same is true in the emergency setting, too. If providers aren't meeting their minimum quota for number of patients per shift, they're simply fired because that means they're not bringing enough money into the system.

As medical providers establish relationships with their patients, there is often pressure placed on the provider to keep their patient (the customer) happy. Medical systems and offices typically give their patients customer satisfaction surveys in attempts to hold their providers accountable, and if the provider isn't rated high enough, again, they're fired. If providers aren't making everyone happy and doing it in record speed, the system kicks them to the curb. Why? Money.

Most patients are also paying at least something out of pocket up front to see their doctor as well, and this further fuels the patient's expectations that their doc owes them something in return. With the increasing amount of medical information and data available to the general public online, it is now common practice for patients to approach their providers with preconceived opinions about what treatment they want and when they want it. To the patient, the doctor's office is now looked at as a retail store that is simply providing a service; and to the medical provider, the doctor's office is now looked at as a way to simply rack in the money. The original goal of medicine was simply to keep people healthy and treat disease, but as our society grew and developed, it became all about the money. In my opinion, this setup is hardly conducive to our health, our well-being, or our safety.

Let's look at antibiotics as an example. The CDC states that at least 30% of all antibiotics prescribed aren't even warranted. That's about 47 million prescriptions written each year that aren't necessary, putting patients at risk for side effects, secondary infections, and allergic reactions, all for no reason. Furthermore, it is fairly easy to become resistant, or immune, to antibiotics with repeated exposure, which then results in them not being effective with later use. This excessive exposure to antibiotics is a harmful practice, and most practitioners are well aware of this. So why do they still do it? It's a two-fold answer. The patient (customer) feels sick, thinks they need an antibiotic to fight the infection, and they simply go to their doc expecting to get one. Again, since the patient commonly pays up front, they want to leave with something tangible. On the other side of the fence, providers feel pressured to keep their patients happy so they don't get terminated, and feel pressured to keep the cash flow coming in. Rarely will you hear a provider say, *"...you're just experiencing a common cold so just run down to the pharmacy and pick up some over-the-counter cold medicine."* In reality, the doctor will usually send the patient home with a script for a needless antibiotic and tell the patient, *"If you don't feel better in 5 to 7 days, call the office and come see me again."* This is driven by a need to maintain positive ratings from their patients as well as a drive to maintain their for-profit business.

This same scenario plays out over and over with pain medication. The patient complains about their pain with the expectation that the doc can, and will, give them a pill to fix their ailment in exchange for payment. All too often, that's exactly how it transpires, too. The prescriber simply sends in a prescription for opioid painkillers, gets their cash, and calls it a day. The pain is resolved, the patient is satisfied, and profits go up. The goal commonly becomes to simply keep the patient satisfied so they come back time and time again, no matter the risk.

To track the trends of overzealous prescribing and acquisition of controlled substances, the state of Ohio did successfully develop a prescription drug-monitoring program in 2006 call OARRS, which is an acronym for Ohio Automated Rx Reporting System. This system

153

requires every pharmacist in the state to document all controlled prescriptions into a centralized state database. This system was implemented to monitor controlled substances, such as opioids, and specifically aimed to reduce the practice of "doctor shopping," which I have witnessed first hand many times. Doctor shopping commonly

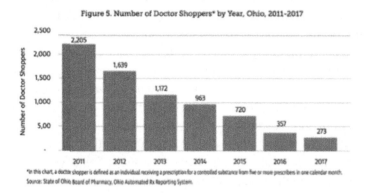

Figure 5. Number of Doctor Shoppers* by Year, Ohio, 2011-2017

*In this chart, a doctor shopper is defined as an individual receiving a prescription for a controlled substance from five or more prescribers in one calendar month.
Source: State of Ohio Board of Pharmacy, Ohio Automated Rx Reporting System.

occurs when a patient develops an opioid addiction and desires to get more pills than what their doctor is willing to hand out. They simply go to another doctor, get another script, and repeat the process until their cravings are tamed. When this happens, it's common that their tolerance to opioids will increase, and thus the patient needs higher and higher doses just to maintain. The OARRS system has done a pretty good job at putting this aspect of the fire out, as the number of "doctor shoppers" decreased from 2,205 in 2010 to 273 in 2017.

All prescribers in Ohio are supposed to check the OARRS database before writing a prescription for a controlled substance of any kind, whether it is Adderall or Oxycontin, to assure their patients aren't displaying signs of diversion or dependence on the given substance. Compliance with this program has been positive, as Ohio was ranked by the American Medical Association as the top state in the country for the most queries to a prescription drug-monitoring program (PDMP). This could be a sign that providers are become more aware of the addiction issue, however, I think it's more likely an indicator that the number of controlled scripts written in the state is astronomical. If they're required to check OARRS before writing each and every controlled script, and the number of "checks" is the highest in the country, it's easy to do the math there.

The OARRS mission statement also states that it should be used to monitor the opioid dispensing habits of prescribers, too. However, the program very rarely, if ever, utilizes this feature and typically only does so in the event that a particular clinician is being investigated or is involved in a medical malpractice case. There is no routine monitoring of medical providers that prescribe controlled substances, largely a result of a few specific roadblocks put in place by the medical community itself.

After Daniel's passing, I was asked to be a member of the Montgomery County Community Overdose Action Team (COAT), and I was assigned to the Prescription Opioid Team. On this same team was an investigator for the Ohio State Medical Board. I asked this guy, *"How do we get information on specific cases of docs who overprescribe opioids within our state or county?"* He replied, *"Scott, unfortunately we have to wait for someone to make a formal complaint before we can investigate a prescriber. We don't just do it proactively."* I stared at him as if he were speaking a foreign language. Our own medical board investigators have access to the OARRS database, which could feed them all of the information they need to address providers who are out of line, yet they choose to be "complaint driven." This specific gap in oversight seems like a no-brainer area for legislators to step in and force their hand, but as you'll discover in the following chapter, our government won't force much of anything on the medical community.

Medical providers hate being told what to do, and in a sense, I completely understand that. They fight for their right to exercise clinical judgment, in other words, their ability to tailor treatment to the individual without restraint. This is the main reason why there is so little red tape when it comes to prescribing medications. The medical community is trusted to make the right and safest decision, so theoretically, there is no need for legal barriers. Makes sense in concept, but in practice, not so much.

Let's look at clinical judgment with an analogy. In order for a police officer to issue a traffic ticket for speeding, there must be a set speed limit. If there is no speed limit, then the officer is wasting his/her time looking for people who violate the law. With prescription opioid dispensing, there is no set limit! A licensed clinician is permitted to use his or her own clinical judgment for deciding the dosage, how many pills to dispense, and for how long! If they feel it is appropriate for a patient to have excessive amounts of opioids for excessive amounts of time, all they have to do is write the script. That's it. How does this make any sense?

It can be difficult, however, to make blanket statements regarding regulations on opioid prescribing since there are so many different opioids, each with a different potency and dosing schedule. To help address this issue, we can use a tool called the MED calculator, which can be found on the OARRS website. Because each opioid has a

different potency and formulation, it would be arbitrary to set a limit for the number of pills or a given milligram number, so morphine was chosen to be the standard, and from there, a calculation was created to convert the dose of every other opioid to what this would equate to if it were morphine. The result is measured in MED, or morphine-equivalent dose. For reference, I utilized this calculator and chose hydrocodone (active ingredient in Vicodin) at 5mg each. The guidelines for prescribing opioids at the time of Daniel's death suggested an upper limit of about 80 MED to give prescribers a reference as to where to draw the line. With this standard, you could prescribe sixteen hydrocodone 5mg tablets *per day*, or 480 pills per month, before the guidelines even suggest that you should slow down. Wow. No wonder we have an issue.

To this day, there has yet to be a hard limit set on prescription opioid dispensing. The argument remains that there are some extreme cases that may require higher doses, and again, I agree with that. Inpatient hospital patients, major operations, cancer pain, end of life care, and emergency room traumas are all reasonable scenarios where high dose opioids are sometimes more than necessary. I don't think anyone really argues that. It is my position, however, that excessive dosing is never appropriate in the primary care setting, specifically. I strongly believe that there must be limits set in primary care, dentistry, and even some outpatient surgeries, of which are actually mandatory and not mere suggestions, but to-date, this has not happened.

According to Alan Mozes of HealthDay News, 99% of doctors prescribe more than the federally *recommended* three-day dosage limit, and nearly 25% of those docs exceed that by a long shot, giving out 30-day scripts at a time on a regular basis. Taking opioids for thirty consecutive days has been shown to be sufficient to induce the brain changes that we have seen in the disease of addiction. 1 in 4 physicians are prescribing at rates that can, and often do, cause a medical brain disease! If that doesn't scream for reform, I don't know what does.

The 2018 annual OARRS report revealed that from 2010 to 2018, the number of opioid pills per prescription went down by a whopping 1 pill. I wish I were kidding, but that is a fact. From 2010 to 2018, the average opioid prescription remained right around 65 pills. This is a shocking number of addictive drugs, and they're so easily being dispensed to the public. No wonder medicine cabinets all over the country all stocked full. The dosing, which is what matters most, only minimally decreased as well. It dropped by a minuscule 14 morphine milligram equivalents, a far cry from how we used to dose these medications back before the epidemic began.

Table #1 - Opioids* Dispensed to Ohio Patients, by Year				
Year	No. of Prescribers	No. of Patients	Average Quantity per Prescription	Average Daily MED per Prescription
2010	55,895	2,733,066	64.37	53.35
2011	66,554	2,761,707	64.55	48.58
2012	66,649	3,053,090	65.38	47.89
2013	65,452	2,686,169	65.20	46.66
2014	63,178	2,650,078	64.15	45.34
2015	57,673	2,615,768	64.59	44.92
2016	56,287	2,359,175	65.48	44.43
2017	55,107	1,998,846	66.48	43.23
2018	56,221	1,850,561	63.43	39.23

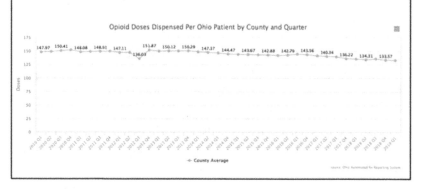

Opioid Doses Dispensed Per Ohio Patient by County and Quarter

Medical providers continue to prescribe at rates that are astronomical. The governing bodies in the medical field and within our state legislature have been quick to tout data which suggests that we are trending in the right direction, as opioid dispensing has recently began trending downwards, albeit to a very mild degree. We are not even close to being at pre-epidemic numbers. We are still prescribing at nearly three times the rate at which we saw before this whole nightmare began. I would strongly caution the powers at work to reserve their worshipping of the medical community until we are back to reasonable figures, as this will likely do nothing but hinder progress.

One of the medical advisors to the National Safety Council, Dr. Donald Teater, stated, *"Opioids do not kill pain. They kill people. Doctors are well intentioned and want to help their patients, but these findings* (referring to the research which found 99% of docs are exceeding recommended opioid guidelines) *are further proof that we need more education and training if we want to treat pain most effectively."*

During the past couple of years, the medical community has publicly stated that they feel as though they already have the knowledge they need to educate their own, and would prefer to avoid having their hand forced to implement better education. They promised to make sure that prescribers understood the power that opioids have, and assured that providers would know how to safely prescribe them. In theory, that is an ideal situation, but clearly we haven't seen that be effective. It is always preferred to fix issues without unnecessary regulations if possible, but we are well past that now. With the rate at which people are dying, we cannot afford to have blind trust for this to happen and simply expect that to be sufficient. Human life should not be held in the hands of unfounded promises.

In 2012, Arron Haslem, one of the senior staff members to the former Ohio AG, became the lead prosecutor in a case that went after the physicians in Ohio who were operating opioid pill mills. He recognized that there was a significant problem with overprescribing opioids, even back in 2012 when it wasn't getting much attention. Mr. Haslem's words were chilling back then, and they are even more disturbing now, in 2019. He said in a public message:

"When we look at opioid prescribers in Ohio, there are three groups of doctors to consider. The first group is comprised of only 4-5%. They are specialists and do it right. They take care of their patients and know when to treat with opioids, usually as a last resort. They prescribe only the amount needed and slowly increase the dosage only if necessary. The second group consists of 2-3% and they essentially say, 'I have a license to make money selling these little pills and I don't care if I harm a patient or not.' Again, that's only 2-3%, but this is who operates the so-called pill mills. The group that scares me the most is the last group, which is comprised of 90% of the doctors practicing medicine in our state. These practitioners have the ability to prescribe, but they lack education about opioids and the harm they can do. Unfortunately, the only education this group receives is from the pharmaceutical reps pandering their products and meandering through their offices."

The 90% of prescribers who are undereducated when it comes to opioids are among the top reasons why Daniel, and so many others, ended up six feet under. Daniel wasn't going to pill mills or pain management clinics. He was simply going to an ordinary primary care doc to get his fix. Daniel didn't need another source; he had a more than sufficient flow of pills straight from the trusted family doc.

We have raised a generation to believe that if a doctor prescribes a medication, it must be safe. That's what we've let the medical industry do to our young people - everyone that went through their teenage years during the years 2000 to 2016. We trusted the medical industry to do what was right, to look out for our best interest, and to keep us healthy - what a mistake that has proven to be.

A dose of reality:

Back in 2013, we had another round of opioid dispensing incompetence with Daniel. At the time, Daniel had been through two residential rehab efforts and was doing ok. A minor physical problem came up, which would require him to have a routine surgery and an overnight hospital stay.

I was very concerned. Not necessarily about the procedure, or even what caused it, but for the potential of another relapse if he were to be administered opioids.

I talked to the physician about this the day of the surgery and informed him about Daniel's opioid history. *"Please do not give him opioids,"* I pleaded. *"Or, at the very least, use them minimally."* He told me that he understood and promised me to be conservative in his dosing, if they were even needed in the first place.

Once the surgery was over and Daniel was settled into his hospital room for the night, we went up to visit. We walked in and saw Daniel awake and doing well. A nurse was injecting a medication into his IV as we walked in the door, and he greeted us with a smile. The dry-erase board next to his bed listed the following information: patient name, today's date, doctor's name, nurse's name, etc. In the medication section of the board, it read, *"Dilaudid every 4 hours."* Dilaudid is a very strong IV-administered opioid. I was stunned and fear immediately swept across me like a raging river.

Daniel was discharged 24 hours later, after getting legal opioid injections every 4 hours, and was still sent home with a rather large supply of opioid pills, just in case the pain returned. This was a huge medical misstep, which unfortunately happens all the time. Not only was this someone that has a severe history of opioid dependence and strong family history of addiction, but he also wasn't even complaining of pain! Nevertheless, he was given more and more without even asking.

My heart sunk. I knew this was going to reignite Daniel's addiction, and within days, it did just that. Daniel struggled for much of the next year. It nearly cost him his life, all triggered by a legal prescription pad in the hands of a provider who didn't give a shit - a provider who didn't take the time to understand the true power behind their pen.

Once the supply of prescription opioids ran out, Daniel simply made an appointment with his primary care provider and the refills kept coming - for months at a time, in fact.

As my own father has gotten into the later stages of his life, I have also witnessed multiple similar scenarios involving the reckless dispensing of pain medications with him as well. Back in 2016, he fell and cut his arm, which resulted in an infected wound so we took him to the hospital to have it assessed and treated. As I sat there in his hospital room, I got another dose of reality. The nurse entered the room and the dialog between the nurse and my dad went something like this:

Nurse: *"How is your pain Mr. Weidle?"*

Dad: *"It's okay."*

Nurse: *"On a scale of 1 to 10, where is it?"*

Dad: No response.

Nurse: *"How about a 4, does that sound right?"*

Dad: *"Okay."*

The nurse walks out of his room and returns with a syringe fully loaded with morphine, a very high strength opioid, and administers it, taking nearly two minutes to fully empty the syringe. She then proceeds to open a pill pack of Ativan, another addictive, controlled substance for anxiety, and tells my dad he can take those between the morphine injections, as needed.

I was witnessing with my own eyes the very thing I had been fighting so hard to stop - the overprescribing of opioids and addictive medications! My dad didn't need all this pain medication. He clearly indicated that his pain level was "okay." The nurse *had* to get an answer based on the pain scale of 1 to 10 so that she could document a certain level to justify the pain med because the bureaucrats up above force her to do so, even when it's not always clinically possible. So, instead of relying on him to tell her, she did it for him. This all goes back to the practice of using a government-approved pain survey to "keep patients happy," and keep insurance invoices churning. Again, the for-profit medical system is alive and well, influencing both medical decision-making and the resulting outcomes.

This was actually a mild story in comparison to what would happen several months later. My dad called and asked us to take him to the hospital because his back was hurting. He had just gotten a new mattress the day before, so I knew this was likely the source of the pain and wasn't overly concerned. However, he does have numerous heart-related health concerns and he typically isn't one to complain, so when he says, *"We're going!,"* we go. Carrie picked him up and took him to the ER where he was then transferred to an inpatient bed for observation. They wanted to keep him on a heart monitor to make sure his mid-back pain wasn't an atypical heart attack. The nurse comes into the room with pain medication for him and it's a syringe loaded with fentanyl - the strongest opioid in existence, originally only utilized for major traumas, significant surgeries, and cancer pain! Carrie looked at the nurse and said, *"Umm, you do realize this man is here for observation because he has a backache from sleeping on a new mattress, don't you?"* The nurse nervously replied, *"Well we'd like to keep him as comfortable as possible."*

I was livid. We had reached a point where we weren't just jumping to Vicodin for a toothache; we were now jumping to fentanyl for a stiff back! It seemed like everywhere we turned, we were running into providers that handed this stuff out like candy. I had spent so much of my life respecting physicians for their intelligence and selflessness, only to have that challenged by the repeated disregard I saw when it came to the care of my own loved ones.

I discovered a news article a couple years back in *Medpage Today* that detailed the findings of a paper published by professors of economics at Princeton University. It determined that physicians who studied at lower-tier medical schools prescribed nearly three times as many opioids per year compared to physicians who studied at top-tier universities. The researchers used the *U.S. News and World Report* to set their parameters for school rankings, and used prescribing data from 2006 to 2014. These findings were consistent even when you took into account the variations of different practice specialties. They were also able to conclude that general practitioners accounted for about 50% of all opioid scripts written during the study period. That figure makes me cringe. In no way, shape, or form, should that be accurate, but it is. Opioids must be restricted to settings where they are absolutely necessary, and I can think of little-to-no scenarios where this is reasonable in the primary care setting.

If we ever desire to truly reach the core of the epidemic that is claiming the lives of about 130 Americans every single day, we must attack this at the source. Like I have said in the past, this starts with education. Not only do we need to educate ourselves as a general public, but we also must hold our medical community accountable to assure that the people with whom we trust our health are thoroughly and adequately educated.

Although education starts in the schools, medical providers are continuously learning and educating themselves on the constantly evolving field of medicine. It seems as though new medications are coming out at a weekly rate, and in order to keep up, providers need to be continually educated on what's new. Somehow, much of this ongoing education is provided and spoon-fed to prescribers by the pharmaceutical companies that make and sell the medications. Since we live in a consumerism-driven and for-profit world, why wouldn't we trust these drug companies to give us reliable and unbiased information? What could possibly go wrong?

In the early 90's, we began to see pharmaceutical sales reps, who act as spokespeople for the various drug companies, flood medical offices to educate providers on the medications in which they sold in an effort to increase the number of scripts written, and therefore the amount of money generated. Most of these sales reps have next to no formal medical education, but rather, blindly trust the drug companies in which they work for to provide them with thorough and reliable information about the medications. After a few short trainings, they are trusted to pass this information on to prescribers, and prescribers readily accept this information as unbiased fact, just like it were coming straight from their medical school textbooks. Furthermore, if you lined up all of these sales reps in a room, it would be unavoidable to see a few trends - don't forget that we're taking about the art of sales and the end goal is to make money. The unspoken first requirements for the job are beauty and charm. I would venture to bet that most male docs are more likely to listen to the marketing pitch for a drug if the rep is a blonde bombshell, and therefore would be more likely to prescribe the medication and generate revenue for the pharmaceutical company that makes it. This isn't always the case, but we all know it happens.

The pharmaceutical companies that produce most of the prescription medications in the United States are commonly referred to as "Big Pharma." These are multi-billion dollar per year companies. The producer of OxyContin, a potent opioid, made over 2 billion dollars on this medication alone over the course of only one year! That kind of money has power that is inconceivable to most of us. Knowing this allows us to see the extent to which these companies can go to dictate and control our system.

As more and more pharmaceutical sales reps disseminated information to physicians about opioids, much of which was misleading and inaccurate, we saw the direct rise in prescribing rates. Docs began to dose opioids until the patient's pain was completely gone, a practice that hadn't been common practice prior to that. It was also in this same time period that physicians began dispensing opioids for long-term chronic pain as well, another change in the methodology of how medicine was being practiced. Big Pharma told providers that opioids with extended-release formulations weren't addictive, and therefore could be dosed long-term, without an inherent increased risk of addiction. For the first time, the medical community had been given the green light to consider opioids for chronic pain management. Prescribers all across the nation assumed this information to be accurate, and almost overnight, we were off to the races. According to Bill Whitaker, correspondent for *60 minutes*, Purdue Pharma has since admitted in federal court (back in 2007) that it had misled doctors and consumers about just how addictive OxyContin can be.

"That was a costly mistake," according to Dr. Kessler, former head of the FDA. A mistake that Big Pharma capitalized on to increase their bottom lines, by billions of dollars. Coincidence? I doubt it.

The state of Ohio has openly admitted that our safety was put at risk because of the inappropriate promotion of opioids for long-term use, yet little to nothing has been done about it. Our safety is still at risk. The only change we're seeing is in a national movement for state and local governments to go after Big Pharma, in hopes that this will push the drug companies to help solve and fix the destruction caused by their greed. While doing this does in fact help us address the results of the crisis, it does nothing to address the men and women behind the prescription pads. Nothing will change if we don't cut it off at the origin, and our government has the power to do this. Yet, here we are, over a decade into this thing, and not a damn thing has changed.

Attorney Mike Moore, the man who took down the major tobacco companies, was hired by current Ohio Governor Mike DeWine to take on Big Pharma. Mike Moore's battle against Big Tobacco resulted in the major tobacco companies paying out 250 billion dollars to help mitigate the damages they caused. If the same plays out for the role in which Big Pharma played in the opioid crisis, we could potentially see billions of dollars poured into treatment for the disease of addiction, a heavily underfunded effort. However, it is my strong belief that much of this money should be geared towards the regulatory efforts within our government to take back control of our policies and safety. Prevention must not be forgotten or we will forever be treating a preventable disease.

In a *60 minutes* special on the opioid crisis, which aired in June 2019, Mike Moore stated, *"Ohio is losing 4-5 billion dollars per year to the opioid epidemic, and 5-6 thousand people per year to overdose deaths. So when a jury hears the evidence in this case, they're not going to award just a couple hundred million dollars, it may be a hundred billion dollars, and whoever amongst these companies think they can stand up against that... good luck."*

Also to blame, according to the same *60 minutes* segment, are the distributors and pharmacies. Since these medications are _controlled_ substances, they must be _controlled_ from the time they are manufactured until the time they are in the patient's hand. As a result of the Controlled Substance Act, the data is very thorough in exactly where these pills are made, distributed, and sold. It was discovered, according to one of the lead attorneys working with Mike Moore, that the drug companies and distributors were all well aware of how extreme this issue had become. In fact, it was the drug companies' own data that was utilized to draw these conclusions. For example, it was discovered through DEA investigating that a single pharmacy within a small town in West Virginia comprised of only 400 people, received **nine million** opioid pills in the span of only two years! There is no way in hell anyone can convince me that Big Pharma wasn't aware of this and didn't consciously choose to turn a blind eye.

I have seen this play out in the life of my own father as well. One day back in the early-mid 2000's, my dad went to the local pharmacy to pick up a prescription that his doctor had called in for him. He brought it back to our office, opened it up, and called me into his office. He said, *"Scott, I don't know what this medication is for."* It was just a bit smaller than a mason jar, and it was full of opioids! I was shocked. My father and my brother both share the same first and last name, and as it turns out, my father had picked up my brother's prescription by mistake. Is there any wonder why my brother battled a drug addiction? All the pharmacy had to do was *control* the release of a *controlled* substance to assure that it was going to the right patient, with the correct date of birth, yet they failed to do this simple task. It was that easy to legally obtain controlled meds in my very own hometown, one of the worst hit in the nation.

I remember telling Daniel about what had happened. I still hadn't linked prescription opioids to heroin use at the time. Again, I thought they were completely different issues. Daniel informed me that he wasn't surprised at all, and that he knew several people personally that had tapped into this type of pill source to suffice their addiction. I didn't know at the time that he was among those on that list. It is stories such as this that reveal just how polluted and awash our society has become, not only in addictive opioid pills, but in loopholes, corruption, and greed.

In the summer of 2017, the Ohio AG filed a lawsuit against five of the major pharmaceutical manufacturers. This is a step in the right direction, but no action has been taken on the case as of yet. The 103-page legal complaint can be summarized with this statement: pharmaceutical companies fraudulently promoted opioids as being safe for the treatment of chronic pain and are at least partly responsible for the opioid crisis that has ravished our state.

The CDC, the U.S. Surgeon General, and many others, support Ohio's position that opioids are not safe for long-term chronic pain. This new way to utilize prescribed opioids has clearly triggered a resurgence of Ohio's heroin epidemic and resulted is catastrophic damage throughout every county in our state. The legal complaint filed against the major pharmaceutical companies is accessible to the public, and I encourage everyone to read through this as it reveals allegations that are astounding to me. The state of Ohio clearly and thoroughly lays out the exact ways in which Big Pharma manipulated the medical community in order to make insane amounts of money. I knew it was bad, but while reading this, my jaw nearly hit the floor.

There are a handful of quotes in this document that are extremely powerful and I would like to take a second to share these with you in the bullets below. They expose the true corruption and malice within Big Pharma, which has driven our medical providers to practice medicine in a way that doesn't increase the well-being of our community, but rather increases the bank accounts of Big Pharma.

- "In 2012, the total cost (of unintentional drug overdose) to the state averaged *$5.4 million per day* in medical and work loss expenses."
- "Each Defendant spent, and continues to spend, millions of dollars on promotional activities and materials that falsely deny or trivialize the risks of opioids while overstating the benefits of using them for chronic pain."
- "Defendants also worked through third parties they controlled by: (a) funding, assisting, encouraging, and directing doctors, known as 'key opinion leaders' (KOLs) and (b) funding, assisting, directing, and encouraging seemingly neutral and credible professional societies and patient advocacy groups (Front Groups). Defendants then worked together with those KOLs and Front Groups to taint the sources that doctors and patients relied on for ostensible 'neutral' guidance, such as treatment guidelines, CME programs, medical conferences and seminars, and scientific articles."
- "...Defendants' deceptive marketing campaigns deprived Ohio patients and their doctors of the ability to make informed medical decisions and, instead, caused important, sometimes life-or-death decisions to be made based not on science, but on hype."
- "Defendants spent more than $14 million on medical journal advertising of opioids in 2011, nearly triple what they spent in 2001.
- "One ad described a '54-year old writer with osteoarthritis of the hands' and implied that OxyContin would help the writer work more effectively. Endo and Purdue agreed in late 2015 and 2016 to halt these misleading representations in New York, but they may continue to disseminate them in Ohio."
- Pharmaceutical companies paid various doctors to speak at programs where… "these speakers give the false impression that they are providing unbiased and medically accurate presentations when they are, in fact, presenting a script prepared by Defendants."
- "APF (American Pain Foundation) received about 2.3 million from industry sources out of a total income of about 2.85 million in 2019; it's budget for 2010 projected receipts of roughly $2.9 million from drug companies, out of a total

income of about $3.5 million.... APF held itself out as an independent patient advocacy organization.... Within days of being targeted by Senate investigation, APF's board voted to dissolve the organization due to irreparable economic circumstances."

- "Second, Defendants falsely instructed doctors and patients that the signs of addiction are actually signs of undertreated pain and should be treated by prescribing more opioids."

Not only has the epidemic of overprescribing, largely secondary to the impact of Big Pharma, cost our state millions of dollars and thousands of lives, the ramifications will continue to be felt for many more years to come. Ohio University published a study in 2019, which revealed that cumulatively, between 2009 and 2018, over **one million years of life were lost** at the hands of overdose deaths in the state of Ohio alone. Think about just how much life we are now missing out on because we let a preventable, man-made epidemic run wild while we sat on our asses and did nothing. Not only could these lives have contributed to our society with their talents and resources, but more importantly, also with the happiness and love they would have brought to the many families whom loved them. Families like mine.

Certainly someone, somewhere, has done something. In actuality, there has been a whole lot of talk, but very little to show for it. The medical industry is immune to reform, resistant to change, and refuses to come down from their pedestal to initiate new policies. They use their money to influence control over our state government and most of our legislators just let it happen. I wish this weren't the case, but I've been in the trenches with this stuff for the past 10 years, and I'm confident in saying that this is actually our reality.

These pills have power, they generate massive amounts of money, they destroy lives, break up families, and put our children in caskets. Is it any wonder that opioid overdose is one of the leading causes of death in America today?

At times, I become extremely discouraged that anything in our system will ever change. It almost seems impossible to facilitate progress when you're going up against companies that make billions of dollars from a single drug, medical associations that have what seems like unlimited funds to achieve their agenda, and against legislators who operate at the mercy of these two giants.

After Daniel passed away, I spent much of my time at the Ohio Statehouse in Columbus. I honestly had no idea what I was getting myself into, but I knew that reform was absolutely necessary if we were going to get anywhere. I doubted that any of the white collar politicians up in Columbus really understood just how devastating the opioid crisis had been in small rural villages like Germantown, and I thought Daniel's story was powerful enough to spark change. Our leadership needed to know just how dangerous these pills were, and how hard it had been for us to find him treatment. I wanted these politicians to simply hear me out. I will share this story in much greater detail in Chapter 13, but what I learned throughout this experience was infuriating. I discovered, with a few exceptions, that politicians are even more corrupt than I had imagined. Generally speaking, most of them don't usually have the greatest reputations in the first place, but what I learned after months of rubbing shoulders with the big shots in office, would make even the most optimistic person skeptic. Never in my wildest dreams did I think it would be so difficult to get our "for the people" system, to actually work for the people. We essentially have a deadly killer on the loose, and our leaders are walking around like their hands are tied.

I came to understand that the medical industry has an enormous lobbyist force inside the capitol building, and thus they largely determine what laws get passed, and which ones don't. With their constant flow of political campaign contributions, the medical community can easily keep necessary and critical reform from happening. Simply put, if it causes an inconvenience to medical providers, the legislation is squashed before it even stands a chance. Medical associations have more than enough power and influence to stop any and all reforms in their industry, and that is exactly what is happening. They have control over local, state, and federal politicians, and it doesn't appear likely that substantial change will happen anytime soon as long as politicians continue to be used as puppets and pawns. I went into the Statehouse wanting to get common-sense legislation passed to reduce the number of opioids scripts in the primary care setting, yet I left with an ever-growing skepticism of the entire world that we live in.

In 2010, the Ohio Department of Alcohol & Drug Addiction Services, alongside our elected officials, promoted a Public Service Message (PSM) called *Little Pill, Big Problem, Ohio's Opiate Story*. This PSM stated that opioid dispensing had increased over a 13-year span, from an average of 7 opioid pills per prescription to 67 pills **per prescription** for every man woman and child in our state. It asked, *"What are we doing to solve the problem?,"* and stated, *"The Cavalry*

has arrived!," referring to the Ohio governor at the time, John Kasich, and his crew. The viewer is left to believe that war had been declared against Ohio's opioid epidemic. Governor Kasich went on to develop a specialized cabinet to address this issue, however rates continued to skyrocket over his tenure. The end of the story still needs to be written, but as you will continue to learn throughout this book, the government has done more to fail their constituents than to save them.

Not to my surprise, *The Cavalry* has done very little to enact change with Ohio's opiate story. They failed to develop mandatory restrictions for the overzealous prescribing crisis in our state, and as a result, people continue to die at astounding rates.

It is a simple fact that no industry wants more regulations. I get that. I don't want them in my gravel industry, and the medical community certainly doesn't want them in theirs. But folks, this is entirely different. Prescription opioids have been killing innocent people every single day for years, and the medical community has remained steadfast in their stubborn view to keep the field unregulated. The root cause of this epidemic, which has killed more people than all of the wars in our country over the past 50 years combined, has been left untouched. If there were ever a time for regulations to be mandatory, it is now.

The leadership in the state of Ohio, from the executive branch to the legislative branch, has pumped the brakes on every reform effort that involved mandatory restrictions, of which could have allowed us to return to a more reasonable pre-epidemic level of prescribing opioids. As you will come to learn through my experience in Columbus, our state leadership is more interested in keeping their political power and money streams, than protecting our citizenry. They're more focused on campaigns and image than effective change. It pains me to admit that, but I witnessed this corruption firsthand over and over, and very few people seem hopeful that this will ever change.

Learning the truth about our government and healthcare system infuriates me to no end. In my mind, it is completely illogical to address this issue from any other angle than opioid prescribing in the primary care setting. Instead, legislators often jump at chances to sponsor bills that offered tougher criminal penalties on people struggling with addiction, and divert attention to the southern border as a means to place blame elsewhere. Legislators also jump at the chance to sponsor bills that improve the treatment of addiction after it has already developed, while still avoiding the chance to address the source. It's like they're striving to check the campaign box of addressing the opioid crisis with involvement like this, when that's only putting a Band-Aid on the end of a fire hose. If you have the opportunity to turn off the source of the water completely, why wouldn't you!? Don't get me wrong, we need better access to treatment without a doubt, but that can't be the sole focus of our approach.

Well-meaning campaigns - whether it was Ohio's Little Pill Big Problem, Nancy Reagan's "Just Say No," or Nixon's "War On Drugs" approach - often did more harm than good. Campaigns don't achieve much of anything if they don't result in real, tangible change in policies and legislation. The "Just Say No" slang suggested this disease was a simple choice, as easy as 1-2-3, further fueling the stigma that we have yet to overcome as a society. However, the lack of success we saw with this message actually reinforces the fact that addiction is truly a disease. The victim is powerless over all-sounding logic and reason, and simply doesn't see "no" as an option. It's naive, uninformed, and harmful.

More recently, instead of focusing attention on the real culprits, everyone wants to point blame at the Mexican cartels and border security, which in my opinion, is backwards. The cartels simply took advantage of the problem we had already created within our very own healthcare system, and only after the fact, hopped on the opportunity to make millions supplying illicit opioids to a population already hooked on legal ones.

Real progress has been lost because individuals in power, both politically and medically, lacked the ability to understand the complexity of the issues at hand - both addiction and the prescription opioid crisis. We continue to see an absence of meaningful action because money buys political influence, and political influence directly impacts the way in which the medical community is allowed to operate. It's all about the money now, and it has always been all about the money. This applies to medical consumerism. It applies to education. It applies to legislative reform. It applies to the development and distribution of medications. It's all driven by money. I remember Daniel telling me back in 2015, *"...You know it's all about the money, don't you, Dad?"*

You were right, son.

It's all staggering, mind-blowing madness.

Chapter 11

The Forgotten Oath

The Hippocratic Oath

I swear to fulfill, to the best of my ability and judgment, this covenant:
I will respect the hard-won scientific gains of those physicians in whose steps I walk,
and gladly share such knowledge as is mine with those who are to follow.
*I will apply, **for the benefit of the sick**, all measures [that] are required, avoiding those*
twin traps of overtreatment and therapeutic nihilism.
I will remember that there is an art to medicine, as well as a science, and that
warmth, sympathy, and understanding may outweigh the surgeon's knife or the
chemist's drug.
I will not be ashamed to say "I know not," nor will I fail to call in my colleagues when
the skills of another are needed for a patient's recovery.
I will respect the privacy of my patients, for their problems are not disclosed to me that
the world may know. Most especially must I tread with care in matters of life and
*death. **If it is given me to save a life, all thanks. But it may also be within my power to***
take a life; this awesome responsibility must be faced with great humbleness and
awareness of my own frailty.
Above all, I must not play at God.
I will remember that I do not treat a fever chart, a cancerous growth, but a sick human
being, whose illness may affect the person's family and economic stability. My
responsibility includes these related problems, if I am to care adequately for the sick.
*I will prevent disease whenever I can, **for prevention is preferable to cure.***
I will remember that I remain a member of society, with special obligations to all my
fellow human beings, those sound of mind and body as well as the infirm.
If I do not violate this oath, may I enjoy life and art, respected while I live and
remembered with affection thereafter. May I always act so as to preserve the finest
traditions of my calling and may I long experience the joy of healing those who seek my
help.
- Modernized by Louis Lasagna, 1964

On the day each medical practitioner dawns their long white coat for the first time, they recite the Hippocratic oath before their families, friends, and educators. This has long become a token of promise to the communities in which they serve, that they will practice medicine to the best of their abilities for the betterment of the sick, as opposed to themselves. It acts as a public acknowledgement to the power in which they are bestowed with, and a formal decree that this power will not be taken lightly. One of my proudest moments as a father was watching my son, Wes, stand up to recite this same oath back in 2017 when he graduated from physician assistant school. I have all the trust in the

world that he is, and will continue to, abide by these words because that is just the type of person he is. I raised him under my roof for over 18 years, I have seen him at his best and at his worst, and so I have full confidence in saying that he was made for the field of medicine.

However, I couldn't help but be confused when I had the realization that so many of the providers who played various roles in Daniel's treatment journey took this same oath, yet went on to practice medicine in such selfish and neglectful ways. It seemed like we met more careless and money-hungry physicians than ones who genuinely gave a shit, and it aggravated the hell out of me. Why did it seem like it was easier to find a needle in a haystack than a quality mental health professional? Heck, at times, I didn't even care about the quality, I just wanted to find someone who was willing to simply give us the time of day. Thinking back on the places we had been, and the people we had met, I can only think of two or three providers that I would trust with my son's life if I had another shot at this. I understand that nearly every medical practitioner has sacrificed years of their time, blood, sweat, tears, and a lot of money into learning the art of medicine, but this doesn't guarantee that all of them are in it for the right reasons. My intention is not to harp on the many selfless individuals that go above and beyond to practice quality healthcare, but when you're on the receiving end of an underserved, stigmatized specialty, it's only natural to become a little frustrated. I wish I could say that I was just unlucky in the providers that we came across, but that is simply not the case. Clinic after clinic, physician after physician, rehab after rehab, it was the same story nearly everywhere we turned - physicians that were either driven by greed or who lacked the basic knowledge of addiction medicine. In either case, there was a common denominator that I only came to understand after the fact. There was a pervasive discrimination in the medical community towards the disease of addiction, and it was preventing millions of people across the globe from receiving care; people just like Daniel.

We did, however, become lucky enough to find a medication that was a godsend in Daniel's life, as long as we had access to it, anyways. I specifically recall the night before we discovered Vivitrol for the first time, which was in early 2015. Daniel had been staying in his old bedroom at my house for about a week. Even though Daniel had his own place at this point, he would periodically come and stay with us when he didn't want to be alone and knew that he needed to be proactive in protecting himself. I was more than ok with this because it made me happy that he felt comfortable enough to stay with his old man, and because he had the insight to know when he needed the extra support to stay clean.

As I was preparing to head to bed that night, he was in the kitchen making a supersized late-night meal. I would often poke fun at him for the amount of food he piled on his plate, and this night was no exception. I can still hear his voice and laughter echo off the walls of our kitchen when I think back to moments such as this. I could tell he was probably under the influence of something as I sat and observed him making his food, though. Most other people would have probably missed the signs, but I knew them all too well. I had spent so much time with Daniel that I knew him like the back of my hand. I contemplated whether or not I should say anything to him about it. I didn't want to risk an argument, and I didn't want him to feel attacked. I contemplated what to say, and how to say it, if I were to even bring it up in the first place. I went back and forth in my mind 100 times. Was it even worth it?

I decided to say something, but tried to be extremely cautious to avoid conflict and keep an open dialogue between the two of us. I simply said something like, *"Daniel, what can we do to make this stop?"* I made sure to use a calm voice to assure he knew I was offering him a helping hand, and not a judgmental, roundabout jab.

He stopped, turned, and looked at me without saying a word and began to cry. He lowered his head onto the counter and just sobbed. After a minute or so, through the tears, he said, *"Dad, I wish I could make it stop, I hate it and I don't know why this keeps happening."*

I felt so terrible for him. I had not realized the depth of the current battle he was fighting with the disease. This terrified me because his actions that night took us both to a much deeper level of concern. The disease was whittling away at him slowly and he was desperate for a break. We had already been through so much in the quest for hope that it was easy to feel like it would never come. I always believed that if we continued fighting, one day, we would find something that would help him beat this disease, but on that night in particular, Daniel was struggling to convince himself of that.

Little did we know, as we stood there in the kitchen crying together that evening, we were less than 24 hours away from finding the answer we had been searching so desperately for.

After his first Vivitrol injection, and during the next eight consecutive months with this medication, things were consistently good for Daniel to a significant degree. No heroin and no prescription opioids. His anxiety and ADHD were finally being adequately treated, and he felt a hopeful sense of confidence in his stability. This was his longest consistent streak of freedom from opioids since we had started this whole process. He was working, paying his own bills, and was making strides in his pursuit of long-term sobriety and remission of this deadly disease.

Although Daniel maintained consistent abstinence from opioids during this period, he wasn't perfect. I could easily glance over the fact that he would still occasionally dabble with marijuana and alcohol, but I don't think that would be doing a service to those whom may be reading this book in the midst of their own battle. Very few people can just cut out all addictive substances cold turkey in the presence of a diseased brain and never at least gradually reduce use. It's a process, not a decision. As much as I wished that Daniel were abstaining from alcohol and marijuana at the time, I was accepting of it because opioids were out of his life, and in comparison, they were so much more likely to result in his death. We had seen so many people lose their life at the hands of opioids, and so I knew damn well the gravity of the situation. When I saw Daniel drinking or smoking pot, it didn't even register as much of a concern on my radar because I knew they weren't going to put him in the grave with the amounts in which he used, and at that stage, that was my only goal. Maybe that's wrong of me, but I was just desperate to keep my boy alive. If that meant he substituted the pills for a beer, then so be it. Nobody is perfect, and we were nevertheless making progress in the right direction. That's all that mattered in my eyes.

I felt Daniel was safe as long as these injections of Vivitrol occurred every 30 days. I went to the extent of attending some of his medical appointments with him because I honestly just didn't trust his doctor, a man who basically owned and operated an OBOT pill mill. However, Vivitrol providers were few and far between, so we took what we could get. We had finally found a medication that kept him alive, allowed him to be a functioning member of society, and so I didn't really care where it was coming from.

It was during my experience of attending these Vivitrol appointments with Daniel that I learned just how low the quality of care in addiction treatment was. I watched in disgust, knowing these clinics were solely profit driven, as they were frequently doing an enormous disservice to an extremely vulnerable population. I had to write a check to the doctor for $250.00 per injection; all the while they were still billing Medicaid for the medication and service as well.

This OBOT clinic, like most others, was required to make each patient attend numerous IOP therapy sessions each week on top of medication management appointments. Theoretically, that makes a lot of sense. But as we discussed in Chapter 5, the way this is carried out in practice is wildly poor. Because of the drive to make a profit, rather than truly help cure a disease, these offices commonly have patients wait for 2+ hours in their waiting room, at which time the office is charging the patient for "therapy." Between the time the patient is checked in and out of the electronic medical record, there is no way for the insurance company, if billed, to prove that the provider is actively providing therapeutic interventions during that time, so offices can actually just make their patients wait in the waiting room while they sit on their ass.

If it is a cash-only operation, all they have to do is document how long the patient was in the office, just in case the state regulatory boards issue an audit, an extremely rare occurrence.

This place was a classic example of how easy it was to work around the system. During my first visit to this clinic with Daniel, the doctor stepped into the waiting area and announced that the time spent in the waiting room was all a part of the services they offered, as there were addiction-related reading materials on the tables, and soft, "therapeutic" music playing in the background that patients were to be meditating to. I sat in disbelief when I heard this. I was aware of stories about stuff like this, but never had it been so obvious in front of my very own eyes. God forbid someone actually take the time to invest in, and care for, someone with addiction. I felt as though that wasn't even a realistic expectation anymore.

What a travesty! This arrogant and criminal son of a bitch could be doing so much to help so many, yet he is sitting here abusing the system at the expense of my son, I thought to myself as anger consumed me. This quack believed his own bullshit that he was actually providing the "integrated care" that SAMHSA (Substance Abuse and Mental Health Services Administration) states should be provided when dispensing medications for addiction treatment. I hated that my son had to be subjected to this world of unregulated medical treatment, but we were desperate to keep him alive, and if that meant putting up with this crap, then so be it. I would walk through fire for Daniel, so this wasn't anything I couldn't handle.

In 2015, 98% of OBOT clinics only prescribed buprenorphine, or Suboxone, as a treatment option because they could churn out more patients faster, treat them all the same way, and therefore leave with a fatter paycheck. It's not real medical care. Offering one medication option, which is still chemically an opioid and requires intentional daily dosing, isn't a super logical way to address the core root of addiction. On top of that, they require all of these patients to return to the clinic three or more times every week for hours of "therapy." It's not hard to see how a medical provider with a business mindset would be all over this. How have we reached a point in our country where it is more common for a medical provider to be driven by the dollar sign, than to

179

be driven by a true desire to help cure the disease of addiction, which is claiming lives at rates which many of us have never seen before?

Commonly, these clinics hire a certificate-trained speaker to yap for 3+ hours to a group 20+ patients in the same room about basic lifestyle changes, triggers, awareness, etc. They then get to bill insurance for all 20+ patients individually, or charge each patient cash, while only investing in three hours of service by a speaker who is typically highly undereducated. It's a real, true life, screw-the-government scam.

Could this possibly be the main reason OBOT clinics don't usually offer Vivitrol? Could it be a cash flow/profit issue? You decide. I already know the answer.

In which other disease states would a medical facility only explain and offer one treatment option for a disease that if left untreated, is often fatal? In what other aspects of medical care would this be reasonable and persist on for years without anyone raising concern? None.

Again, Big Pharma profits on both sides of the opioid epidemic. Teach the doctor to prescribe until the pain is gone, and also long-term if their clinical judgment feels that's appropriate. If the patient develops an Opioid Use Disorder, then treat them with another opioid-based medication like buprenorphine, which is also addictive and commonly abused. Yet the people in charge turn a blind eye and let this madness continue. It's such a shame. All I'm asking is for us to step back and look at this system from a macro-level perspective because it makes no sense.

By the time Fall of 2015 rolled around, when Daniel was successfully about eight months into his treatment process with Vivitrol, we began to feel the ground shake beneath us. One Saturday morning in September, we read in the newspaper that his doctor at this OBOT clinic had been arrested for various medical practice-related problems.

We were instantly worried sick that Daniel would lose his Vivitrol source. We hadn't heard a peep from the doc, or his office, but had about two weeks before his next injection was due. Two weeks went by and we continued to be in the dark, not knowing what was to come of this doctor. Daniel drove to the office for the next scheduled appointment, and fortunately, the doors were still open and his appointment was still on the books. However, instead of walking into the waiting room with 10-20 other people waiting for 2+ hours, there was only one other patient and Daniel was seen within 10 minutes. What happened next still makes my blood boil.

Once in the office, the doctor told Daniel, *"Well, I guess you heard, I was arrested, but it's fine, I'm clean... nothing will come of this."* The doctor then puts his leg on the desktop and brags about his court-ordered GPS ankle monitor. *"This will be gone in a week's time,"* he said.

Daniel said it was surreal. The appointment was all about the doctor's problems, ranging from the arrest to issues within his personal life; not a single concern about Daniel.

When it came time for Daniel's Vivitrol injection, the doctor got the medication out himself - no assistant. He told Daniel to expose his hip and prepare for the injection. These injections go into the deep muscle and they hurt significantly more than most shots, so Daniel was always a little on edge before getting them.

The doctor cocked back and dove the needle into Daniel's hip, at which time he yelled, *"Oops!"* Daniel told me the doc had forgotten to load the medication into the syringe, so he then unscrewed it from the needle, which stuck out of Daniel's hip, and proceeded to draw up the medication. He then reattached the syringe to the needle and completed the injection. Daniel said it went from being the typical 20-second injection, to a three to five minute excruciating process, and Daniel left really pissed off.

I wanted Daniel away from this clinic, but I couldn't locate another provider. I was spending hours everyday on the Internet searching for someone to take this guy's place.

Three weeks later, the same facility called and left us a message. They said they needed to cancel the next appointment, which was only one week away, because the doctor was unavailable. They recommended we call back to reschedule. Ok, fine, no big deal, I thought. But deep down, I was worried this was just another red flag that the rug was about to be pulled out from under our feet.

Daniel called back a few days later and was told that they didn't know when the doctor would return. Daniel was again asked to call back in a couple days to reschedule.

After Daniel told me about the run-around he was getting, I told him I wanted to be present on the next phone call. At this point, the Vivitrol was simply sitting in the fridge at their office, but they had no one available to administer the injection.

"We are going to get your medication away from this doctor," I told Daniel. Vivitrol is an expensive medication, about $1,000 per month at the time, without insurance. The standard procedure is for the doctor's office to order the medication several days prior to the patient's appointment as they only put in orders on a per-patient basis. We had discovered this innocently a few months prior. One day Daniel went home from work to find a package left at his front door. He opened it and discovered a vile of Vivitrol with his name on it. It also said, "keep refrigerated" on the label. The office had ordered the medication in advance and accidentally sent it directly to the patient, and not the prescriber!

That is the level of care inside these clinics - careless mishap after careless mishap.

On Daniel's next call to the clinic, I was on the line as well, but let Daniel do all the talking. After he was given the run-around yet again, he asked the office manager to release his medication to him so that we could take it to someone who was capable and willing to administer it, as his injection was now past due and he was vulnerable to an overdose.

The office manager paused, and then stated, *"I can't schedule you, and I'm not sure where the medication is kept so I can't release it to you."*

Daniel quickly replied, *"It's in the refrigerator with my name on it, please check there."*

She returned to say that it was, in fact, in the refrigerator, but she still couldn't let Daniel pick it up. That was the end of the discussion. She hung up and the line went dead.

I couldn't believe what I was hearing. *"Shit!,"* I yelled in disbelief.

Here we were again, left in the dust. Daniel was left hanging without medical care by a state-licensed medical provider at a time where all he needed was a simple routine injection of a non-controlled medication that was FDA approved to treat his life-threatening disease. My mind was still unable to wrap itself around why this was such a hard thing to accomplish.

The next day, I called our county addiction agency, commonly referred to as CADAS (Center for Alcoholism and Drug Addiction Services). I talked to a person by the name of Gail. Gail knew my father, myself, and even Daniel. I told her of our desperate situation, she said that she understood, and offered to help us find a physician to provide Daniel's next injection. Two days later she called me back and said, *"Scott, I'm sorry, I can't find a doctor to provide Daniel with his next injection."*

I couldn't believe it. If a county addiction agency can't find a provider to administer this benign medication, how was I going to find one? This was yet another medical system failure, but this time by a county-funded public health department. By this time, I was in full-blown panic mode. My son was at risk, and I was grasping for straws.

The day I got the call from Gail at CADAS, I took this photo of Daniel. Daniel and myself had been doing property improvements at the old historic home on the land that we discussed in Chapter 6. I gave him the terrible job of paint removal on the entrance to this 1853 timeless home. Right after I took this photo, I got the return call from Gail.

I told Daniel the news while he was on top of this scaffolding. He slowly stepped down and we walked around the backside of the bank barn to sit down and talk it out. Daniel and I talked about more than that, though. We discussed the home, the barn, and the projects we envisioned for the property.

I asked Daniel, *"How are you handling things right now?,"* referring to his stability and sobriety.

He said, *"It's a struggle, Dad, it really is, but I will be okay."*

A several minute pause went by, as we were both at a loss for what to do next.

I turned to him and said, *"It's your turn to live in this home, if you want it. By spring time, we could make that happen if we stay on the right track and work hard."*

Daniel replied, *"Dad, you don't know how great that makes me feel,"* with his magnetic smile stretching from ear to ear.

If only I could have that day back, I would have done so much more in that moment. I would have made it a point to not put off this search for another day. I would have made it a point to let Daniel know that I was dead serious about making him feel loved and valued - a regret I can now never resolve.

A day later, we got a call from a physician who we will refer to as "Doctor Black." He had been a part-time provider at the clinic where Daniel had been receiving his Vivitrol injections for the past 8 months, and had even administered one of Daniel's shots when his typical provider had been out of town. He told Daniel, *"I understand you may have been left without a provider."* He continued to inform Daniel that he had since left that facility and moved into another practice that was allowing him to see patients.

"I'm willing to take you on as a patient," he said. Without hesitation, Daniel responded, *"Yes, please!"*

He told Daniel he could see him the following Tuesday, and they quickly set up the appointment.

The very next day, Doctor Black called Daniel back and canceled the appointment without reason. I was feeling such a vast array of emotions at this point I could barely keep up. One minute I felt safe and secure, the next I was overcome with fear that Daniel was going to lose his battle.

I called Doctor Black back within the hour. I had met this doctor before and had greater respect for him than the doctor who owned the clinic. For all we knew, Daniel's original doc may have been sitting in a jail cell again, so I figured this guy was just scrambling to absorb all of the abandoned patients. I assumed it was just going to be a money issue that I could defuse very quickly. Money was NOT going to get in the way of my son's life.

"Hey doc, I hear you canceled Daniel's appointment, what's up?"
Doctor Black stated that the office he had moved to wasn't set up for
Medicaid paperwork, and therefore they were no longer going to take
Daniel on as a patient. I told him that this shouldn't be a problem, as I
was willing to pay cash on Daniel's behalf. Doctor Black stated that
they couldn't do that either, and hung up the phone.

I was furious. Why would this doctor do that? Didn't anyone
understand that we were dealing with a potentially fatal brain disease
and that without this medication, Daniel could relapse and overdose at
any moment? Daniel wasn't just another invoice; this was my *son* we
were talking about!

It wouldn't be until after Daniel passed away that I was given an
"answer" as to why Daniel was refused treatment by Doctor Black. A
few days after the funeral services, I was sitting in my living room and
the home phone rang. I was not taking any calls at the time, as I had no
reason or desire to talk to anyone. I wouldn't even answer the door.
Carrie was back at work, and I was alone in the house. I had
disengaged every aspect of my past life at that point. I was slowly
dying inside, simply waiting for God to take me. There was no reason
for me to pretend that I could overcome this grief.

I glanced at the TV screen out of habit because our phone company
links the caller ID to our cable provider. I had no intention of
answering regardless of whose name popped up.

It was Doctor Black. I jumped off the couch and grabbed the phone.
This doctor's refusal to treat Daniel was a responsible party to the
medical discrimination that had cost Daniel his life. I had dreams of
running into this guy in a dark alley and making him pay for Daniel's
death.

I answered the phone coldly.

The voice on the other end of the line said, *"Hello, this is Doctor
Black, is this Daniel's father?"*

"Yes, it is," I replied.

"I'm calling because I just heard of Daniel's passing and I want to offer my condolences."

At that moment I was clear headed enough to understand how hard it would be for this person, in his position, to make this call. I knew he meant it, so I let him continue. Once he was done with his condolence speech, I decided to take advantage of this opportunity to get some answers.

"You have to answer me one thing, doc," I said. *"Why did you refuse to give Daniel his Vivitrol injection in November when you had given him an appointment at your new practice, had treated him before, and knew what was at stake?"*

Doctor Black replied, *"Because the new practice I had relocated to was operated by a medical group that did not want the hassle of disposing of used needles."*

Disposing of used needles was a hassle for a medical practice?!

The room began to spin. I don't recall anything else. I assume I hung up on him.

This devastated me. A medical professional that had previously given Daniel a Vivitrol injection was well aware of the risks Daniel faced without the medication, and still knowingly denied lifesaving treatment because he worked for an entire group of medical providers who also thought the handling of needles was too inconvenient. Wow. There was no excuse he could have offered to make this any easier to deal with, but saying this occurred because of something as trivial as needle disposal was simply infuriating to me. My gut ached, my heart pounded, and the tears flowed.

After Daniel was refused treatment by the OBOT clinic and Doctor Black, he was able to get an appointment for the first week of December 2015 with his primary care provider, who operated out of an office in a nearby town. This doctor had been dispensing the anxiety and ADHD medication Daniel took, and understood Daniel's personal and family addiction history. This doctor had known our family for years, but in my opinion, had done more to start and contribute to the development of addiction in our family, than help our situation. Regardless, we didn't have any other medical providers near Germantown, so we were out of alternative options.

I told Daniel, if necessary, to plead and beg this doctor to administer the Vivitrol injection. *"Whatever it takes at this point,"* I told him. All we needed was someone with the capacity to write the script and give their nurse the orders to inject the medication, which I knew they had the power to do. After the appointment, however, Daniel told me that he asked repeatedly to get back on Vivitrol, but was ignored. The doc was willing to write him two scripts for controlled medications for anxiety and ADHD, with known addictive potential, but refused the non-controlled medication to treat his addiction, which was keeping Daniel alive.

After Daniel's death, I spoke with the office manager at this primary care practice and asked why the doctor didn't give Daniel the Vivitrol injection he had begged for. She said she would check into it and get back with me. The manager contacted my wife a few days later and informed her that it was their medical group's business policy to not treat addiction. All individuals struggling with the disease of addiction, whether or not it was caused by their own aggressive opioid prescribing, would have to be referred out - passed on for someone else to deal with.

My personal primary care physician told me that he had even tried to discuss this professionally with the provider who treated Daniel, but to no avail. No explanation was ever given.

Take a step back and look at this from another perspective. If you were to develop diabetes from eating predominantly carbs and sugar your entire life, your primary care doctor will likely be happy to assist you in getting the correct diagnosis, recommend different treatment strategies, and even treat the side effects of the medications chosen, if any. Even if you slip up on your new diet plan, they will continue to treat you and work with you to find the best solutions. Imagine, though, that you returned to your doc after messing up on your diet and your doc replies, *"Sorry, you relapsed, I can't help you anymore."*

This happens with the disease of addiction on a daily basis and I saw it time and time again with Daniel. 75% of heroin users start with a legitimate, legal prescription opioid supplied by a trusted medical provider. These patients subsequently become opioid dependent, and then can't get help from the same provider that was responsible for triggering their addiction in the first place. It's insanity and it makes my skin crawl.

This is clear and blatant discrimination towards the disease of addiction. There is no other way to put it.

SAMHSA, a federal agency with a 40 billion dollar budget, developed protocols for the use of naltrexone (Vivitrol) in the primary care setting in an effort to encourage more family docs to utilize this. Instead, most of these providers have made it their "business choice" not to offer treatment for opioid addiction, even if caused by their own reckless prescribing of opioids, and even if the treatment is non-controlled and FDA approved. Out of the roughly 900,000 physicians in the United States that are able to prescribe controlled substances such as opioids, less than 4% are certified to prescribe buprenorphine to treat the possible addiction that can occur when they prescribe such medications. If this medication only requires an 8 hour certificate, why do so few physicians even attempt to right their wrongs?

I've received numerous roundabout answers as to why it would be in the best interest of a medical practice to avoid addiction treatment. As I've noted, almost all reasons are centered around money. However, I've had providers tell me straight to my face, that they don't treat addiction because they simply don't want their waiting rooms to be "filled with junkies," as this would give their practice a bad reputation and make other people uncomfortable. Others have told me that most people with addiction are on Medicaid, and this doesn't reimburse as well as private insurance. Others stated that people with addiction don't show up to appointments as consistently, and this results in missed revenue for the practice. See the common thread here? Money over health care; stigma and discrimination over humanity. This must change or we will never recover from this devastating epidemic.

Daniel's last Vivitrol injection protected him up until mid-November 2015. After this date, Daniel was at risk of relapse, and this would remain the case for the remaining days of his life.

Around December 15th, Daniel relapsed. He called me the following morning while I was settling into my fake trial run at being semi-retired in my RV on the beach in Florida, with the intent to come clean about it. I was very glad to hear from him. Daniel asked me how things were going, and wanted to know if I was enjoying myself. He said, *"You deserve a break so please try to enjoy things, Dad."*

He then muttered, *"I need to tell you something, but I'm afraid to."*

I quickly replied, *"Well you've already went too far now, spill it."*

"I don't know, Dad...." he stammered, amongst a nervous shake in his voice.

I was sitting in the living room of our RV and decided to go lay down on the bed in the back. I was worried about what Daniel was so hesitant to tell me, yet he felt was important enough to initiate a conversation about. I knew where this conversation was heading, but tried carefully not to jump to conclusions. I braced myself.

He said slowly, *"Dad, I relapsed yesterday, and I made it to the other side. It was calm and peaceful. I'm not scared of dying anymore...."*

"...I hit the floor," he continued. *"The person I was with called a friend who had some Narcan. He drove to my house and gave it to me, bringing me back. I was gone for quite awhile they said."*

I was shocked, scared, angry, and speechless. I was truly unable to reply with words and my hands instantly began to shake as I tried to hold the phone to my ear. He was knocking on death's door, quite literally, and I was hundreds of miles away.

Since I arrived in Florida, I had been in daily contact with Daniel. The night he relapsed and "crossed over," I hadn't heard from him, so I had asked Wes and his Uncle Mitch to head over to Daniel's house to check

190

on him. I hated doing this, as I knew it was potentially setting up Wes to walk into something that would forever scar him, but I also knew he was always willing to drop everything to check on his big brother, and he was as resilient as they come. They went to Daniel's house and saw him lying on the couch, watching football by him self, awake and alert. They said he seemed fine, and Daniel promised them he was ok.

While I was still on the phone with Daniel, I asked him about Wes's visit that night and he said they had stopped by after the overdose had happened, and he pretended everything was fine because he didn't want to scare anyone or stir up attention.

Before hanging up, Daniel said, *"Dad, I will be okay. I'm glad I got that urge to use out of my system and I survived."*

The following day, Daniel was to report to his probation officer. What we have not touched on yet was that about 13 months prior, during one of Daniel's downward cycles, he had gotten into an argument with the mother of his youngest son. During the argument, Daniel verbally threatened her, and the police were rightfully called. Daniel was arrested for the threat of domestic violence, a mandatory policy in the state of Ohio. The outcome was that Daniel was required to report to a probation officer for periodic random urine drug screens and to assure that there was not a developing pattern of violence in Daniel's behavior and relationships.

His next random check-in date was set to be the day following his relapse. This meant that he was more than likely going to "piss dirty" as it would pick up on the heroin in his system, and he would be thrown in jail for violating probation – and that's exactly how it happened. He was thrown into county jail on December 17th, 2015.

I was in touch with his probation officer the day Daniel showed up. I knew jail was probably imminent, but I also knew this was potentially a pathway to finding a Vivitrol provider again. I had heard the court system in our county had just started implementing an early release program with Vivitrol treatment, and so I thought maybe this could turn into a positive outcome. Never have I been so wrong.

While Daniel sat in a jail cell, the plan was to get him out in two or three days with a court-ordered Vivitrol injection. If Daniel agreed to this, he would be released and free to go before Christmas. I knew that wouldn't be an issue.

The medical staff in the jail is supposed to first obtain a blood sample to do their standard labs and screen him for other drugs of abuse, and then the jail will hand him off to the medical facility they partner with to handle the Vivitrol. The medical facility then transports Daniel from the jail, directly to their facility for the injection, and then releases him to a designated family member.

Daniel called me each day during this process saying that no one had come to collect his blood, and he was becoming increasingly anxious that this wouldn't be done in time for him to get his injection. He was rightfully upset and we were both beginning to panic. I complained to the judge handling the case and to his probation officer as soon as I learned of this. The probation officer told me she would check into it, and got back with me the following day to inform me that Daniel was supposedly refusing blood work. I confronted Daniel and he said, *"Why would I do that, Dad!? That's a lie! They're just covering up for not doing their job!"* I made a second complaint to both the judge and probation officer, and received the same typical response... *"We will look into it."*

After about a week in county jail, the judge intervened after talking with Daniel personally. Daniel was scheduled for a videoconference court hearing with the judge, who was familiar with our family, and was well aware of the pain our family had already endured. I sense that he foreshadowed the path Daniel was on. He called Daniel's attending family to the front of the courtroom so that Daniel could see them through the video monitor.

He said, *"Daniel, look at your grandparents. Look at your little brother. Look at your mother, and your aunt, and your uncle. Do not make them bury yet another loved one. You know what can happen if you remain on this path. Do you want to get help?"*

Daniel, visibly shaken and tearful, replied, *"Yes! I want help more than anything. I keep telling people that in here, and no one listens."*

The judge agreed to let Daniel out on December 23rd, 2015 on the condition that he would be given his ninth Vivitrol injection through the court-appointment OBOT clinic later that afternoon. Daniel was released from jail straight to the medical facility and sat patiently, waiting to be seen by the physician. In the meantime, the medical assistant collected a urine sample from Daniel for the standard drug screen. The assistant asked Daniel what medications he was currently prescribed, and he informed her of his low dose anxiety medication, Ativan. All of Daniel's past providers, including the OBOT clinic where he had been getting Vivitrol from for the past eight months, as well as his probation officer, knew this part of Daniel's mental health care. It had shown up on all of his monthly probation drug screens, and no issues were ever raised. The OBOT clinic associated with the jail, however, told Daniel that he was not permitted to be on both Ativan and Vivitrol. Daniel proceeded to explain that he had been on Ativan for nearly a year, and all the while he was also on Vivitrol. If it was such an issue, why had he never run into a problem before?

The assistant took Daniel's file to the doctor's office across the hall from where the assessment was done, and told the doctor that Daniel was on a benzo. The doctor replied, *"Then I'm not going to see him. Tell him to come back when he is off his benzos."*

He knew that addiction is a chronic, progressive, and often fatal disease.

He knew that the overdose rate is significantly higher for someone recently released from jail.

He knew that the holidays could also be an added stressor, given the fact that many families judge and shame those who battle addiction.

And he knew that this was a court-ordered medication.

This physician decided that Daniel was not worth seeing under the false assumption that there is a contraindication between Ativan and

Vivitrol. Such contraindication does not exist. It was later exposed during a court deposition, which we'll discuss in the next chapter, that this doctor, we'll call him "Doctor X," had never even treated a patient using Vivitrol before. Daniel would have been his first. Not only was he uninformed, but he wasn't even willing to give Daniel the time of day.

The physician released Daniel without his court-ordered medication, just days before Christmas. The judge had ordered Daniel's release on the stipulation that he be given Vivitrol, and when that wasn't done, this doc decided that it would be best practice to just let Daniel go home, unprotected.

Wes picked up Daniel from the medical facility and spent the majority of the following days with him to ensure he had the love and support he needed to stay sober. Daniel's maternal family was actively engaged with him at the time too, as they were all well aware of the situation and what was at stake. Just three months prior, Daniel's cousin on his mom's side, Andy, lost his battle with the disease of addiction unexpectedly. I knew Debbie's family understood what Daniel was struggling with and that brought me some comfort, but I was still in frequent communication with Daniel and Wes to keep tabs. I was desperately trying to calm my nerves, as I knew this had the potential to become the nightmare I had so desperately been trying to avoid.

I attempted to have Daniel accounted for at all times because all I could think about was the worst-case scenario. I felt completely helpless as though I was watching a car accident unfold before my very eyes.

He had been shunned and rejected by numerous medical providers who had the power to simply write a prescription for a lifesaving medication, but refused. Just two months prior, for the first time, Daniel had finally started to see what life might be like after addiction. Prior, he wasn't sure if life after addiction even existed. But because of the medical discrimination towards the disease of addiction, Daniel was left in the wake, naked and exposed, alone and hurting. Daniel lost his battle three days later.

A few weeks after Daniel's passing, the judge that had ordered early release with court-ordered Vivitrol wanted to understand what had happened, so he set up an appointment with the medical CEO of the facility to discuss the situation. I attended this meeting. When I told the CEO there was no contraindication between the two drugs, he told me that there was. He was also later proven wrong in deposition.

I asked the CEO if Daniel and I could have walked into this facility as a private walk-in patient to obtain Vivitrol. He answered, *"No. We only use Vivitrol for county jail patients."* When pressed for a reason, he straight up said it was because of the money.

I later contacted the cellmate Daniel had shared his cell with while in jail and asked him if Daniel had ever refused his blood work. The gentleman replied, *"Hell no, he didn't! He was upset the entire time. He wanted it because that was his ticket out of jail."*

I believed him. The fact that the jail staff told the probation officer that Daniel was refusing the blood work speaks for itself. To this day, the judge and probation department stand firm that their actions and system did the best they could for Daniel, when in fact they failed him miserably.

It was clear to me that the medical discrimination of the disease of addiction was not only rooted in the medical community and legislative system, but also the criminal justice system - all the way from the judge to the local police force.

In early 2016, during a period of time when opioid overdose deaths were continuing to skyrocket, I was in my beginning stages of trying to facilitate change to prevent this from happening to other families. I would occasionally attend the meetings of our local drug-free coalition, which had been started by Daniel's maternal aunt after the passing of her son, Andy. After Daniel's death, it was named The Andy Genslinger and Daniel Weidle Drug-Free Coalition, but later changed to the Valley View Community Drug-Free Coalition, to reflect the name of the school district in which we live. Their aim is to raise awareness within, and advocate for, four different populations within our town: law enforcement, faith-based groups, schools, and community members at-large. They have regular public meetings to educate and provide services to our community, and have done an excellent job at bridging a few large gaps within our small town. One of the first issues at hand involved improving access to Narcan.

Narcan is an immediate-acting opioid blocker, which can reverse the effects of lethal doses of opioids within seconds. Commonly, when someone overdoses on opioids, they don't die instantly. They usually pass out and gradually over time, their breathing and heart rate both decrease until they are too low to sustain life. Because of this, there is a small window of time where someone can still be saved after they lose consciousness. Time is of the essence, so medications that work as quickly as Narcan are of vital importance.

Most law enforcement agencies at that time required their officers to carry this on patrol as they are commonly the first to arrive on the scene when someone calls 911 in the event of an overdose. It is extremely simple and easy to use, as administration is given via nasal spray that anyone can go to his or her local pharmacy to purchase. To-date, this antidote has saved thousands of lives. Although it isn't doing anything to prevent the epidemic, it saves lives and if Daniel had been found sooner, it would have saved his, too.

At the time I attended my first coalition meeting, our own local police department was stuck in the stone ages and refused to require their officers on patrol to carry Narcan. When they were questioned about this, one detective stated, *"Our officers are often by themselves on patrol and we feel it is unsafe for them to administer this nasal spray, as victims can become combative once the effects of the Narcan kick in and the victim wakes up."*

This response caused more anger inside me than I knew how to deal with. To them, the risk of aggression towards a police officer, who is heavily trained and physically protected to handle this sort of thing, was more important than saving a human life. This is the same police force that failed to address the two main heroin dealers in our town that I confronted face to face. I handed them the names and addresses of numerous hard criminals who were feeding opioids to our young people on a silver platter, yet they did nothing. I didn't have much hope this would be any different, but thankfully, they soon caved and took our advice. I don't necessarily think this was because we changed any viewpoints, but rather had more to do with the spotlight they found themselves to be under because of the coalition.

In our neighboring town of Farmersville, however, the police department was even more backwards. I waited a couple of months after Germantown established their new policy thinking that Farmersville would soon follow suit, but that wasn't the case. To address this, I decided to go to a city council meeting, as the police department answers to them. I stood up and made my case. The mayor responded to me, *"Mr. Weidle, our rescue squad carries Narcan and they normally arrive five to ten minutes behind the police department and we feel that is adequate."* I couldn't tell if he was being serious or if this was some sort of sick joke.

When we're talking about life and death, every second matters. Five to ten minutes could easily be the deciding factor on whether or not someone lives or dies. Didn't he know that? Again, it was viewed as too inconvenient although the training is very simple and the resources required are minimal. To make it even more absurd, our county police department, as well as the largest nearby city, had both already been carrying Narcan for more than a year. They each had hundreds of stories surrounding the many lives in which they had saved because they were able to administer this simple medication in a timely manner. How was this not enough evidence in and of itself to make common sense updates in policy? Could it have anything to do with the shallow opinion that individuals struggling with addiction don't deserve to be saved? I'd bet my money on it.

After the mayor made that comment to me, I knew it was going to be a long, hard battle to change opinions. This type of discrimination ran deep, and I felt like I was the only person in the world who saw how detrimental that can be.

Daniel paid the ultimate price because our system failed him. He was doing everything in his power to fight this disease. He tried the rehab route more than once. He tried Suboxone several times. He attended and participated in AA group meetings consistently, and worked the

12-steps to the best of his ability. He tried off-label medications and alternative treatments. Daniel was putting in the work and trusted in the process, but in the end, it was a system failure that caused him to be without the medication that kept him safe from the lethal effects of opioids. The disease of addiction cost Daniel his life because the medical community and our legislative system turned their backs on him and denied him the decency and medical treatment needed to keep him alive - medical treatment that would have allowed him to live the healthy and productive life of a 30-year-old father, son, and brother.

Discrimination towards addiction has heavily permeated the medical community, our government, and our communities to the point where innocent people are dying daily because of it. We must reflect on our past, analyze the ways in which we have failed, and be open to rethinking this entire thing. If our system and our society have been built on the foundation of stigma, misconceptions, discrimination, and stereotypes, we must tear it down and start over.

Chapter 12

Wrongful Death

"We've got to start also holding people accountable, and we've got to reward people who succeed. But somehow… greed is rewarded, excess is rewarded, and corruption - or certainly failure to carry out our responsibility - is rewarded." - John McCain

My family had become a statistic - another tragic story in the mounting casualties of a broken system. I had lost my son, and this was now close to costing me my own life, too. After several months of not wanting to wake up, I slowly began to want justice, and as time went on, my depression and anger morphed into an overwhelming *need* for justice.

After attending the meeting with the judge and OBOT clinic CEO, it was pretty obvious to me that the clinic had made some grave mistakes. They had blood all over their hands. They breached the standard of care, neglected basic human decency, and it had cost my son his life. I began talking with my family members about my desire to file a medical malpractice case. None of them supported it. They all simply wanted to put this behind them and focus their energy on the future. I couldn't let it go, though. I couldn't ignore it. I had no future to look forward to. If it was still possible to stand up for Daniel and get justice, I couldn't pass that opportunity up. Daniel had been my responsibility for thirty years and that didn't stop because he was now gone. I owed this effort to Daniel.

Furthermore, I wanted his sons to know the facts, as I understood them, and not just the rumor mill stories that would be passed down. The only way I could prove what happened was to get the facts, and the only way I could do that was by force. Legal action would require depositions of the parties involved, which would expose the details of what had happened, therefore shining a direct light on the faults and errors of the clinic.

Money meant nothing and winning wasn't about money. I wanted public record of the disgraceful actions taken by those who contributed to my son's death. I knew this would cost a small fortune, and it was hard to even find an attorney that was willing to take on a case of medical malpractice based on a percentage of the settlement. Doctors are afforded a lot of clinical judgment protection and very rarely lose. This is one of the main issues with our system - hardly anyone can afford to hold the medical profession accountable! If I wanted to file suit, it would require me to pay hourly rates out of pocket, but I didn't care. It was worth every penny to me if it meant that the truth would be illuminated because I knew this truth had the power to spark change on a much bigger scale.

I finally found a law firm that accepted the case, and it wasn't long before we were off to the races.

In most cases, when someone files a medical malpractice suit against a physician, the physician's insurance carrier steps in and takes over the legal representation at no extra cost to the physician. This meant that I would have to take on a major, national medical insurance carrier with very deep pockets. They're skilled at knowing how to drag out a case in order to weaken their opponent, both emotionally and financially. So of course, they wanted to hold depositions for any and all of Daniel's friends and family. With each one, another two thousand dollars floated out of my bank account.

During the 10-month lead-up to deposition, we went through the "discovery process." In a civil suit, this period of time allows both sides to demand, by subpoena, everything you can imagine: medical records, emails, letters, text messages, voicemails, etc. They want any and all information in attempts to find supporting information for their side and incriminating information on the opposing side.

Once the documents are all compiled, which is an overwhelming process in and of itself, they are reviewed and the cases for each side are built. Once each side is ready, it comes time for sworn testimony and depositions. This all happens behind closed doors before it is even decided on whether or not there will be a courtroom trial. Depositions are where cases are made or lost, where the stress really escalates, the cost skyrockets, and the stakes are the highest. In Daniel's case, the depositions lasted for approximately three months, which began in late 2017.

Depositions are pretty unforgiving and some people just can't stand up under the strain and pressure. Imagine being hooked up to a lie detector machine and your worst enemy is permitted to ask you questions for seven straight hours in hopes of tripping you up and catching you in a lie or misstatement. If that happens, you're done, case closed.

The pressure, the pain, and the re-opening of wounds, which will likely never heal to begin with, are so great that it's hard for me to put into words.

I was the first to be deposed by the opposition, or more accurately referred to as the defendant. In a high-rise office building overlooking the neighboring city of Dayton, I underwent more scrutiny than you can imagine. It was a plush attorney's conference room, but I felt cold and miserable. There was a court stenographer at one end of the long mahogany table, two county jail attorneys from where Daniel had been held, Dr. X's medical attorney (Tony), and my attorney (Tom).

Tony walked in and took the seat to the right of the stenographer. He and I were now sitting face to face and I couldn't help but feel hate for a man that I didn't even know. At that time, I was sworn in, and Tony then opened with a polite introduction of himself. He offered his condolences over the loss of Daniel's life. I sat there thinking to myself, *"How dare you. You're such a fraud. You could care less about the loss of Daniel. He's just another name on your legal pad."*

Tony then said, *"I understand your pain. I just lost my daughter 8 months ago in the same way."*

The room started to spin. I couldn't believe he had just shared this. Looking back, I don't even recall the first thirty minutes of my deposition because I was trying to process what he had just told the room. Was this the attorney's tactic or was he genuinely trying to connect with me on a human level? How could he be on their side if he was basically walking in my shoes? Was I misjudging this man? All of my preconceived notions about him were called into question. I can't say what his intentions were with any certainty, but it was enough to distract me from why I was there. Either way, he had a job to do and so I tried to disconnect from my feelings to just focus on the facts; easier said than done when you're forced to sit in a room full of strangers and talk about the details of losing your own child.

After it was all over, I walked out of the room, ready to fall over from exhaustion and emotional overload. My knees were weak and shaky, barely able to support my frame. If the defense was going to make a case for themselves, they had to blame a grieving father, or anyone else for that matter, and that didn't bother them at all. The alternative was to take responsibility for their actions, and we all knew that wasn't going to happen. Tony did this for a living and he was good at it. Fortunately, I was confident that they gained nothing from my deposition that would hinder our case. I delivered the facts, kept my answers short and to the point, and avoided their traps. The key to deposition questioning is to look at the questions and situations through the eyes of the defense. You can be 100% truthful and forthcoming without feeding them unnecessary information, which they then typically twist, turn, and manipulate against you.

The timing of this process was terrible for Wes, in particular. He was in the final weeks of physician assistant school as depositions began, and was scheduled to graduate and take his board exam in mid-December of 2017. He had endured the entire grief process up until that point while being stuck in an intensive 27-month long master's degree program, and was finally starting to see the light at the end of the tunnel. He had told me once that this journey - grieving the loss of his brother for the second time in the setting of a high-stakes medical program - was like swimming in the middle of the ocean with weights on his feet. The only goal was to keep his mouth above water to stay alive. He knew that once he graduated, the weights would come off and allow him to float, but he would still find himself in the middle of the ocean. His deposition was scheduled for two days after the final examination of his medical education. I hated doing this to him, but it wasn't in my power to get around it at that point. The attorneys for the defense were ruthless and scheduled it anyways.

Wes has always been a rock in the face of adversity, but I could tell he was hanging on by a thread during this deposition. He seemed numb, almost hardened, throughout most of the questioning. He answered the questions honestly, bluntly, and with a matter-of-fact tone. I was proud of him for mustering up the strength to do this, as I know he has struggled with significant guilt for leaving Daniel alone on the night of his death. Wes was the one to pick Daniel up from Dr. X's office and was with Daniel more than anyone in his final days, so Wes's deposition was beyond detailed. They wanted to know every conversation, every interaction, and every move Wes had made as it pertained to Daniel in the final hours and days of Daniel's life. Forcing Wes to relive those moments in this bleak and harsh setting was gut wrenching. He made it through the questioning, but I thought he was also going to collapse as he left their office that day. It was only then that the weights came off his feet, allowing him to swim to safety and begin processing his grief.

During the deposition of Daniel's probation officer, who we'll refer to as Julie, emotions ran high yet again. It was clear she was nervous and emotional. This young lady had worked closely with Daniel over the final year of his life. While my attorney was asking her questions, I could often see her lips begin to quiver as commonly happens when you're on the verge of breaking down. She would frequently pause to compose herself. Many people, including myself, would do anything to have the chance at a do-over regarding the events of that year, and I believe Julie was one of those people. Her deposition was painful and pointed out numerous mistakes that were made in monitoring Daniel and attempting to get him the care he needed.

Next up was the deposition of Dr. X, the physician who refused Daniel his court-ordered Vivitrol, of which would have prevented his death that occurred only three days later. I wasn't going to let this go unpunished or undocumented. When we arrived to the attorney's office for the deposition of Dr. X and his assistant, I was feeling so many mixed emotions. I was about to be face to face with the man who I felt was most guilty for Daniel's wrongful death; the man who did nothing to save my son, but had the power to do so. I was angry as hell, depressed, nervous, but more than anything, determined to see this through.

It was a blistering cold wintery day. As I walked alone across the parking lot that led up to the attorney's office building, it was dark and the wind whipped through the buildings with a sting. This is where the truth-finding mission would be carried out. The day had finally come - the day for justice, or at least the beginning of it. My mind raced back to the day on the beach when I had received the text message that would change my life forever. The doctor I was about to encounter had set all of those events into motion. The pain was just as fresh on that day as it had been on that sunny warm day in Florida just two years prior, the only difference being that along with that pain, there were now feelings of hope that justice would be served.

How utterly alone I felt. No one was there for support. This was something only I could do. I was still dealing with the depression of Daniel's passing, fighting for reform in the state capitol, and now I found myself knee-deep with this medical malpractice case. I know the only thing that kept me from imploding under the pressure and intensity of these emotions was the thought of Daniel watching down, proud of the fact that I was still fighting for him.

The following are excerpts from the actual deposition of Dr. X and his certified medical assistant, Miss C. There will also be made reference to Miss W., who was the nurse in the clinic working that day. The manner in which the doctor answered my attorney's questions sickened me. It was as if he was totally devoid of any feelings and compassion. No wonder the medical system is so broken with men like this in charge of care.

Deposition: Doctor X

QUESTION: Is it a correct statement that opiate addiction is a disease?

ANSWER: Yes.

QUESTION: Is it a correct statement that the prognosis in opiate addiction is generally poor absent treatment?

ANSWER: Yes.

QUESTION: Is it a correct statement that other disease processes can exacerbate or make the addiction disease worse?

ANSWER: Yes.

QUESTION: And those other diseases that can make addiction worse can include things like depression?

ANSWER: Yes.

QUESTION: How about anxiety?

ANSWER: Yes.

QUESTION: What was your first exposure to Vivitrol as a medication for opiate addiction?

ANSWER: I'm not exactly sure but the case with Mr. Weidle might have been the first one.

QUESTION: When you're going through this list of questions are you as the physician directing those questions to a nurse or are you directing them to the patient?

ANSWER: To the patient. The nurse is in the other room.

QUESTION: So, at that point where you're going through that list of questions that you just gave me, the patient is sitting in your office across your desk and the two of you are having a dialogue?

ANSWER: Yes, sir.

QUESTION: Did you ever do that with Daniel Weidle?

ANSWER: No. I never saw Daniel Weidle.

QUESTION: All right. You made a comment a few minutes ago when you were ticking through things that needed to be looked at before the patient is given Vivitrol that one of the issues for you is whether they were on benzos?

ANSWER: Yes.

QUESTION: Right?

ANSWER: Yes.

QUESTION: Which is a short or abbreviated term for a class of medication?

ANSWER: Benzodiazepine medications.

QUESTION: And that includes things like what?

ANSWER: Valium, Xanax, Ativan, Restoril, things of that nature.

QUESTION: And those medications that we're going to continue to refer to loosely as benzos –

ANSWER: Benzos.

QUESTION: -- are prescribed by physicians from time to time for the care of their patients?

ANSWER: Yes.

QUESTION: Among other things those medications can be prescribed for treatment of anxiety?

ANSWER: Yes, sir.

QUESTION: For treatment of depression?

ANSWER: Just for anxiety.

QUESTION: Where did you get the information that there was some contraindication for the administration of Vivitrol if the patient was taking benzodiazepines?

There was an objection here, but the doctor was told to go ahead and answer.

ANSWER: The only thing I recall I talked to a drug rep when I was at that meeting in Dallas and he said there was no contraindication to give Vivitrol to someone who was on benzos.

QUESTION: Other than your experience over the years with seeing patients who were on benzos did you get any specific education from any source that said you can't give Vivitrol to somebody who's on benzos?

ANSWER: No.

QUESTION: You mentioned that when you were in the meeting in Dallas and you talked to one of the drug reps from the Vivitrol manufacturer they told you that there is no contraindication for Vivitrol.

ANSWER: Right.

QUESTION: -- and the use of benzos?

ANSWER: Right.

QUESTION: Did the drug rep give you any educational material in support of that statement?

ANSWER: No.

QUESTION: So, as we sit here today have you read any treatises, articles, discussions of any sort that address the question of whether Vivitrol and benzos are inconsistent with one another?

ANSWER: No.

QUESTION: So, did you ever look at any of the paperwork that had been prepared by Miss C. or by Miss W. before saying anything about what medication this fellow should or shouldn't get?

ANSWER: No.

QUESTION: Did you look at the paperwork prepared by Miss W. or by Miss C. after you told Miss W. the patient wasn't to get Vivitrol?

ANSWER: No.

QUESTION: When's the first time that you looked at the paperwork that ███████ prepared concerning Daniel?

ANSWER: Probably when the lawsuit was filed.

QUESTION: After this case was filed?

ANSWER: Yes.

QUESTION: So, am I correct then, sir, that at that point where you told Miss W. not to administer Vivitrol to Daniel you didn't know that he had been on a course of Vivitrol before that?

ANSWER: Right. I didn't know that at that time.

QUESTION: And you didn't know that he had been without Vivitrol for more than thirty days?

ANSWER: I didn't know that.

QUESTION: Did you know anything about the patient's level of anxiety about his addiction and the fact that he hadn't been receiving Vivitrol?

ANSWER: No.

QUESTION: At that point where you told Miss W. that Mr. Weidle was not going to get Vivitrol because there were benzos in his urine did you know that Mr. Weidle was being prescribed benzos for treatment of an anxiety disorder?

ANSWER: No.

QUESTION: *At the time that you made the decision that Mr. Weidle was not going to get Vivitrol that day were you aware that he had been ordered to ████████ by the court for the express purpose of getting a Vivitrol injection?*

ANSWER: *No.*

QUESTION: *Do you recognize these four pages to be a portion of the written record concerning Daniel Weidle from December 23 of 2016?*

ANSWER: *Yes, sir, 12/23/15.*

QUESTION: *It goes on to say at that time he had been on Vivitrol injection from -- I can't quite make out that word. Do you know what that word is, ████████?*

ANSWER: *I think that's misspelled. I think that was ██████ practice, but I believe it started with an █.*

QUESTION: *Was ██████ the name of the practice?*

ANSWER: *Yes.*

QUESTION: *It says Vivitrol injection from ██████ for eight months. Do you see that?*

ANSWER: *I see that.*

QUESTION: *Which would suggest eight injections of Vivitrol.*

ANSWER: *That would suggest that.*

QUESTION: *And am I right that you did not read this document before you made your decision about whether to treat Mr. Weidle on December 23?*

ANSWER: *That's correct.*

QUESTION: Did you talk to Miss C. about what she had learned and what she knew about Mr. Weidle before you made your decision?

ANSWER: No, sir.

QUESTION: The next page of the exhibit which is upper right corner Weidle-000509 is entitled Encounter-Office Visit, Date of Service and so forth. Do you see that?

ANSWER: Yes.

QUESTION: And at the bottom of this document under Patient Notes it starts out saying client is actively taking benzos. Do you know who puts the information into the system that produces this patient note?

ANSWER: I don't know.

QUESTION: Then the next sentence says Dr. X refused to see client due to positive urine screen for benzos. Do you see that?

ANSWER: Yes, sir.

QUESTION: Is that true?

ANSWER: No, sir. That is the way she interpreted it.

QUESTION: So, you deny that you refused to see the gentleman?

ANSWER: Right.

QUESTION: You didn't see him?

ANSWER: I didn't see him.

QUESTION: Do you know what his reaction was when he was informed that he was not going to be getting a Vivitrol injection?

ANSWER: I believe he was upset.

QUESTION: How did you know that?

ANSWER: I think from the record later. I didn't know that night.

QUESTION: You didn't listen to the discussion between Miss W. and Mr. Weidle about --

ANSWER: No, sir.

The next to be questioned was Miss C., who was present at the time Daniel was taken to Dr. X's office for court-ordered treatment. Although she was not as detached as the doctor, she clearly dropped the ball in advocating for Daniel's treatment. I'll never forget how she did her best to avoid all eye contact with me. She was scared and wanted to be anywhere but this room.

Deposition: Miss C. (Dr. X's certified medical assistant)

QUESTION: Based upon your conversation with Dr. X did you understand that Dr. X knew that someone like Daniel was at risk of relapsing if he didn't have medically assisted treatment?

There was an objection here, but the witness was instructed to ahead and answer.

ANSWER: Yes.

QUESTION: Did Dr. X say anything else to you that you can remember about Daniel?

ANSWER: No.

QUESTION: Dr. X never saw Daniel while he was there?

ANSWER: No.

QUESTION: How far from the room where Daniel was, was the room where Dr. X was?

ANSWER: Within earshot.

QUESTION: But are we talking about next door or three doors down the hall, what?

 ANSWER: Probably two doors down.

QUESTION: Did Dr. X have anyone else with him at the time that you went in to talk to him about Daniel?

ANSWER: No.

QUESTION: Daniel was the next person that was on the schedule to see Dr. X that evening?

ANSWER: Yes.

QUESTION: And when you went back to the room where Daniel was located what did you tell him?

ANSWER: I told him he wasn't going to be able to get his Vivitrol injection because he had benzos in his system.

QUESTION: Did Daniel respond to you?

ANSWER: Oh, yes.

QUESTION: Was he unhappy about that?

ANSWER: Very.

QUESTION: Did you carry Daniel's unhappiness back to Dr. X and say hey, wait a minute, the patient is upset about this decision, can we do something?

ANSWER: I don't recall if I did that or not.

QUESTION: Would that be your typical practice that you'd go back to the doctor and say gee, we've got a problem here?

ANSWER: Yes.

QUESTION: But you don't remember whether you did or didn't?

ANSWER: I don't remember.

QUESTION: Once you and Daniel wrapped up your conversation how did Daniel leave your facility?

ANSWER: Very upset.

QUESTION: How did he physically leave? Do you know how he was transported in order to get from where you were located to where he needed to be?

ANSWER: I'm not sure.

QUESTION: In your training and experience involving addiction disease what role does stress play in relapse?

There was an objection here, but the witness was instructed to ahead and answer.

ANSWER: Heavy.

QUESTION: It's been your experience in your training that the more stress the patient is under the greater the likelihood of relapse?

ANSWER: Yes.

There was an objection here, but the witness was instructed to ahead and answer.

ANSWER: Yes.

QUESTION: Have you also learned through training and experience that other medical conditions or disorders can enhance the risk of relapse?

There was an objection here, but the witness was instructed to ahead and answer.

ANSWER: I'm not sure.

QUESTION: Are there any conditions that you know of from which a patient might suffer that would put them at greater risk of relapse than anybody else?

There was an objection here, but the witness was instructed to ahead and answer.

ANSWER: Okay. Just anxiety and stress.

QUESTION: Did you have any experience with whether the holidays all by themselves, the Christmas holidays, were potentially a stressor for addiction patients?

ANSWER: Yes, they've told me.

QUESTION: When you met with Daniel on this day in December 23 of 2015, I gather from what you've told me that he appeared to be stressed?

ANSWER: Yes.

The deposition process was almost unbearable. The doctor was so arrogant and smug. At one point, my attorney stopped the deposition in order to have a private moment with me.

He said, *"Scott, I don't know how you are able to contain yourself after hearing this type of information. I can proceed and you do not need to stay in the room to hear all this."*

I politely replied, *"No, I'm staying."*

The doctor was unwilling to acknowledge how his lack of efforts contributed to Daniel losing his battle; unwilling to even consider the fact that he may have been wrong. His ego was the main problem and he had clearly sat himself on a high pedestal that he didn't think could be reached.

Nevertheless, the truth was now documented. The doctor had never used Vivitrol to treat addiction before, he never laid eyes on Daniel while he was in his office, and he wasn't aware of any specific contraindications between Ativan and Vivitrol, yet he still refused to treat Daniel's disease. To me, this documentation was what I wanted in order to show how the medical discrimination of addiction played a significant role in Daniel losing his battle with addiction. It further shows how dysfunctional and unregulated the licensed, state of Ohio opioid addiction treatment clinics and providers truly are. Reality was now exposed, and the doctor left the room in disgrace, whether he allowed himself to show it or not.

After only the first few depositions, I was ready and willing to take this case to court. I felt we already had everything we needed to win by a landslide, but I had two big problems.

First, I was now more than $100,000 into this effort, all out of pocket. It was extra money that I didn't have just lying around. Going to trial was probably going to cost another $100,000 minimum. No wonder most medical providers can't be touched - most average Americans could never afford this insanity! In the back of my mind though, I knew that if I could take Daniel's story into the courtroom, the exposure alone would have been worth every cent. If we won the case, I would be reimbursed, but more importantly, it would provide a substantial monetary value that would be exclusively left to Daniel's children. This would set them up for opportunities with furthering their education in the future, and help bridge the financial gap left by the fact that they no longer have a father for provide and support them throughout their childhood and adolescence.

Secondly, those family members that had went through depositions, including Wes, Debbie, Carrie, and the mothers of Daniel's children, would now have to be interrogated yet again, but this time on the witness stand in a more public setting. They had been through so much already and this would be yet another pain-staking process. In trial, a skilled attorney makes sure that they uncover sensitive and damning information about each witness in attempts to discredit them. We've all got stuff in our past that we aren't proud of, and I feared the damage this could do to our remaining skeleton of a family. Almost everyone on our side of the case strongly urged me to avoid trial at all cost. Not only was it going to take thousands of dollars, but it would also inevitably result in much more costly emotional turmoil that no one wanted to endure, and rightfully so.

I'll never forget the deposition of Audra. She was Daniel's first love. They had met in high school, lived together for a decade, and had two beautiful sons, Dylan and Landon. Once Audra and Daniel had split, things became very hostile for a period of time, but slowly things between the two of them settled down and they focused on raising the boys as best they could, while each living separate lives. Tony was inquiring about the last time Audra had talked to Daniel, which was on December 25, 2015, less than 24 hours before he died. Daniel had called her to talk about when he could see the boys again. She said they had a very calm, nice conversation. Audra's answer to Tony's final question made my heart break into a million more pieces.

He asked, *"What were your last words to each other?"* She hesitated, as tears began to gather in her eyes, but then replied, *"Daniel said, 'I still love you', and I replied, 'I love you, too'."*

These words brought me to my knees, and I'm sure they were difficult for Audra's new boyfriend to hear, as he sat there in the room with us. Depositions bring out the truth and make it public, whether we like it or not - truth that most never intend anyone to know, let alone be made public knowledge. I know this was the case for Audra.

It was because of moments such as this, ones filled with such raw emotion and pressure, that I decided to take a step back. I decided to settle out of court to avoid trial, not because we couldn't win or because Daniel wasn't worth it, but because I felt the risk of potential damage to my family was too great. The thought of forcing Wes and Carrie to sit in front of a jury and be interrogated seemed torturous to all of us, and so in the end, we bowed out.

After everything was signed and compromises were made, I was able to recover my legal costs and still got a little extra that we could put into a trust for Daniel's children. More importantly, I walked away with the evidence from the depositions and that meant more to me than money. Daniel's sons would one day understand what really happened to their father. I also now had the legal documentation to prove our mainstream medical community was, and still is, a disaster. I had record to show exactly how the discrimination towards the disease of addiction directly contributed to Daniel's death, and how this can easily be applied to cases all over the country. As the case closed and we attempted to right some of the wrongs in Daniel's story, it became obvious to me that there was a bigger narrative here - bigger than me and bigger than Daniel's story. I didn't want to be finished yet. I had only just now exposed a corrupt system, so what was going to be done about it?

No one else was going to do anything, so why not me?

Chapter 13

Man on a Mission

"The only thing necessary for the triumph of evil is for good men to do nothing." - Edmund Burke

Grief is a complicated thing. I'm still not sure I really understand it, but everyone likes to put definitions and parameters to it as if there is some normal and abnormal way to handle the loss of a loved one. I don't see it that way. It's messy and dark and can change at the drop of a hat. Everyone experiences it differently because grief is a personal process that each individual works out in their own time, in their own way.

In that first year, I frequently thought back to the way in which my mother must have felt in the moments leading up to her death. I tried like hell to remind myself of the pain it left behind. I thought back to that night after Debbie and I separated when I laid under the stars and wrestled with the idea of throwing in the towel. If the pain of divorce had pushed me to my limits, how was I ever going to survive the loss of a child? I was now living with a pain so monstrous that I didn't feel like I stood a chance. Back then, I was motivated by the fact that I had two boys who relied on me to teach them resilience and grit, and so I knew giving up wasn't an option. If I gave up then, I feared the cycle would continue. But now, with Daniel gone, what did I have to live for? Yes, I still had my youngest son and my wife, but this grief was so consuming it blinded me to anything outside of my own body. By the grace of God I made it out of those first few hellish months alive, and very slowly began to regain the motivation to keep living.

As the fog lifted, I gradually came to the understanding that this was going to be a constant battle for the rest of my life. I would have to be proactive, deliberate, and mindful. If I was going to actually survive my own personal grieving process, I had to get away from my own mind and that meant constant action. If I wasn't busy, I was engulfed in sadness, and I knew eventually that was going to suffocate me. There was no more time for stagnation, I had to saddle up and find a reason to live.

It wasn't just the mere act of keeping myself busy that allowed me to keep my head above water, however. I still found myself obsessed with the fact that Daniel's death didn't make sense to me. It shouldn't have happened and I couldn't live with myself unless I did something about it. The tires of my mind spun endlessly in the mud as they were desperate to find solid ground, desperate to find answers.

It was during this time that I began searching the Internet feverishly to learn more about opioids and the epidemic that seemed to engulf our country. It was in these dark days that I began to wrap my head fully around the gravity of the situation at hand. I dug through records, news articles, research, and personal stories. I already knew the country had an opioid problem, but it wasn't until I did my homework, which included hundreds of hours in front of the computer, that I realized just how much of this crisis was preventable. There were certain charts and articles that I read over three or four times repeatedly because I didn't think an entire nationwide epidemic could actually be so easily caused by human error.

When you think back to the major medical epidemics in our country's history, very few of them are caused by synthetic medications or mishaps. It's much more common to see random superbugs or viruses, largely out of our control, pop up and ravish neighborhoods, than it is to see a man-made medication do the same thing. Yet, here we are, experiencing an epidemic that is entirely our fault. If we caused the epidemic, however, shouldn't it be easier to control and stop than the others? How was it, then, that we're a decade into this epidemic and reform has yet to happen? Were people just consciously turning a blind eye? Did they not care? Or did they just not know the facts?

Don't get me wrong, this epidemic has deep roots, winding roads, and has a complexity that took me months to sort through. But once I understood our reality, two things became prominent. First, the blame always came back around to the unregulated dispensing of opioids, and secondly, the most logical and guaranteed way to fix the issue in a timely manner would be to actually enforce real regulations on the overzealous prescribing in inappropriate settings. Couldn't we better control the parameters of dispensing so that in the long run, we have fewer patients to treat? Prescription opioid reform was easily at the top of my list regarding what needed to be done to prevent more people from dying, and so I laced up my boots and set out to do just that.

From my perspective, almost every effort that had been initiated up until that point was focused on treatment and reaction, with no mention of what was to happen on the front end. I understand the need for treatment, but why would you wait to extinguish a fire when you could simply prevent it from happening in the first place?

By the time I had accumulated all of the data already shared in this book thus far, I knew where I needed to start. If other people knew the information I had come to understand - the statistics, the figures, the trends, etc - they would easily be on board, or so I thought. I felt an overwhelming force pushing me to get out and begin sharing this critical information with anyone and everyone who would listen. I realized that the only way we were going to promote change was to advocate for the thousands of people like Daniel, Zac, Andy, and Ron Jr. This would also provide me with an outlet to distract myself from my own pain and depression by attempting to make something good come from something so terrible. If I was busy making sense of Daniel's death, I found that it was easier to tolerate each day that passed.

As an introvert, I don't cold call or knock on doors. That type of advocating and marketing has never worked on me, and I cringed at the idea of doing it to others. I don't speak in group settings, and I don't enjoy crowds of people. My nature is to internalize, wrestle with my thoughts, and put that into direct action. I'm a "straight to the point" type of guy and that's exactly what I wanted to do with this opioid crisis. Regardless of the fact that it is a complex issue, there are still causes and consequences just like most problems in the world. It seemed simple enough - identify the issues, implement solutions, and outcomes are naturally going to improve. In my mind it all just came down to figuring out the details of how this would be executed.

Over the years, I had made a few political connections that I felt might come in handy now that I found myself having thoughts and dreams of changing the system we live in. In past years, my company had the opportunity to host a few political meet and greet fundraisers for county and state politicians, and through this process I met Sandra. Sandra was now the southern Ohio liaison for Governor Kasich. I reached out to her and informed her of Daniel's passing, and noted a few ways the governor could help the issue. Sandra promptly asked me to come to her office to share Daniel's story in more detail. Carrie and I did, and Sandra was deeply touched. Tears rolled down her face and I knew she understood just how many things were wrong with our medical and legislative systems.

At the time, I didn't realize it, but *this* was advocating. It was one of the first times I had taken Daniel's story to anyone who associated with politics, but would become something I routinely did throughout the following months. This issue would force me through doorways, into offices, and in front of public testimony hearings - all places I had no real desire to be. In fact, I would have previously done anything to avoid situations like this.

After the initial meeting with Sandra, she contacted me a week later. She had arranged a high-level meeting in the Rhodes State Office Tower in the heart of Columbus, and put me on the agenda as the sole order of business. All the significant state agency heads would be in attendance. The Ohio State Medical Board, The Ohio State Pharmacy Board, The Ohio Mental Health and Addictions Services Board, a few legislators, and several other key individuals. I was shocked to get this kind of opportunity this quickly, but jumped at the chance.

We gathered in a large conference room overlooking the capitol building. After a simple one minute introduction, I was given the uninterrupted opportunity to tell Daniel's story.

It may have been naive of me at the time, but I assumed all of these people had good intentions and would be on my side if they simply knew the truth. In reality, most bureaucrats simply want to protect themselves and make sure the agency they represent does not get negative media attention. If their agency gets too much of that, shit hits the fan. This was a CYA (cover your ass) type of meeting. After I shared Daniel's story to the heads of every major medical board involved, not a single one of them did anything about it, and not a single one even bothered to contact me.

Anyone that knows me well would agree that talking in front of all these big wigs was extremely out of character for me. Hell, talking in general is out of character for me. I would never have done any of this for any other reason, but if it involves my boys, then my own comfort zone doesn't matter. I had strong beliefs that an injustice had been done which cost Daniel his life, and if this is what it took to fix it, then bring it on.

When I shared Daniel's story that day in Columbus, there were visibly mixed reactions. It brought tears to a few state agency heads. It brought blank stares from a few of the legislative policy makers. I could even sense the medical board director's blood pressure spike as I went into detail regarding the role in which prescription opioids played in all of this. I witnessed a few jaws drop when I mentioned that I had gone on the government addiction services website the day prior, in attempts to see if Vivitrol had gotten any easier to access, only to be turned down by all ten offices on their list.

"*This* is what killed my son," I said as I tried desperately to hold back tears.

"*It's one hundred times easier to get prescription opioids - legalized heroin - than it is to get a non-addictive, non-controlled, safe medication like Vivitrol.*"

You could have heard a pin drop.

That experience in Columbus drained me. I was completely out of my element. I had no idea what I was up against, and maybe that was a good thing. All I knew in the back of my mind was that I was going to fight for justice on behalf of Daniel. I was ready to throw the entire playbook at this crisis and I wasn't going to give up until something was done to ensure that this would never happen to another parent's child again. I had fought for Daniel's life while he was living, and now I was ready to fight in honor of his memory. I wanted to do whatever I could in order to spare one more family from going through the hell that our family experienced with these lousy broken systems.

Sandra had elevated me, and this issue, to the highest level in state medical leadership and government, all in a week's time. I felt empowered and more hopeful than I had felt in years. I strongly believed I could make a difference. Regardless of how uncomfortable I felt, I would walk through every doorway in Columbus and share Daniel's story over and over to fight for this cause. I'm typically a big planner because it eases my anxiety to have structure and clarity, but this was happening at such a whirlwind speed, I struggled to keep up. I wanted to have everything perfectly articulated and prepared ahead of time, so it took awhile for me to let go of that control and realize that I just had to show up. I already had a story and I knew this stuff like the back of my hand. The rest should fall into place naturally, I hoped.

Throughout the next six months I pushed myself to the limits of my comfort zone. I attended and spoke at numerous meetings with various groups and organizations at the continued help of Sandra and many others I would meet along the way. I couldn't believe this was actually happening. My only option was to go with the flow and improvise along the way. I picked up on what people responded to, and what they didn't. I picked up on what was "socially acceptable" in politics, and what wasn't. I was learning a whole new culture, all the while being thrown to the wolves.

One of the first one on one meetings Sandra set up was a nightmare; not to her fault by any means, but politicians can sometimes be wildcards and this was one of those times. She told me that she had scored a meeting with a member of the Ohio House of Representatives who was considered to be *the* representative leading the effort inside the capitol to address opioid reform. We'll refer to him as Mark.

We were scheduled to meet at a restaurant on the top floor of another high-rise overlooking downtown Columbus. I arrived, and to my surprise, found the restaurant completely vacant of any customers. I advised the hostess that I was there to meet Sandra and was immediately taken to a small private dining table near the back of the room.

Mark entered a few minutes later, and after some brief pleasantries, we were all seated. Sandra looked at me and clearly saw that I was a bit nervous, but was coping well enough with the situation to go forward. In her own gentle manner, she asked me to share Daniel's story. Sandra was always so perfect at opening these meetings and trying to put me at ease.

I shared Daniel's story with Mark, as Sandra listened. It was becoming second nature for me to do so, but I could never tell the story without a fresh and overwhelming awareness of the tragedy. Without fail, I knew the tears would come and there was little I could do to keep them from coming.

I guess because of Mark's reputation as a "champion" for the cause, I was more than surprised at his reaction as I finished sharing. His face was completely blank and expressionless. I remember him looking at his watch several times while I was exposing my deepest pain. When I finished, with no emotion, he simply asked, *"So, what do you want us to do?"*

My immediate response: prescription opioid reform.

At that point, he stood up and said he'd give it some thought, and then excused himself by stating that he was late for another appointment. *"Nice to meet you,"* he said as he walked away.

I was stunned by his lack of empathy, lack of comments, and absent suggestions.

I never heard from him again.

The following year, I watched Representative Mark sponsor legislation to enhance the state of Ohio's One-Bite Reporting Exemption - a rule which allows medical clinicians who may have become addicted to a substance themselves, avoid the obligation of reporting the problem to their licensing boards on the first offense, as long as they are actively seeking treatment.

I wondered why other industries and professions don't also receive this type of free pass. Are professionals outside of the medical community obligated to report addiction to their licensing boards? Of course! Could you imagine if the teacher's union or the police union pushed for legislative reform that protected them from having to report addiction in their industry!? So why is the medical industry unique? Could it be their excessive influence in the state capitol? I think that goes without saying.

I also watched Mark support legislation that would require pharmacists to offer special pill bottles with plastic locking lids for all opioids dispensed - yet another grand effort to reduce the prescription opioid epidemic by Mark. *What a joke,* I thought. That was a real life effort to curb an epidemic that has killed hundreds of thousands of Americans.

I recall witnessing the lobbyist assigned to this plastic locking lid enter the private office of Senator Bob Hackett. I was in Senator Hackett's lobby waiting next in line to get his attention and essentially do the same thing, but with suggestions for real reform that would make a substantial difference. Senator Hackett had already met me at this point, and saw me waiting next in line.

He walked out of his private office with the plastic lid in hand, and asked me, *"Scott, what do you think about this?,"* as he handed me the product. *"Do you think this would reduce the opioid problem?"*

I looked at him and half jokingly asked, *"Are you serious?"*

He took the bottle back and said, *"Ok, that's what I thought, thanks."* He then walked back into his office and one minute later the lobbyist pushing this concept walked out. Stuff like this happens inside the offices of just about every single state senator and representative on a daily basis.

Within a few short months I was already growing frustrated by the lack of response to my efforts. After repeatedly wearing my heart on my sleeve in front of complete strangers, I was already starting to doubt the system. I couldn't understand why no one wanted to get involved. I had a lot of positive feedback, yet no action. Everyone admired the ship I was on, but nearly everyone in those first few months let it sail on by. *"Not my problem,"* I could almost audibly hear so many of them saying in their minds.

Rather than giving up in the face of this type of rejection, I used the lack of concern to push myself towards a legislative effort as opposed to a state agency effort. I had to strategize. Grassroots movements are commonly effective to get the attention of the people at the top who have the power to facilitate change, and that's what I sought to do. Our state legislature had clearly not been handling opioid reform with any efficacy, and if they wouldn't listen to me, maybe they would listen to an army of people all echoing the same thing. I began reaching out to everyone who would listen, not just in Columbus. *Let's take a step back, start from the bottom, and assemble the real everyday people this crisis actually impacts,* I thought to myself.

At around the same time this was happening, I was attending the Thursday morning men's group gatherings that I discussed in Chapter 8 through Southbrook Christian Church. I was honored to have been invited to join the group, but I knew I was again walking into something far outside my comfort zone. However, I knew it was an opportunity not only for myself to heal, but to continue my advocating efforts. If you recall, it was here that I met a man who was very active in supporting those battling addiction, but his position on addiction was old school and outdated. It was his belief that addiction was a "thinking problem," not much different than addictions to pornography or gambling. This is completely illogical, but I did not see the point of debating him in this setting. I gained some spiritual strength from attending this men's group, but didn't received much support towards my goal of fighting the real cause of medical addiction. I sensed that the guys in this group understood what I was trying to tell them, but none of them seemed to have the motivation to do much about it.

It was also through Southbrook Christian Church around this time that I met a guy named Joe, who owned a professional advertising agency and was extremely talented in documenting stories on film. It dawned on me that putting Daniel's story into a video format could potentially be a good way to reach a larger audience, and would spare me the pain of repeating it over and over. Every time I was forced to go down memory lane, it was like ripping the scab off again, and that had worn on me significantly over time. I contacted Joe and he was eager to help me. I felt he had a passion for what I was doing and he was very good at his trade, so I hired him on the spot.

After a few days of filming, he produced a great 10-minute video that I still commonly use to get my point across. It can be viewed at www.DanielsStory.org, along with a wealth of other information Joe helped me accumulate and organize. It brings out a solid message and has become an easy way for me to relay the information I have gathered to anyone that is interested in learning.

One of the Southbrook leaders who had originally invited me into the men's group was the lead pastor, Charlie. He had been the officiate of Daniel's funeral service, and I still have a great deal of respect for this man. Charlie was aware of my efforts in Columbus and he wanted to somehow bring attention to this epidemic through his resources. After several months of anticipation, Charlie informed me he was going to insert part of the video I had created with Joe into his sermon that week. This meant that Daniel's story would be presented during three services to an estimated 5,000 people! I was hopeful this would be pivotal in finding new support and could lay the groundwork for our grassroots effort.

I was set up in the lobby of the church after each service concluded for people to get more information and give me feedback. I witnessed 75% of the congregation very touched emotionally, and many were brought to tears. It was already appearing likely that I would have strength in numbers, and they were the kind of numbers required to put pressure on the state legislators, which in turn would bring about big, much needed, formal change.

In the weeks following these church services, however, nothing happened. I had called thousands of people to action by contacting me through our website so that I could assemble a solid list of supporters and organize them into our grassroots effort, yet I got crickets. Nothing ever materialized from this magnificent opportunity, and again, I felt defeated.

Here I was battling with the state of Ohio about the prescription opioid crisis, yet I can't even get the support I was hoping for from my very own church and men's group. Everyone had heard of addiction in some capacity, but it was obvious there was no true understanding of the details. If I couldn't organize the people in my own community within Montgomery County, the hardest hit county in the entire country, how would I ever make a difference in our state's capitol?

I started brainstorming my next moves and decided to reach out to a government affairs employee to see if they had any suggestions on ways in which I could get involved. I was told that I would need the help of a formal lobbyist if I wanted to actually change the laws and regulations. I had no idea where to even begin the search for a lobbyist, and was honestly turned off by the sound of working with one.

It was my understanding at the time that every lobbyist just tries to sell their new and improved idea, plan, or product, in order for the signers of their paycheck to become more successful and profitable. It doesn't matter if they actually believe in it or not, they're being hired as salespeople in the world of politics, and their job is to make deals. It seemed almost like I would be working with a used car salesman, just in a different setting with more at stake. I hesitated, but if that's what it took to get the job done, then that's what I was going to do.

It wasn't long before I was given the contact of a non-traditional lobbyist - a well-respected gentleman that had termed-out of the Ohio House of Representatives and Senate after 16 years inside as an elected state legislator. I was also informed that this guy had been the chairman of the Ohio House Health Committee during his last term - a committee I would have to convince that prescription opioid reform was needed. He had recently made the transition from inside legislator to private lobbyist, and it looked as if this would be the perfect man for the job.

I blindly reached out to this seasoned politician, Lynn Wachtmann, and within 48 hours, he walked through the doors of my office at Weidle Corporation in Germantown. I was floored that he would go so far out of his way to sit down and talk with me about my mission, but at the same time, I understood he was now working for profit. If he wanted to make money, he now had to do stuff like this. Regardless, within ten minutes of meeting this guy, I knew I found my lobbyist. He was not your typical politician. He said what was on his mind and he didn't use a filter. He was rough around the edges, but that's what I liked about him. He gave me a sense of confidence that he could get shit done. I signed a retainer with Lynn at the end of 2016, just 12 months after Daniel lost his battle.

On January 4, 2017, I drove the 90-minute trip to Columbus. It was swearing-in day for the newly elected legislators - The 132nd General Assembly.

I was so new to all this that I honestly didn't know where to go, so I found a coffee shop across the street from the Statehouse and ordered a drink. I simply had an internal need to be present in our capitol that day, and I knew I would figure it out somehow. In many ways, that's how my life had always been, whether I liked it or not. Sometimes you just have to go with your gut and figure out the rest as you go.

As I sat there hovering over a lukewarm cup of overpriced coffee, I called Sandra. *"Hey Sandra, can I go inside the capitol building or do I need an invitation?"* She replied, *"Scott, that's the people's building! Walk in any door!"* And so that's what I did.

Once inside, I found the chambers for the House of Representatives and walked in during their individual swearing-in ceremonies. I watched for about ten minutes as I scoped out the order of events and the flow of the process. After each legislator was sworn in, they would exit down a side hallway, each with a pep in their step as if they had just won the lottery. I planted myself at the end of this hallway to get my face seen. If they made eye-contact with me, I reached out my hand to congratulate them. I know this doesn't seem like much to most people, but it was a big step for an introvert like me.

For the next year I drove to Columbus on most Tuesdays and Wednesdays when the House or Senate were in session. Most of these days I had no schedule or appointments, I just went looking for opportunities to connect. It gave me purpose, and looking back, a reason to get out of bed each day. Sometimes I would go to Lynn's firm where they allowed me to use a spare office when it was available. I would wait for Lynn to get up from his desk and then ask him to go across the street to the Statehouse to see who we could run into.

I would follow him around like an apprentice intern. Every time we made this trek from his office, it would take us 20-30 minutes even though we were right across the street. This was because Lynn knew everybody on those sidewalks. Lynn took advantage of chance meetings. Most of the legislators that had been in state politics for more than four years would call out to him, *"Hello Chairman!,"* as we walked by.

There were other days when Lynn was busy with other duties, or not in Columbus at all. I went up anyway. I just wanted to observe, learn the faces, and get my bearings in this foreign world I was trying to infiltrate. I wanted to figure out who was there to feed their own ego, and who was there for reasons other than self-promotion. What I learned was about ⅓ are there because it makes them feel like a celebrity and it fuels their self-esteem, ⅓ are there because they genuinely want to make a difference and care about the people they represent, and ⅓ fall somewhere in the middle.

When I went to watch the House of Representatives in session for the first time, I was amazed by what I observed. As a spectator, you sit in the balcony up above - a birds-eye view. During the session, when other representatives have the floor to make a case to their colleagues, many of the observing legislators are completely disengaged. Most of them don't care to hear about an issue that doesn't pertain to them, and most won't give anyone the time of day who differs in political opinion

229

from their own. I watched many of them surfing the Internet or scrolling through Facebook, paying no attention to their fellow legislator that had the floor.

Meanwhile, I'm walking the halls with a guy who had put in over 15 years of tireless effort into fighting for causes that he was passionate about, and he didn't even know what Facebook was. He cared about policy and reform, and I could easily see how he held a seat in our state government for as long as he did. He was effective and I know he wouldn't have been that guy in the audience with a lackadaisical attitude.

Because of Lynn's respected recognition, we were not forced to make appointments with most legislators. That wasn't the case for most lobbyists. Most freshman legislators and some democrats required formal appointments, but not those that were familiar with this seasoned leader. Lynn walked right into most offices and they immediately gave him their time and attention. Lynn also knew the committee schedules and session schedules. He planted himself in those meetings or in the hallways at strategic points intentionally. Chance meetings were his style and he was good at it. Lynn also made it a point to know each legislator's staff, to call them by name, and to treat them with respect. It was details such as this that made him so impactful. By being in good graces with the people that mattered, he had almost unlimited access to anyone that he wanted, or needed, to meet. Lynn taught me a lot as I watched his people skills in action - skills I had never developed.

When Lynn would get inside of a legislator's office, he would make small talk for five minutes or so, then he would introduce me and then say, *"Scott, I don't feel right telling your story, so if you would, please do so."* It was the perfect introduction.

I learned to compress Daniel's story into about three minutes of the tragedy, and about three minutes pertaining to prescription opioid reform. I would conclude by saying, *"Ohio is the leading state in the nation for prescription opioid deaths and I'm here in a grassroots effort to spark a much needed change in our legislature."*

90% of the time, legislators would respond with their own stories of family or friends that were overprescribed opioids and how that had led to larger problems. One representative's wife had developed an addiction to opioids and was even arrested after stealing them from her pharmacy; another high-ranking official had two sons who struggled with opioid addiction; and one staff member to another high-ranking leader overdosed and died. In many ways, these politicians knew the issue, knew the damage, and knew what was at stake - human lives. Yet the opioid crisis rages on and on. Clearly that wasn't enough.

I had one legislator, Michele Lepore-Hagan, hand me a tissue while tears streamed down her own face as she listened to me share my message. She pointed her finger at me and said, *"You need to keep doing what you're doing, we need more people like you in this building sharing what you are sharing."* I was deeply touched by little comments and gestures such as that. She was crying, but was still handing me the tissues. I've come to pick up on genuine empathy like that much more since Daniel's passing.

Within six weeks of shaking hands alongside Lynn as he lobbied on my behalf, we had significant support. The next step was to zero in on who exactly we wanted to sponsor our bill. It would have to be individuals who had the backbone to stand up against the medical associations and had the respect of their colleagues. In just one amazing week of searching for the right legislators, we ended up selecting one state representative and two state senators who all endorsed our message and formally joined our mission.

They were Senator Jay Hottinger, Senator Bob Hackett, and Representative Jay Edwards.

We had solid support in both chambers, and it was Lynn's call that we would simultaneously introduce a bill in the Senate and in the House that were identical. These are called companion bills. I was told this was a rare position to be in, but Lynn felt we had enough support behind us to make this happen. I was energized and I desperately needed this kind of positive sign as I was hurting emotionally. This process was difficult for me. Yes, it provided purpose and kept me busy, but it also required me to relive the tragedy of losing Daniel on a daily basis. With each office meeting and each chance sidewalk meeting, I had to re-open and expose my broken heart. No easy feat for a socially backwards guy from small town USA. I was relieved to be moving forward onto the next step.

The ensuing move was to come up with the proper language for the bill – to build the details. I had concepts in mind, but I felt they needed refined. I developed a very crude outline of topics that I had come up with throughout the preceding months, and etched them onto paper. I gave them to Lynn, thinking that he would take my draft, pick out a few key points, reword it into legible english, translate that to formal political jargon, and then submit it. Instead, my outline was used verbatim as the formal proposal for the bill, and submitted to the Legislative Service Commission. I was stunned by this originally, mildly mortified, but also felt empowered that they respected my ideas enough to submit them unfiltered.

What goes in rough, typically comes out rough, and this was no exception. I have always struggled in my ability to articulate my inner thoughts, let alone put those thoughts into a grammatically correct document, so when it came to the topics of addiction and the opioid crisis, I found it especially difficult. Since I had so much I wanted to say and so much I felt necessary for the world to know, I found it difficult to be concise without leaving out crucial details. Luckily, Lynn didn't care much. He trusted that I knew what I was talking about and felt every point I made needed to be addressed with legislation. I appreciate that respect very much.

Shortly after, we met with Representative Ryan Smith in his office. Representative Smith was the chairman of the Finance Committee at the time, and has since served as the 103rd Speaker of the Ohio House in 2018. In state government, you don't become the chairman of a committee unless you're extremely close to the leadership. Chairmen are basically one position below the Speaker of the House, so at the time, being in front of him was a big deal.

Lynn and I went to his office and had a rather casual meeting. It felt like old buddies getting together. Lynn and his boss, Andy, made the pitch to Representative Smith, and he said, *"Hell yes! We need to do this."*

In the same conversation, Representative Smith even suggested that we make the suggested reform tougher because he knew there would need to be room for negotiations. I had taken the propositions in the bill pretty far already, in my opinion, but I was more than pleased to meet someone that felt this was an issue significant enough to go after substantial, but necessary, reforms in the way we allowed medical providers to prescribe opioids.

Having leadership support at this level was a substantial step. I was honored to be in the same room as some of these men, not to mention the extent to which they let me be involved in the process of drafting a bill. Most people seeking reform never even get to this stage.

A day or two later, we met with the House Speaker's legislative policy guru, Shawn. Ironically enough, we met in the same coffee shop I had sat in on swearing-in day when I didn't even know which door to enter the capitol building through. When we gave Shawn our overview, he said, *"This is perfect, we need this, I can't believe how great the timing is."* He said he was going straight to another meeting to establish a legislative opioid organization called HOPE. *"This will be perfect for this group,"* he said. He went on to say, *"We'll fast-track this bill, Scott. It'll get done."* He was literally giddy with excitement, and so was I.

Ten minutes later, I was surprised to see the Ohio AG, Mike DeWine, walk by our coffee shop meeting. He stopped because he knows Lynn and Andy very well. They told Mr. DeWine a short version of my efforts and introduced me. He reached out his hand and smiled, thanking me for my efforts. I happened to have a few binders of information I had put together, so I gave him one.

At that moment in time I had goosebumps. I couldn't believe I was rubbing shoulders with the heads of the state, and not only that, but I had their support, too. Support I couldn't even get back home in my local community. I didn't think that day could get any better at the time, but it did.

Later that afternoon, as Lynn and I were exiting the capitol building on the east side, we saw Governor Kasich and his security detail walking up the steps to the building. We stopped, and Lynn yelled out, *"How are you, you SOB!,"* jokingly. Governor Kasich headed right to Lynn and shook his hand as if they were the closest of friends. They exchanged words and Governor Kasich said, *"Lynn, do you remember coming into my office beating your fist on my desk that one time?"* Lynn smiled widely and said, *"Hell yes, I do!"* They both laughed.

At that point, the governor's handler pushed himself into the conversation. He looked at the governor, pointed to his watch, and said, *"We have to go, Sir, we're late."*

Governor Kasich gave him the look to back down, and the handler immediately did so. I will never forget that. The governor spent another five minutes with Lynn, just chatting, before Lynn pulled me into their conversation. He said, *"This is Scott Weidle, and Scott lost his son, Daniel. He has launched a grassroots effort regarding the opioid epidemic."*

I pulled out another copy of the information I had handed to Mike Dewine earlier that day and gave it to the governor. I had two minutes to tell him Ohio's prescription opioid dispensing was a significant problem. He agreed. He told Lynn and I to take this information straight across the street to his office. He said he would call ahead to make sure his staff would be waiting for us. Governor Kasich then politely said his goodbyes and headed into the capitol building.

Two weeks later, we got news that the governor has pulled together an opioid reform proposition of his own, and the press conference for it was scheduled to be the following week. We had already scheduled our press release for that same week, just three days before the governor's. At the time, Lynn and I believed the governor was trying to get ahead of our legislative effort by developing an executive rule instead, as he feared we were about to steal his thunder. He may or may not have already had this in the works previously (I've been told conflicting information on this), but I think it's no coincidence that his press conference popped up out of nowhere the same week we decided to go public with ours, and this all happened within two weeks of us sharing our proposal with him. If this was something that had been mapped out and planned for months to years prior, why didn't any of the GOP legislators around me know about it?

We were hearing that the governor's new proposition was to develop a new "rule" for prescribing opioids. This rule wouldn't be mandatory, however, but rather would act as loose advice to the medical community. In essence, these guidelines set recommendations for the max number of days in which a provider can prescribe opioids for acute pain, but allows the clinician to disobey the rule by simply "explaining why in the patient's medical record." The guidelines set no limit for the long-term use of opioids in managing chronic pain either, which is really where the bulk of the opioids on our streets are coming from. The Ohio Academy of Family Physicians even states on their own website that, *"These prescribing guidelines are intended to supplement – not replace – clinical judgment,"* which reinforces the fact that the sky is still the limit, technically. There is no oversight and no enforcement.

As I read through Kasich's plan, I was baffled, wondering where the remainder of his proposal was, when in actuality, that was it. Those guidelines were his grand plan to address the entire opioid epidemic. The governor created an entire cabinet to deal with the biggest epidemic our country has ever seen, and that's all they came up with. An epidemic that is killing people every single day, in a state that has seen more opioid deaths than every other state in the union, including all 33 states that are bigger geographically, and the big solution to abolishing this problem is a narrow-scope prescribing suggestion to the medical community? Give me a break.

Regardless of when his plan originated, we surmised that this effort by Governor Kasich was at least somewhat driven by a desire to pump the breaks on our efforts to legislate mandatory reform. We went forward with our press release, now with the knowledge that we probably would not have the support of the governor - a significant blow.

Because we had already been promised the support of numerous legislators repeatedly for several weeks, we expected everyone to follow through with their end of the bargain. We naturally assumed that even though the governor was rolling out his own plan, support for our plan would not change. If someone tells me they're going to see something through, I usually believe them. Maybe it was just me that had this expectation though, because in hindsight, I probably shouldn't have so easily trusted a politician's empty words until I saw action. Rookie mistake.

On March 29th, 2017, we unveiled our bill in a formal press conference, which can still be watched by going to The Ohio Channel link in the resource section of this book. Emotions ran higher for me on that day than I knew how to comprehend. I was happy and proud while being simultaneously overcome with constant tears and sadness, as the only reason we had gotten to this point was because it was too late for Daniel.

I made the opening remarks and briefly introduced Daniel's story. I shared stats and figures about the opioid crisis and shared the reasoning behind why we felt it was necessary to legally change the limits on prescribing opioids. I remained calm, cool, and collected, even though internally I wanted to scream this stuff from the rooftops.

Representative Edwards took the floor next to introduce the bill.

"The bill, which I'm calling Daniel's Law, after Mr Weidle's son, will make three changes…" He went on to detail our goals. First and foremost, we needed to address prescribing rates. We simply proposed that the CDC guidelines, which were already in place, be followed legally, however, we would continue to allow physicians to have the autonomy to practice outside of those limits as long as they offered treatment programs to those patients that were receiving opioid doses in excess of that. Our aim was to reduce the overall dosage per day of 80 MED to 50 MED. If we had seen death rates increase with every year that dosing increased, it's only common sense that death rates should decrease if dosing decreased.

The remaining two changes that we targeted with Daniel's Law were treatment related, developed directly from the gaps that Daniel and I discovered throughout his pursuit of sobriety. The first issue sought to fix the fact that so many profit-driven OBOT clinics only offered buprenorphine as a treatment option. The issue being that bupe is a controlled substance as it is merely a regulated form of an opioid, and isn't really allowing the patient a chance to free themselves of opioids entirely. Because of the way it's dosed and the cost of the drug, it produces more revenue for providers, and so they commonly ignore the other safer, more logical treatment options, such as Vivitrol. Patients need to be given options and have access to medications that can be lifesaving, end of story. Both medications have their time and place, however when the non-controlled, longer-acting option (Vivitrol) is harder to get your hands on than heroin, we have a problem.

Secondly, I wanted to address the issue of required group therapy in the context of addiction treatment. Because Daniel had experienced so many problems in group therapy settings, which are usually a requirement in these clinics, I just wanted there to be another option. Group therapy can be great, however in the context of addiction medicine, there are significant potential pitfalls when you put a bunch of people in a room together that are typically very early on in their treatment process, many of which are still actively using and selling. So we proposed that an online IOP therapy module be established to give patients safer access to therapeutic interventions. This would also allow patients to take the material home and learn at their own speeds in whatever environment they learn best in.

After the bill overview was given by Representative Edwards, Senator Hottinger approached the podium and gave a statement which surprised many. For the first time, he shared that his father-in-law had lost his life at the hands of addiction, which was the result of being prescribed excessive amounts of addictive, controlled medications following a work-related injury. This guy was successful, drove a corvette, owned and flew his own airplane, and had a family whom he loved dearly. He was driving home the fact that no one is immune to this disease. It doesn't discriminate, and he wanted the world to know that it's not just the Weidle family struggling with this. I appreciated that very much.

Ohio Secretary of State Jon Husted also showed up to the press conference as well, and proclaimed his support for Daniel's Law. We never specifically asked Mr. Husted for his support, but we appreciated it and welcomed it with open arms. He was a respected state leader and

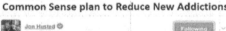

I was impressed by the fact that he was on board. Representative Larry Householder was also in attendance and stood on the platform in our support, yet we never specifically asked for his support either, but again, we welcomed it. I mention that because it's easy to assume that legislators are coaxed into supporting various bills because it will look good for their image and reputation. Although that does indeed happen often, we had acquired the unsolicited support of high-ranking legislators because, in my opinion, our bill made logical sense and was providing answers that would directly save the lives of thousands of Ohioans. If it wasn't a realistic bill, they wouldn't have wasted their time.

COLUMBUS—On Wednesday, State Senator Bob Hackett (R-London) joined Governor Kasich and a coalition of state leaders to discuss legislative efforts aimed at battling Ohio's drug epidemic through prescription drug reforms.

Senator Hackett is the sponsor of Senate Bill 119, also known as Daniel's Law. This legislation would make Ohio law consistent with the prescribing guidelines set by the Centers for Disease Control (CDC). Additionally, it formally acknowledges that addiction often originates from overprescribing certain medications for the treatment of acute pain.

Two days before the Daniel's Law press conference, an avid supporter, Representative Ryan Smith, said that he could not be in attendance due to a scheduling conflict. I was later informed this was not the case. He was told to walk away from supporting our effort by someone above him - someone at the "top." I had a hard time understanding the way power was used in the Statehouse, and this was my first real world peek at how this influence trickles down to control outcomes. From the governor's office, down to the legislators, committees, lobbyists, medical practitioners and organizations, everyone was in someone else's pocket to some degree. This was proven to me over and over again throughout this process. Despite this, I felt we were still in a strong position because nearly all of the legislators supported our concepts and ideas. Unfortunately, I was mistaken.

It appeared to everyone involved that Governor Kasich had pulled legislative leadership away from our effort for a couple of reasons. First, he wanted the spotlight and credit for addressing the issue, and secondly, he was under the manipulation of the medical associations whom were opposed to our bill. As we've already discussed, the medical community is opposed to reform if it involves an increase in regulations or restrictions to the clinical judgement of providers. If the medical associations get wind that there is a bill in the pipeline which could result in either of those scenarios, they go straight to the leadership to assure it gets squashed. I had numerous people inside the Statehouse telling me that this was indeed happening to our legislation. Power and money rule the world even when people's lives are hanging in the balance.

Daniel's Law went from a top legislative issue on March 29th, 2017, to falling flat. After a bill is drafted, it then must go through the appropriate committees for revisions, negotiations, and review. Our bill sat on the floor of the House Health Committee for months without being picked up. Every week, in every committee, the designated chairman selects which bills they will debate, and which bills are left lying on the floor. Our bill was left lying on the floor. If you don't have the support of the leadership (ie the chairman of the committee), your proposals aren't even listened to. A significant portion of submitted bills never even make it to the committee floor, and the leadership controls that. It was because of this that we realized revisions were going to be required ahead of time if we wanted to even be picked up and heard in a formal fashion. The rug had been pulled out from underneath everything we had worked so hard for, just like that. It was that easy to get around necessary, common sense reform. I'm sure it didn't help that the chairman of the House Health Committee was a practicing state-licensed physician himself.

The next six months were an all-out fight to regain support. We revised Daniel's Law six times and failed with each revision because leadership would not allow it to advance. As long as a revision included restrictions on opioid prescribing, even though we were using the CDC guidelines as the basis for our content, it was ignored.

I did realize throughout these revisions that there was a segment of the population that my effort to restrict opioid prescribing could actually hurt, if we were successful - those folks who had already become dependent on prescription opioids for chronic pain and had remained under a doctor's care for long-term opioid prescriptions. Although we already know this is not good medical practice, it would be ignorant to ignore the potential impact of cutting people off from an addictive medication that their body has grown dependent on. This is how many heroin users are made, and I wanted to avoid that at all cost. If early versions of Daniel's Law would have been successful, these individuals could have been forced to turn to the street for their opioids in order to avoid the debilitating physical withdrawal that would inevitably ensue. Once I realized this, we changed our approach. In the subsequent revisions, any existing chronic pain patient would be grandfathered-in, and no opioid reduction reforms would apply to them. Our goal for opioid reform was not to take opioids away from those that were already dependent under medical supervision, as that could do more harm. Our goal was to stop the escalation of exposing *new* patients to what has been described by the former head of the FDA as one of the greatest mistakes in modern medicine.

Regardless, by December 2017, the effort was all but dead. Not because it wasn't needed, but because of the influence and power exerted by the medical industry. It was becoming ever so clear to me that the medical industry is *the* most powerful influence in state politics.

How does one get influence in the capitol? It takes money - big money. Each of the many medical associations - and there are many - employ full-time lobbyists to control what gets passed and what doesn't. By way of their lobbyists, the medical associations can simply overwhelm legislators with campaign contributions, incentives, and roundabout manipulation. If a legislator endorses or supports a given association, that association has the power to influence all of their members to vote for that legislator in their appropriate elections, and the legislator now becomes indebted to that association and acts as their puppet.

According to The Center for Responsive Politics, in 2017, the American Medical Association (AMA) spent over 21 million dollars on lobbying to control the industry, which ranked as the ninth highest in the country. So far in 2019, the AMA ranks sixth highest for most amount of money spent on lobbying nationwide, and that's just talking about one medical associations effort to control practice reform via one route – lobbying!

When it comes to the way in which politicians are controlled and influenced by Big Pharma, it's even worse. The pharmaceutical industry has about two lobbyists for every one member of Congress, according to *The Guardian*, and these companies spent over 150 million dollars in 2016 alone to specifically influence legislation. 90% of the US representatives and 97% of the senators have accepted political campaign contributions from pharmaceutical companies (McGreal, 2017). According to the *Associated Press*, makers of prescription opioids and their allies have specifically poured over 3.5 million dollars into Ohio political funds throughout the course of the opioid epidemic. Among state candidates, guess who topped the list for most money accepted from the Pain Care Forum - Governor Kasich (Smyth, 2016). AP and the Center for Public Integrity investigated the issue as a whole, and found that the Pain Care Forum consistently worked in Washington to quietly derail efforts to curb consumption of opioids. Is it any wonder why common sense reform can be so difficult to achieve? If you don't believe that this kind of money directly results in the way these politicians vote, you're living under a rock.

In the case of Daniel's Law, the medical associations at work used the governor, along with other leadership in our state government, as their roadblocks to prevent restrictive reforms in their industry. I vividly remember the anger I felt when I thought about how our governor allowed himself to be used as a pawn in this way. I had been an avid supporter of him for years and never expected to run into this issue with him at the wheel. Didn't he realize that his decision would directly sentence hundreds of Ohioans to death by opioids?

Feeling defeated and conflicted, I was unsure of where to turn next. I felt as though the power of politics was too enormous and daunting to overcome. How was I going to change a broken system if the way in which you enact change is broken? Was this all just a pointless game?

During a small group meeting with Lt. Governor Mary Taylor, I sat beside a member of the House whom I had come to trust and develop a great deal of respect for. I said to him in frustration, *"Why is the medical industry so immune to any needed reforms? I just don't get it."*

He looked me straight in the eye and said, *"It's simple, Scott. It's because they own us."*

I was floored by his honesty. Most, if not all politicians, will deny or diminish the amount of influence exerted by the medical industry because it is a roundabout way of admitting the ways in which they're being played. He was right, and I admired him for that honesty. It gave me hope that not everyone in the capitol building was in denial and there were still some people, at least, that recognized the behind the scenes power struggle.

I sat in the Ohio Statehouse on a bench one afternoon in late 2017 trying to process and understand the many different variables at play in our attempt at Daniel's Law. A state senator, who I had several meetings with, sat down next to me and said, *"Scott, I know for a fact your effort in the capitol this year caused the governor to scramble and issue his executive new rules for opioid dispensing."* He went on to say, *"...I know this is not what you wanted, and it fell short, but know that you did cause Kasich to take some sort of action. You can be proud of that."* He patted me on the back, shook my hand, and walked away. I felt a mix of emotions in that moment, mostly frustration. Daniel's Law had support, yet big money and big power stopped us dead in our tracks.

As 2017 came to a close, Daniel's Law seemed like a lost cause - dead on the legislative floor of the 132nd Ohio General Assembly. Through the course of trying to get our bill through committee, it died six separate times, and with each defeat, I felt like I was dying along with it. All the endless days of advocating had proved unsuccessful. The language in our bill just couldn't get past the power of the politicians who would rather keep their office and campaign money flowing, than keep Ohioans alive. The holidays were upon us, and with them, came overwhelming sadness. December was once my family's favorite month of the year, a time of togetherness and joy. Now, it was only a stark reminder of Daniel's absence.

With the new year, however, came new hope. The story of Daniel's Law wasn't over, to my surprise.

During my time inside the capitol building when Lynn wasn't with me, I found a very small circle of folks that I felt I could trust - not an easy task in the world of politics. With everyone I had come into contact with during these many long days in Columbus, I found only a few true confidantes. These contacts proved to be immensely helpful in assisting me to make sense of what had happened and what was going to be done about it. In early 2018, I received some encouragement from my allies in Columbus to continue the effort and keep fighting. Although I was weary and skeptical, I kept going, and I'm glad I did.

It would be much to the credit of Senate Chairman David Burke, and the Director of Government & Public Affairs for the Ohio Pharmacists Association, Antonio Ciaccia, for reviving Daniel's Law in spring of 2018. They would take it upon themselves to redraft what would be the 7th version of Daniel's Law.

Finally, we had something that we felt could get across the finish line. However, both the House and Senate bill propositions were nothing like what we started with. We were forced to completely change strategies if we desired to do anything that would address the opioid crisis in some way. Most of the bite had been taken out of each bill and I wasn't happy about it. They were doing their best to keep Daniel's Law alive though, and I was just pleased to see someone care enough to give it the time of day.

They drafted a bill that granted pharmacists in the state of Ohio the authority to dispense and administer the medicated-assisted treatment of naltrexone (Vivitrol) without a doctor's prescription, as long as the patient had previously been on this medication. This would improve access to treatment and addressed the biggest, and final, gap in addiction treatment that Daniel and I had discovered in his pursuit to beat this disease.

It may seem outlandish to some, but think about it in the context of other medications. Years ago, everyone had to go to their primary care doc in order to receive their flu shot. Over time, however, pharmacies were awarded the authority to administer flu shots right inside the pharmacy, and now it is common practice - second nature almost - to automatically get our flu shots in this way. If we proposed the same type of legislation for a simple medication like naltrexone, we could pave the way to eventually be in the same position as the flu shot several years down the road. Many times it's small changes like this that accumulate over time to result in real, meaningful change. Furthermore, if this type of law had already been established before Daniel passed, he would still be alive. Instead of running around frantically trying to get his ninth Vivitrol injection to no avail, we would have been able to simply walk into the pharmacy to get the injection, which would have bought us another thirty days to find a new provider.

The redrafted version of the bill would also require physicians to briefly screen patients for addiction potential before prescribing them an opioid of any type. Along with this, it allowed the Ohio State Medical Board the freedom to develop the standards for performing this evaluation, and by doing this, we would establish a new standard of care.

We wanted to bring the medical community into the conversation as far as developing the specifics of the screening process in attempts to lean on their expertise, but at the same time, hold them accountable to assure their power to prescribe was not done with disregard. This portion of the bill would lessen the dispensing of opioids to the most at-risk populations, and therefore would reduce the incidence of addiction and death. To me, it seemed like a very logical step. We weren't putting limits on the amounts that they prescribed, and we weren't telling them when they could and couldn't prescribe. We were solely asking them to be mindful and diligent with *who* they prescribed opioids to.

I don't think anyone in their right mind could convince me that it isn't good practice to avoid prescribing unnecessary opioids to someone with a significant personal and/or family history of addiction. For example, Wes was in the Emergency Department several years ago with a sport-related injury and rated his pain as a 5 out of 10 on the severity scale. He knows his family history suggests that he has an insanely high chance of addiction if exposed to opioids, and so he actively refused them, although they were offered immediately upon arrival. He took some Tylenol instead, and his pain was reduced to a 2 out of 10 within an hour. Without screening, however, the ER doc taking care of him could have easily triggered the brain disease of addiction, which could have been avoided by simply giving safer pain relievers. Wes now proactively lists opioids as an allergy in his medical chart because he knows he won't be screened for addiction, even though he is high risk. If screening for susceptible individuals, such as

Wes, became a new standard of care, we could easily reduce the incidence of addiction.

By now, I'm sure you can probably guess what happened to this logical clause in our new draft. The medical associations came back and demanded we take it out! Shocking! They were determined to object to the passage of Daniel's Law if that clause was left in place. The medical associations, who should be doing the most to protect lives, wanted nothing to do with fixing this epidemic of seismic proportion. In every way, shape, and form, they refuse to regulate and slow down the stream of opioids that are coming straight from the doctor's hand to the patient's mouth.

Of course, Mr. Ciaccia and Chairmen Burke were then forced to remove our screening proposal in order to proceed with the remaining content of the bill. Once they did, we finally had a piece of legislation that the medical associations did not object to.

The only real victory we had, assuming that we could get the rest passed and signed, was that it would increase the availability of naltrexone. Yes, that was a big deal, it would save lives, and I would rejoice in it, but it's like closing the barn door after the horses have already run out. There was nothing the bill would do to stem the tide of opioid overprescribing that fueled the epidemic in the first place. *That* was the bigger need.

Daniel's Law had the green light in committee and support was in place before the last vote. It appeared Daniel's Law would be ratified, yet it was not the bill I had hoped for. I was given the opportunity to make my last address to the legislators in Columbus before they underwent the final vote. I had so many conflicting emotions. I knew this would be my last chance to be heard in this process and I wanted to say so much. I wanted to call out the individuals and organizations that hindered this bill from having the impact it was meant to have, and I wanted to call out the weak-minded, self-serving politicians who had bastardized the bill. I knew, however, that I couldn't say exactly what I felt internally in this arena, but that's what this book is for.

Here are some excerpts from my final address:

"Chairman Huffman, Vice Chair Gavarone, and House Health Committee Members - Thank you for the opportunity to provide proponent testimony on Senate Bill 119. My name is Scott Weidle.

This bill is named in honor of my son, Daniel Weidle.

Exactly 12 months after my firstborn son Daniel lost his battle to the primary medical disease caused by opioids, I walked into this building for the first time. That day was the swearing in of the new members of the 132nd General Assembly.

I was passionate about what the current Ohio attorney general, our next governor, has been stating publicly, 'The pain med problem is fueling our heroin epidemic!'

I had nothing personal to gain by spending time, energy and money advocating for common sense reforms. Reforms for Ohio citizens that are dying every day because of this issue.

The cost, and the emotional pain that this effort would put me through, would test my will to live. But I had to do it, and I continued to follow my gut and my heart.

By the spring of this same year, I had visited with dozens of the 132nd General Assembly members. At each encounter, I shared Daniel's story, reliving the pain and heartache of losing my son. A pain and sorrow I will never fully recover from.

During these initial visits, the vast majority of people that I spoke with gave me immediate feedback which indicated that they too had witnessed and/or experienced the devastating results from the overprescribing of prescription opioids, and the Substance Use Disorder that often develops from opioids.

I heard stories of families and friends that fell prey to Opioid Use Disorder. Stories about wives, husbands, father in-laws, staff members working inside this very building, school teachers and coaches. People from every walk of life and from every sector of our society.

We were receiving overwhelming comments of support and positive feedback along the way, but I would be lying if I said this experience hasn't been full of frustration and disappointment because we can and should be doing more.

In two short months from my first visit to this building, my crude concepts were submitted to the Legislative Service Commission.

At that time, Ohio was 6 years into an opioid epidemic. Ohio had become the leader in the nation in not only heroin deaths, but also in prescription opioid deaths. Almost every legislator we spoke with understood that we had to face the facts and do something.

So, we submitted the same bill in both the House and Senate, a companion bill.

The title of the Senate Bill 119 is Address Opioid Prescribing and Addiction Treatment. Unfortunately, through multiple versions of the bill, this legislation's ability to 'address the opioid prescribing issue' has been removed. We have experienced resistance from the medical associations in trying to change prescribing practices. It is hard to understand their commitment to the current practice when so many are dying. This crisis needs collaboration from all parties.

The latter part of this bill's title is Addressing Opioid Addiction Treatment; Developing a Common-Sense Pathway to Expand Access to Treatment that Could Save Lives. This legislation is a positive step forward in opening the door to treatment options which 99% of mainstream medical professionals do not offer.

Expanded access to MATs would have saved my son, Daniel.

Thousands are dying each year. I will admit, it took me awhile to fully understand that addiction is a medical brain disease. It isn't a character flaw. This is supported by medical evidence. Medical professionals must not add to the practice of stigmatizing patients looking for assistance to beat this medical disease.

This version of Daniel's Law offers to increase access to life-saving treatment by granting pharmacists the authority to dispense and administer the safe, non-controlled medication, Naltrexone.

This effort can and will save lives. Ohio has been leading the nation in opioid overdose deaths for far too long. It's time for us to lead in solutions, including easier access to safe opioid blockers.

Thank you for your time and consideration today. I urge you to favorably support this important legislation in hopes that it will provide another tool to save lives. I also ask that you continue to prioritize your efforts to change prescribing habits. All parties must remain committed to ending this crisis. No parent should have to experience the pain that I have endured in the wake of Daniel's death.

Thank you for your support of Daniel's Law. I am happy to answer any questions the committee may have at this time."

I was able to get some of what I was feeling off my chest that day. I had wanted so much more from a bill that carried my son's name, but I was up against insurmountable odds. I realized that I, along with the help of some wonderful allies, had done what few accomplish — getting a bill signed into law. That doesn't go unrecognized. Daniel's life would never be forgotten and lives would be saved through this bill. Those two things had always been the driving forces behind my trips to Columbus, and I achieved that, albeit to a lesser degree than I had anticipated.

One of the chief allies I found in the state capitol was Senator Jay Hottinger. He had been a sponsor of the bill since the beginning, and without his tireless efforts, I'm confident the epidemic would be even worse than it is today. I appreciate men like Senator Hottinger more than I can express, for his words encouraged me to keep going on the many days where I didn't think it possible. Senator Hottinger gave an incredibly powerful public testimony in the Ohio Senate and granted me permission to share his words with you in this book.

"One of the worst experiences that this life can offer any parent is the tragedy of burying a son or daughter. I can think of no more difficult task for a mom or dad than to skip the natural order of life and have to say goodbye to a child. It's a grief that never subsides or goes away. The questions of why, and the challenges to one's faith, are often overwhelming.

Likewise, one of the most difficult and sad conversations a legislator has is with a parent in this situation. What do you say? How can you help them channel their pain, suffering and grief into something meaningful and impactful?

Scott, I will always remember the day that you came into my office to advocate for change in Ohio's prescribing authority, and to help slow the pipeline of addiction which tragically took your son, Daniel.

You became a champion through your pain. A tireless crusader for a bill aptly named, Daniel's Law.

I have often said that the easier thing to do when one loses a child is to dig a hole and stay hidden for the rest of your life. However, you were determined and steadfast and worked for change on behalf of Daniel and others. You wanted positive change so fewer families would have to endure the pain that you and your family continue to experience.

The process of enacting Daniel's Law from idea, to bill, to law, had numerous hurdles, disappointments and setbacks. I know you and your family grew impatient, frustrated and discouraged many, many times, but you never gave up. You endured and kept on pushing forward.

Your commitment to make a difference and to help others is so worthy of emulation.

Every time you shared Daniel's story in either private, or in the most public of settings, I know it never got easier. Imagine taking the most horrific event that you ever experienced, that rocked your world and altered the rest of your life, and having to relive that every time you retold the story. Gut wrenching.

The telling and retelling of Daniel's story was the sole driving force in turning tragedy into some triumph; the life saving legislation forever known in Ohio as Daniel's Law.

On the day this bill took a major step forward towards becoming law, I recall you eagerly asking, 'What's next?' What is the next step in our ongoing battle with opioid and opiate addiction, and how could you continue to channel your loss and grief into impactful change?

Scott, your commitment to making a difference in the lives of others is as encouraging and inspirational as your great faith.

Thank you, Scott, for never letting any setback, hurdle or knockdown keep you permanently down. And thank you for daily crawling out of that hole of loss and despair to make a difference."

On June 27th, 2018, the Ohio Senate unanimously passed Senate Bill 119, and on November 14, 2018, the Ohio House of Representatives unanimously passed House Bill 167. Daniel's Law was finally headed to the governor's desk for his signature to become an official law.

On Wednesday, December 19th 2018, Governor John Kasich signed our bill, and Daniel's Law became a reality.

The final versions of our legislation were sponsored by Senator Bob Hackett and Senator Jay Hottinger (SB 116) and Representative Jay Edwards (HB 167). I will always be indebted to these men. By the time the formal bill hit the governor's desk, it was co-sponsored by 71

representatives and 19 senators. I'm humbled to walk away from this with numbers like that.

I am thankful that Daniel's Law will keep other families from experiencing the pain of losing a loved one because they were denied lifesaving medication to treat their addiction, and my hope is that this bill will be an example for states across the country to follow. It's a legacy for Daniel and I know he would be proud.

Ohio, and this nation, still need significantly greater reform if we are ever going to stop this runaway train of opioid addiction. Yes, we will save many lives through the passing of Daniel's Law, but the death train is still fully fueled and traveling with deadly momentum. In the words of Senator Hottinger, *"What started out as an issue 2-3 decades ago, grew into a problem, which morphed into a crisis, which is now a full-fledged epidemic."* This preventable, man-made catastrophe developed because nobody took action during the early stages, and it has only grown because people in power continue to avoid action. This chapter is a call to action. I'm shining a spotlight on the ugly reality that is our system in hopes of igniting change. We can make all the micro-changes we want, but if we don't address this with a macro-level approach, starting at the top, greed will continue to win.

As I reflect back on this journey into the murky waters of state legislation, I'm reminded of several people that I owe a debt of thanks. One person in particular was a lobbyist that I blindly trusted. He gave me great insights and I learned an enormous amount from him. He knew that it was unlikely I would succeed in my efforts, but he never discouraged me. He helped me keep it all in perspective, and that is invaluable.

I also owe a special thank you to the following people who worked a great number of hours, some with little-to-no recognition for their efforts: Lynn Wachtmann, Andy Herf, Casandra Perkins, Stephanie Kaylor, Senator Bob Hackett, Senator Jay Hottinger, Representative Jay Edwards, and Antonio Ciaccia. Your dedication to me during a desperate time in my life does not go unnoticed.

Chapter 14

My Brother's Keeper

"We'll always be brothers. Come rain or shine, through hell or high waters."
- Charlie St Cloud

During the writing of this book, my older brother Ronal Lee Weidle, Jr. also lost his battle with the disease of addiction. I had planned to weave a little of my brother's journey within the pages of this book, but because of his untimely departure and the impact this had on me, I find it appropriate to expand on the great man he was and give him his own chapter.

My brother was so similar to Daniel in many ways. Like Daniel, his relationship with God was paramount in his daily life. Some people tend to think of those with addiction as the scoundrels of society - the guy on the city street corner, the liar, the thief, etc - but that's simply not reality. My brother Ron was a quality guy, through and through. He had a heart of gold and everyone that knew him would agree.

Because I spent most of my life under the false assumption that addiction was a choice, I would frequently tell my brother, *"Just stop using!,"* as he was stuck in the thick of it. I was ignorant to the facts and it kept me from properly helping so many people in my life who were suffering, especially Ron. I have learned that some of the strongest people in this world are the ones who go to war on a daily basis against the disease of addiction, with dreams of simply living a normal life. My brother was one such person.

The dictionary defines the word regret as *a feeling about something sad or wrong, or about a mistake made and a wish that it could have been different.* This is how I feel for so many reasons. If I had only received the knowledge earlier about the truth of the disease that devastated my family, I could have done so much for some of the ones I loved the most. I've since come to learn to use my feelings of regret as a guide in the way I view and treat others. I'm fearful of having too many regrets and the passing of my brother has generated a few more.

We all have positive and negative qualities. None of us are without faults. We're all born with genetic predispositions, personality traits, and the potential for hereditary diseases which are passed down from one generation to the next. As you've discovered throughout this book, my family has been plagued with the medical disease of addiction and battles with mental illness to a very significant degree. My brother was another victim to these genetics, dealt an unfortunate burden that was largely out of his control. Many of our life-long battles are written in our microscopic DNA and sometimes all we can do is hope and pray like hell that the outcome doesn't put us in the grave.

On September 13, 2018, after a lifelong battle with this horrible disease, my brother lost the fight.

Ron went to Dayton Christian High School where he excelled at basketball. He was a sports fanatic in ever sense of the word. He loved playing them, watching them, and especially enjoyed going to see his son and grandchildren play. He was great at memorizing sports stats, something I could never do, and he shared his sports knowledge with anyone who would care to listen – and some who didn't.

Ron was a man with a true passion for life, especially when it came to his four children Heather, Tara, Trey and Taylor. Ron had the gift of giving unconditional love and it naturally poured out of him. He had the ability to look past a person's problems and accept them for who they were, without judgement and without hesitation. I always admired him for that, and I have always wanted to be more like him in that regard.

His sense of humor was something he maintained throughout his entire life, through many tragedies and many triumphs. He could always laugh and make those around him smile. In hindsight, and upon recent discoveries, I know this was secondary to a deep-seated faith in God. Ron practiced what he believed, and he sought to do what he felt God wanted him to do. Despite his disease, Ron never gave up hope, and never stopped believing in God and His ability to help him through the fight for sobriety.

On a Thursday evening in September of 2018, I received a text message from Ron's daughter, Tara. She was concerned because she hadn't heard from her dad that day, and that wasn't like him. He called her nearly every day. He was always so connected to all of his kids. He loved talking with them simply to hear about their day and the updates on their lives. He was the type of guy that you could get on the phone and just talk to for hours because he was filled with stories, jokes, and genuinely cared about whoever was on the other line. Their family unit had always maintained such a degree of closeness and unity, something that I often envied.

Tara asked if I could help figure out where he was. It was already late that night, so I agreed to follow through in the morning. I told her I would stop by to check in with him on my way to a business meeting I had scheduled in Cincinnati for 9AM the next day. A few weeks earlier, Ron had decided that the solitude of living alone in his own place was not helping to maintain his sobriety, so he and our dad decided to see how living together would work out. My dad's second wife had passed away from cancer many years prior, so our dad was struggling with being alone, too.

As I pulled into the driveway at our dad's, Ron's truck was sitting in its usual spot. I noticed the garage door was up. It was about 8:00 AM. My first thought was that my brother was probably somewhere around the house and maybe his phone wasn't working, or he had left it in the pool house, where he often spent the evenings alone reading or listening to music. But in the back of my mind, I feared the worst.

As I walked in through the garage and into the living room, I noticed the morning newspaper lying on the coffee table. I felt a sigh of relief because my brother was usually the one who brought the paper in for our dad to read over breakfast each morning.

I grabbed the paper and made my way to my dad's bedroom. He was asleep and I gently woke him, and said good morning. *"Hey Dad, here's the newspaper. Did Jr. bring this in for you?"* Dad replied, *"No, I went out and got it myself, I think your brother decided to sleep-in this morning."*

My heart began to race. This wasn't like my brother. I told Dad that I was going to go to the kitchen and fix him a cup of coffee and left the newspaper at the foot of his bed. Dad wasn't in good health these days, and I didn't want him to be concerned if there was nothing to worry about. On the way to the kitchen I popped my head into my brother's room, and he wasn't there. It didn't appear that the bed had been slept in.

I took Dad his coffee and then started going room to room, searching for Ron. With each door I opened, my breathing became more labored and my hand trembled as I reached for each door knob.

I hadn't been the one to discover my mother's body all those years prior, but I was all too aware of the lasting impact this had on my dad. Daniel's mother had found Daniel while I was in Florida and she barely survived it. Now, I was searching for my brother and fear was sweeping over me in waves. He had battled the same disease as Daniel and so many of my other family members. I prayed that God would spare me this additional heartbreak.

I found my brother that Friday morning around 8:30 AM. He was poolside.

When I discovered my brother's body, he was lying on the ground by the pool house. Music was playing at a low volume in the background and the pool house light was on. The sound of the waterfall fountain, which was next to the pool, was noticeable. This very calm area created an atmosphere where Ron felt at peace. It was his "woods" and he used it as Daniel had used the forest when he wanted to be alone with God. He would often come here to study his Bible, which he always kept close by. This devotional Bible and his cellphone, which had no battery charge, were both there beside him. I'm sure this printed companion was something he had been reading at some point the evening before.

As these events began to unfold, I started to understand just how deeply Ron trusted in the Lord. When I came across his personal devotional Bible beside him on the ground, it was dog-eared and heavily highlighted. I stood there motionless for a few minutes. My mind was spinning and I hesitated for an extended period of time. I was thinking about Ron's kids and how at this moment in time everything was ok in their world. I was paralyzed by fear, knowing that with my next phone call, I was about to turn that upside down. I knew there was no way to avoid what came next. I walked back to the driveway and stood beside Ron's truck. I leaned against it hoping it would help me keep on my feet. My knees were weak now and my body felt like Jell-O.

I called 911 and made the report. My words were broken and hard to form. How would I muster the strength to share this news with my dad, who was just a few feet away, or even worse, Ron's children?

I walked into the house and sat down beside my father. I told him that Ron was gone, and that he had went on to be with the Lord. He had almost no reaction. Dad was in his mid-eighties now and dealing with dementia. I'm not sure if this made the news harder or easier for him to process. I was just relieved that he didn't fall apart, as I began to have flashbacks about seeing my dad in that same living room in the fetal position after the death of my mother.

I called Carrie, and she started to sob. I asked her to go to the school where Tara worked to give her the news. I didn't want Tara to get this news over the phone. I knew all too well how that felt. Carrie knew I needed her help, and without hesitation, she handle this for me. Once again, she was my rock. I called Wes next, and told him what had happened. Once again, he immediately got in his car and made the trip home from Columbus to console me.

It took almost three hours for the coroner and first responders to finish their work and remove Ron's body from the pool area. Some family members had shown up by this point, and everyone stood on the driveway in disbelief and sadness. As they brought Ron to the front of the house, all of the first responders and the coroner stopped and stood silently with their hands folded and heads tilted downward. One of them asked if we wanted a few minutes alone with my brother. I leaned over his body and laid my head on his chest. I was crying again, and through the tears all I could utter were the words, *"I'm sorry brother. I love you so much."* Shortly after, they wheeled the gurney into one of the rescue vehicles and drove away.

Over the past years, Ron and I weren't that close, but recently we had some meaningful conversations. I'm thankful for those now more than ever. As I stood there next to my brother's lifeless body that morning beside the pool, my mind raced back to our ride together to Mom's funeral all those many years ago. We were together in the family car, silently sharing in the grief of our mother's passing. Now, I was completely alone in the grief of losing yet another family member to a disease that relentlessly made its way through my loved ones.

As I held his devotional Bible, I thought about the times he must have turned to this book seeking answers and comfort. I'm sure that evening poolside he had turned to this book for that very reason. We're all seeking answers. The thought crossed my mind that maybe we should all be spending more time reading the Bible and less time passing judgements onto one another.

I took Ron's cell phone home with me, but I didn't charge it until Saturday evening as I was just too emotionally spent. On Sunday morning, I was awakened at 7:15 AM to the sound of beautiful wind chimes. I didn't know where this was coming from at first, and then I realized it was Ron's cell phone alarm.

Upon further inspection of the phone, Carrie and I discovered this was the only alarm set and it was recurring for every Sunday morning. I'm sure this was his preset wake-up alarm for church each weekend.

My brother Ron, as did my son Daniel, my stepson Zac, and my nephew Andy, all suffered from our society's stigma on addiction. The disease claimed their lives needlessly, as there are viable treatment options that could have prevented this. We, myself included, are all too guilty of using shame as a motivating tool to somehow cause a medical disease to subside or heal. This is done in ignorance. We, myself included, have even shunned these sufferers from our lives and the lives of those they dearly loved, when love and affirmation are actually the very things they desired and needed above all.

We don't have to look any farther than the Bible to understand how Jesus was drawn to those who were struggling. Not to enable them, but to love them and lift them up. He never shunned them nor shamed them. He showered the struggling with forgiveness, protection, and affirmation. He always pointed them toward a means of healing.

I regret that Ron and I weren't closer, that we didn't see eye to eye on many things, and that I didn't do more to help him battle his disease. But, we can't live our lives in regret. It's not healthy and it's not what God would want. I know it's not what Ron would want. We all must forgive ourselves and each other. We must learn from our regrets and not be defined by them. By learning and growing as individuals, we can help others who still wake up each day to face their demons head on.

Anyone who knew Ron, who loved him, who got angry with him, who laughed with him — will miss him. We'll miss the friend who was always quick with a funny line, who was always eager to spout off the latest sports headline, who fought with us, and who loved us with equal passion.

We'll miss the grandfather, the father, the brother, the son, the boy who was prone to pushing limits, and the man who had both won and lost in life over and over.

We'll mourn the man who's gone - whom we lost so tragically - but we'll remember him, and remember that above all, he would want us to remember him as he lived: passionate, full of life and hope, seeking to love and be loved, determined to fight, survive, and thrive in a world where understanding and compassion are often rare. Through tears and sorrow, I shared these same words at Ron's funeral. As I stood on the altar that day, I so desperately wanted to help people see how devastating this disease is and how the stigma and rejection only make it worse. Ron felt that constantly throughout his life and it eats at my soul knowing that I didn't protect him from that.

As you read this book, you no doubt have a "Ron" in your life, maybe more than one. I hope you will reach out to them in love and understanding. Help them battle their disease with education, love, and patience. There is hope. I have often read the following words, and if you, or someone you know, is working through addiction, you are probably familiar with them. I read these at my brother's funeral as well.

Serenity Prayer
God grant me the serenity
to accept the things I cannot change;
courage to change the things I can;
and wisdom to know the difference.
Living one day at a time;
Enjoying one moment at a time;
Accepting hardships as the pathway to peace;
Taking, as He did, this sinful world
as it is, not as I would have it;
Trusting that He will make all things right
if I surrender to His will;
That I may be reasonably happy in this life
and supremely happy with Him
Forever in the next.
Amen.

I have peace in my heart knowing that my brother, Ronal Lee Weidle, Jr., has found his peace, his serenity, and is at this very moment with our Heavenly Father. He no longer fights a battle against the devastating disease of addiction. I have lost so many loved ones in my

family, but understanding that they succumbed to a disease and not a lack of moral integrity has helped me to put it into a better perspective. I hope my experiences and willingness to openly share their battles will help others who read these words. I've yet to encounter a family that is untouched by this affliction on some level.

We must all be our brother's keeper.

Chapter 15

A Light in the Darkness

"Darkness cannot drive out darkness. Only light can do that. Hate cannot drive out hate. Only love can do that." - MLK Jr.

It brings me great joy, along with great heartache, that my two children, along with their half-brother Zac, were also each other's keepers. After we lost my brother Ron, I realized that Wes and I now shared a bond that I never intended to form with him: the loss of a brother. To an extent, it allowed me to step into Wes's shoes as he had already gone through this twice by the ripe age of 25. But it was also a shared pain both of us hated with deep anger. The respect I have for this kid, who has been through more in his 28 years than most people go through in their entire lifetime, is something I can only attempt to put into words. He is a special breed and his brother's knew that. Although Wes was the youngest of the bunch, he was always the leader of the pack and was always willing to set himself aside for the

betterment of his siblings. Wes has been instrumental in the development of this book and so I find it more than fitting to share with you just how much he meant to Daniel and Zac, and just how much he means to me. His strength during these years of our life is something that we could all learn from and strive towards.

Wes has always been an easy kid to raise. He's strong, resilient as hell, intelligent, and independent. Like me, he tends to be on the quiet side, internalizes his feelings, and keeps to himself. I think this is partly because he got my introverted genes, but also because he struggles to find people who understand the pain he carries around on a daily basis. Throughout the divorce of his parents and the loss of his numerous family members, he has seen things that I wouldn't wish on my worst enemy. All the while, he has stood strong in the face of devastating adversity only to come out the other side a very wise and impressive young man.

Throughout it all, Wes graduated from Miami University with honors and a degree in psychology, and went on to obtain a master's degree in physician assistant studies from Ohio Dominican University. He now lives in Columbus and works as a PA-C providing medication management in the outpatient psychiatry setting, and teaches psychiatry at one of the local medical schools. He has made it his life's mission to help bridge gaps in care that we discovered through Daniel's treatment journey, such as treating the risk factors for addiction - anxiety, depression, and ADHD. This is his way of helping to prevent other families from going through what we have gone through, and he is extremely talented in doing this. I know the world has huge things in store for Wes and there couldn't be anyone more deserving.

I have always known that my two boys, Wes and Daniel, are vastly different people. Wes is the intellect, while Daniel was the daredevil. Wes is the introvert, while Daniel was the life of the party. It surprises me sometimes that they came from the same two people, but that is one of the great joys of parenting - bringing a life into the world that has innate parts of yourself mixed with the products of their unique experience and upbringing. Watching them grow up together was nothing short of my most treasured privilege.

Daniel was six years older than Wes, and he loved him very much. As the older of the two, Daniel loved to protect his little brother and kept tabs on him always. Wes and Daniel had a special bond; a bond that was formed through many difficult roads that only the two of them shared. Both suffered through my breakup and divorce from their mother. Both supported me and kept the home together while I put in insane work hours throughout the years. Both clung tightly to each other while they lost their oldest brother to addiction in 2005 and their cousin in 2015. And they both held onto each other as Daniel fought for his life.

To this day, Wes keeps every voicemail, text message, and letter that he received from Daniel saved on his phone. Each voicemail from Daniel begins with, *"Hey, little Brother! It's me....,"* and every single one ends with, *"...I love you, little Brother!"* Daniel was filled with love for his brothers - an unconditional love like I had rarely, if ever, seen elsewhere.

As the middle son in a pack of boys, Daniel was able to enjoy being both the protector and the protected. He was able to learn from and look up to Zac, whom Daniel admired dearly. They inevitably had a special bond being the first two boys, but they had so much more in common than that. Daniel looked up to Zac because of his sensitive heart and keen sense of humor. Zac's humor was next to none. No matter where he went, he had the room in stitches and loved every minute of it because he was bringing joy to the people around him. Daniel typically took the brunt of Zac's jokes, but Daniel didn't care. He was just happy to be laughing and smiling. I remember many nights sitting around the dinner table with our family listening to Zac share story after story, which almost always left us with happy tears and stomach aches. After Zac passed away, there was a noticeable silence that filled the living rooms, the dining rooms, and our family gatherings. Daniel was quick to assume the role of his big brother, once again filling the rooms with laughter and joy.

After looking up to Zac for 20 years, Daniel knew exactly how to be that person we all missed and loved and not many things gave him more joy than seeing a smile on the face of another human. He was a natural. Witty and keen – he never had a filter, and I know he got this from Zac. Although this sometimes came back to bite him, it was the foundation of his unique personality that everyone adored. Whether it was sitting around the dinner table telling us about his day, or giving me gag gifts on Christmas morning, he knew how to light up the room and he wasn't at all shy about doing it.

Although Daniel looked up to Wes in many ways, he also took great pride in protecting and watching over Wes, too. Wes told me a few stories about Daniel coming to his rescue many times that I hadn't heard about until recently. When Wes and I get together, we commonly share stories about the boys. I'd like to think it's our attempt at planting ourselves right back into those moments in time where all was right in our world; moments where our family was whole and pain was a distant concept.

I think these stories paint a perfect picture as to the type of man and big brother Daniel and Zac were to Wes.

Rewind to 2014 when Wes was in 8th grade. Wes had the bright idea to chase after this girl that was well out of his league, and turns out, that wasn't so smart. Supposedly, this girl had an older, much more muscular boyfriend, who lived down the street from us and he didn't take too lightly to Wes trying to steal his girl. Daniel and Zac were the first two out the front door and into the street ready to defend Wes when this guy came knocking. Wes was probably all sorts of embarrassed by their reaction, but I know he also felt a great sense of comfort knowing that he had two big brothers who would never let him get in harm's way. When Wes told me this story he said, *"Daniel didn't even hesitate to fight someone even though that wasn't what I was asking him to do. He didn't laugh at me either, like most older brothers would have probably done. He just stepped up and took me under his wing. He protected me like a big brother should do, and I'll never forget that feeling."*

Fast forward to a very different time in Wes's life - October of 2015, just three months before we lost Daniel. I knew Wes had been struggling with some deeper, darker secrets of his own for some time regarding his sexuality, but it wasn't until he moved out of our small town that he reached a point where he felt comfortable enough to come out formally to his family and close friends. Daniel was one of the first

people to embrace Wes when he did this. Wes still vividly remembers their first conversation about it. Daniel looked at him and said, *"I love you, little Brother, you could have come to me sooner, ya know?"* Wes cracked a smile, and through tears, replied, *"I've never worried about your reaction, bub."*

Daniel never once made anyone feel inferior, embarrassed, or ashamed of who they were. That just wasn't in his nature. After his passing, we found his journal and naturally flipped through the pages. In it, he had created a "gratitude list." Item #7 read: *"Wes: Regardless of his sexuality, I love him unconditionally. Honestly, I would beat someone's ass if they ever talked down to him for that."*

That is who Daniel was. He was a protector and he wore that "Big Brother" badge with pride.

I'm glad that Wes got to share this side of himself with Daniel before it was too late. Towards the end, I know Wes could sense that Daniel was getting closer and closer to the edge, and he feared the regret he would have if Daniel left the world without ever really knowing the real Wes. As painful and scary as it might have been for him to share such intimate parts of himself with Daniel, he did so because he knew it would help Daniel feel more safe in sharing his vulnerabilities in return. That's how the two of them always operated. They leaned on each other and put each other first, through good times and bad, through hell and high water.

Daniel and Zac didn't always take it so easy on Wes, however. Being the baby of the group, Wes took his fair share of "brotherly love." I can recall Daniel and Zac giving Wes wedgies so hard that they ripped the underwear straight off his body! They were all big fans of professional wrestling during their childhoods too, and naturally used Wes as their guinea pig for trying out the famous stunts they would see The Rock and Stone Cold Steve Austin perform on TV. It wasn't uncommon for them to pick Wes up and throw him over their shoulders, only then, to body slam him onto a bed of pillows while everyone involved roared in laughter.

Without a doubt, one of our favorite past times was the many trips to our houseboat on Lake Cumberland. As a family, we would go there as much as possible. It was common practice during the months of May through October to hop in the car on Friday after work and make the 4-hour trek south for the weekend. Daniel and Wes were in their adolescent-teenage years during this period, and both were a little nervous at first to operate the jet-skis by themselves. That quickly diminished as I coached them through this learning curve. I think Wes

had his boating license before he ever even got behind the wheel of a car! It was a special period for me to have this one on one experience with them after all we had been through during the breakdown of our family unit. Daniel was always trying to flip Wes off of the innertube as he towed him around the lake, and they were always having "dunk wars" and competitions to see who could do the coolest flip off the top-deck of the boat. When I think back to the moments where Daniel was most happy, I can't help but envision him out on the lake on a warm summer day with his family present, Wes in particular, because we shared so many laughs there.

Wes's most profound memory of Daniel was in his final days, and illustrates just how big Daniel's heart really was. Daniel most certainly wouldn't want people to think he was a "softy," but he was in fact, just that. He was a big teddy bear with a heart too full to contain. He let his heart and emotions lead him, an aspect of himself that gave him great joy, but also caused him great pain. Daniel hated seeing anyone hurt, whether it be his little brother, or a stranger on the street. Many actions and conversations helped me see this side of Daniel, but I think the most impactful story took place right before he left this earth.

On Christmas Day of 2015, the boys spent the day at their grandparent's home in Germantown. This was a family tradition dating back generations, which they very much enjoyed and looked forward to every year - mostly because of the cooking, but also the company! After their meal, without being asked, Daniel cleaned up after every last person in the room, all 25+ of them. Plate by plate, dish by dish, Daniel made sure that no mess would be left for his grandparents, who were well into their eighties at the time. It was only after this was finished that he accumulated a giant plate of leftovers for the neighbor, an elderly single man that was likely spending the holiday alone. Daniel gave Wes a hug and kiss goodbye, told Wes he loved him, and walked out of their grandparent's house to drop off this plate of food on his way home. That was the last time Wes would see Daniel alive. I will never forget the many selfless acts that Daniel engrossed himself in until his literal last day. *"Even when Daniel was at his weakest, he found purpose in helping others. He found meaning in giving back to*

Daniel and Wes on Christmas Day 2015

those that were less fortunate. Despite all the demons and struggles that Daniel fought on a daily basis, he always made time to make sure everyone else was taken care of first," Wes once told me, when reflecting back onto that day.

Daniel and Wes didn't always see eye to eye on everything, however. In fact, I think it's fair to say that they had more differences than similarities, but selflessness was not one of them. They had the same heart, and as a father, there is nothing that makes me more proud than that. I know that Wes has struggled to process his own grief given the fact that he has taken it upon himself to ensure that the rest of our family stayed on their feet during this time. He didn't have to do this, but he did it anyways. In doing this, he buried his pain, but in writing this book with me, he has been able to journey through that inevitable process in his own way, at his own speed.

It's often the small things that pop up when you process loss that make it hurt the worst. Wes shared with me that he had been writing one day at his favorite coffee shop and it dawned on him for the first time that his future children and spouse will never know Daniel or Zac. In that moment, Wes said the emotional pain took his breath away. In telling me this, Wes expressed, *"My children will never know Uncle Zac or Uncle Daniel. They'll never have sleepovers with their cousins at Daniel's house. And they'll never know the witty sense of humor that enveloped them both. Whomever I marry will never have a brother-in-law that gives them a hard time. And my brothers won't be beside me on the altar, as my best men, to watch me say 'I do'. Because addiction took both of these lives far too early, my future family will miss out on two of the greatest souls I've ever known, and that is a pain I cannot describe."*

Daniel and Zac were incredible human beings with hearts of gold and personalities to match. I mourn for the millions of people that were unable to know them as intimately as we did, and I mourn for Wes as he ventures through life without the guidance and support of his two biggest fans.

The three of them had a unique connection that can never be replaced. They went through life together hand in hand until the disease of addiction took over, and ripped them apart. Even when they were on each other's last nerve, they all knew who to call if they needed someone that could empathize or understand in ways that no one else could.

Wes has always been there for me, and I appreciate his willingness to journey through this book writing process with me. Wes is one of the first people I was able to talk to after I learned of Daniel's death. Wes was one of the first people to arrive at Daniel's house when his mom discovered his body. Wes was the first person to comfort Carrie and I as we arrived back in Germantown after our 24-hour drive from hell. He is, and always has been, the light in the darkness, even when everything around him seemed void.

I'm reminded of the story of the prodigal son in the Bible. One son went out and got into as much trouble as he could - tried everything he could and experienced things he never should have. The other son was always there, always faithful, always did what he should, and never got the lion's share of attention. Wes was that son. He was always there, never failed, never caused grief or pain, and was all too often overlooked as we focused all of our attention on helping Daniel fight for his life. Wes sadly was the forgotten son so many times because he was strong enough to stand up on his own two feet and fend for himself. I love both of my boys equally, but one needed more of my attention, and Wes quietly understood that. He humbly took the backseat because he knew Daniel's life depended on it.

Thank you, Wes. I love you beyond words.

Chapter 16

Threads of Hope

"Even the darkest night will end and the sun will rise." - Victor Hugo

As the days, weeks, months, and years pass by, I find myself continually looking for reasons to push forward. I find myself looking back often, in amazement that I'm still alive. Sometimes I'm not really sure how that even happened. Back when Daniel was struggling, I would often have fears about what might happen to me if he were to lose the fight. To put it frankly, each time this thought came to my mind, I saw an image of myself in a morgue. It wasn't an image that I liked, but I honestly didn't think an alternative was possible. Yet, here we are. It has been over three years since I've hugged my son, and I'm still pushing through. Fighting like hell, but I'm still here. This hasn't happened because I'm a strong guy or because I'm busy distracting myself from reality. I'm alive because small threads of hope have been frequently weaved into my life - random chance encounters, my wife, my son, my dad, and the three little boys that Daniel left behind. *These are the reasons why I move forward each day.*

Around the same time I began my advocating efforts for Daniel in Columbus, I had one of these chance encounters with a complete stranger - one that gave me enough hope on that particular day to push on. I was at work one afternoon on a spring day in 2017 in our retail sales lobby. Business was beginning to pick up as the weather broke and our gravel plant restarted operations for the year.

I remember staring out the front window of our building which overlooked the parking lot. My mind was anywhere but work as my internal battle against depression and grief raged on. I noticed a beat-up construction truck come flying into the parking lot before abruptly coming to a screeching halt in the first available parking spot. The driver's side door swung open and a long-haired man stepped out. He appeared to be a construction worker, sporting a sleeveless button-down shirt proudly exposing several intricate tattoos. He slammed the truck door quickly and headed towards our entrance. I thought to myself, *"Damn, this guy is either about to come in here and raise hell, or he's just really excited to get some gravel!"*

At this point, I had already formed an opinion of this man. He was a redneck laborer, struggling to make ends meet, probably lived a rough life, and he didn't mind if others noticed. He looked liked someone you really didn't want to get into a bar fight with, but he certainly gave the impression that he had been in a few. I had just formulated an entire profile in my mind about this fellow in less than 30 seconds.

I typically let our dispatcher, which used to be Daniel, handle all the retail sales. But because of my preconceived stigma-based opinion, I didn't walk off and hide in my office. I decided I should handle this customer myself.

I was on the customer side of our display counter as he entered the showroom. We stood face to face, toe to toe.

He asked about the various types of gravel and we had a brief conversation about his needs. I thought I had answered all of his questions, when he noticed a brochure on the counter titled, *Daniel's Story*. It was the pamphlet I had created to advertise the information on www.danielsstory.org to spare myself the pain of going through the entire story multiple times per day.

"What's this Daniel's Story all about?," he asked. He quickly followed-up with, *"I thought Daniel's story was something out of the Bible."*

I was a bit startled by his tone. He sounded as though he might have been offended. This was followed by an awkward silence as he stared at the literature. I was not sure where this conversation was headed. I braced myself for his response and for a couple seconds I thought we are about to lock horns. In hindsight, it was probably just my sensitivity to the subject.

I remained composed and simply replied, *"Daniel is my son and he passed away 19 months ago."*

There was an even longer awkward silence.

"I lost my 23-year-old son three years ago," he said as he pulled out a wrinkled up photo of his son from his wallet and handed it to me.

He looked me straight in the eyes and said, *"He was my life and he meant everything to me."* I could hear his voice begin to crack and noticed a tear well-up in the corner of his eye.

At that moment, as we stood there together, all walls crumbled. There was an instant connection and understanding. No words were needed. After a brief silence and a struggle to maintain our composure, he looked down at the picture of his son and said, *"Brother, let me tell you, after three years, it doesn't get any easier. The pain never goes away."*

He put his wallet back in his pocket, we locked eyes once more, and stood there together, motionless. It was clear we were both on the verge of a meltdown. As he turned to leave, the thought of what just happened overwhelmed me. A stranger, a man I had never met before, nor may ever see again, just shared in the most intimate, broken part of my soul. We were in each other's hell - each other's anguish. It was like the reality of the moment was too much. I had to remind myself to breathe. As he was walking away, I knew in my heart that it was my turn to reach out to him. I extended my hand and formally introduced myself. He said, *"I'm Willy....,"* and then, as he looked intensely into my eyes, he added, *"I will pray for you, brother."* Willy turned and walked out of the building and I never saw him again.

This may seem insignificant to you, unless you've experienced it for yourself, but the instant bond that occurs when you meet someone who understands where you're at and what you have endured is a rare occurrence. Even more so when your initial impression of the person you just connected with was totally wrong. It was something I think God knew I needed. It did something in me that day that no number of counseling sessions had accomplished. It allowed me to turn off the loneliness for a split second, and *that* was exactly what I longed for. I prayed for Willy that day also, and at times since. I'll never forget that encounter and what it meant to me. Thank you, Willy, wherever you are.

Stigma is a terrible part of addiction. Everyone in my family that had this disease has been the target of it at one time or another. Even the way I viewed Willy on the day he walked into my office was based on a preconceived notion and stigma. I still find myself struggling to practice what I preach at times because judgement has been ingrained in our beings and into our society so deeply. It is devastating to healing and most often robs us from getting to know people who can greatly bless our lives.

Webster defines stigma as *a mark of disgrace associated with a particular circumstance, quality, or person.* How many times have we missed out on the opportunity to help or connect with a person based on stigma? We simply do not know what is in the heart of a person from looking on the outside. One of my favorite quotes is, "Be kind, for everyone you meet is fighting a battle you know nothing about." It's so true. It has been true for me as an introvert when people assume I am so many things that I am not, it was true for my family members that struggled with addiction, and it's true for many people of every marginalized group in this country. Imagine how much more effective we could be if we stopped viewing people with the medical disease of addiction as merely weak or unable to control their cravings, and actually saw them as champions locked inside a body, fighting for their lives against a fatal disease. In truth, we are all meant to be our brother's keeper. We aren't meant to be their judge. And when I implement this philosophy into my own life, not only do they win, but I win, too. I gain a sense of love by giving love. I gain the hope that it is possible to keep pushing on when I dish out hope to others. It's a beautiful thing.

These chance encounters with strangers happen more often than you'd think, but I welcome them with wide open arms. During my initial few meetings in Columbus with Sandra, I decided that I needed a 3-ring-binder full of information about Daniel to more easily share what an incredible person he was, and detail the overall message I was trying to get across about addiction and opioids. Many times, people don't remember the details of conversations, so my goal was to put together something that people could see and touch as this seems to be more impactful than just verbal rambling. It proved to be very effective, as there were commonly many tears shed as strangers whom I had never met flipped through the pages.

When I went to the local FedEx-Kinko's to make copies for this project, I was barely functioning emotionally. It was one of my first ventures out of the home after six weeks of being cooped up and depressed. I set myself up at a large self-serve copier facing out towards the parking lot. I had my pages all laid out and I began the copying process, which took me a couple of hours. At one point a young lady started using the self-serve copier beside my station. My items were taking up more than my allotted amount of space, so I tried to pull my items closer in order to give her the room she needed. At this stage of my grief I could barely engage anyone in conversation without triggering my emotional pain and tears. I noticed her looking out of the corner of her eye towards the photos of Daniel that I had in line for copying. I was already hoping that she wouldn't ask me, or attempt to make a polite comment, such as, *"Is that your son? He looks so much like you!,"* which I have been told many times. I knew that would instantly bring me to tears.

This young lady soon completed her copying needs, packed up, paid the clerk at the service counter, and walked out the front door. I watched as she got into her vehicle and appeared to leave.

By this time, I was almost finished with my work and piled the newly assembled binders into a box and headed to the service counter to pay. As I approached the counter, the lady I had watched get into her car, who had just spent the past hour next to me at the copier, was now back at the service counter, three feet in front of me. I saw her point to a FedEx-Kinko's Canvas print promotion on an easel display, which was on sale for $90. She then told the clerk that she wanted to pay for this and give it to the man over at the copier. As she turned to show the clerk where I was, she realized that I was right behind her.

I was as shocked as she was at that point. I wanted to know why she felt the need to do this, but I also didn't want to have a conversation in the middle of the copy store about burying my son. It was still just too raw and I was too fragile.

There was an awkwardness as we stood there.

I finally managed to uttered the words, *"Thank you, but I don't understand why."*

She gently replied, *"I noticed the photos and I felt your pain."*

There was another awkward silence as I could not advance the conversation for fear of a melt down in public.

I asked her what her name was and she said, *"Reyna."* I thanked her again, and she walked out of the store. This random act of kindness was very appreciated, but my logical mind sat there in disbelief trying to understand how she had even come to the conclusion that I had lost my son by simply seeing me at the copier. I was deeply touched by this random act of service and kindness. She felt something, even after she got into her car to leave, that propelled her to come back in and provide hope to a complete stranger that was hurting. I choose to call that divine intervention. On that day, Reyna was the reason I had the ability to keep pushing forward.

After using these binders to disseminate information to as many people as I could reach without much of a response, I was pondering my remaining options. The pain was too great and there was no relief in sight. My efforts were not making an impact and I was discouraged to say the least. I had fought a good fight, I was finishing my course, and I tried to keep my faith.

I walked back into the woods where Daniel used to hunt, simply seeking some solitude so that I could sort out my thoughts and think more clearly - the same way my son often did.

On this day in particular, however, I wasn't finding peace out there, but I stayed as I could not face another person or conversation. My heart still ached as if I had just received the text on the beach.

I was neglecting just about everything I could neglect. My health, my marriage, my business, my staff, and my youngest son. I frequently went missing-in-action, and on this day in particular, I spent the entire day contemplating whether or not I had the strength to hang on for yet another dreadful day.

As I laid on a hammock in the woods, my cell phone rang. For months, I rarely answered it, especially if I didn't recognize the number. For some reason, I decided to answer this call and I'm glad I did.

Scott: Hello

Caller: Is this Scott?

Scott: Yes.

Caller: This is Rick Marion (Rick was one of my good high school friends whom I had not had much contact with for nearly 20 years)

Scott: Hi, Rick.

Rick: Scott, are you okay?

Scott: No, I'm not, to be honest. Why do you ask?

Rick: Honestly, I don't know why. You have just been on my mind a lot today and I thought I'd give you a call to touch base and see if you need anything.

Scott: I'm sure you must have seen a sappy post of mine on Facebook or something?

Rick: I don't even have Facebook. I really don't know why I have worried about you today, honest to God.

At this point, I was a bit shell shocked and didn't say much of anything back. I couldn't dump on Rick after 20 years. Where would I even begin? He wasn't calling to be my therapist.

Rick: Scott, you know where I live. I'm here all the time. Please stop by because I would like to see you. Is there anything I can do for you?

Scott: You already did Rick, thanks for thinking of me and reaching out. I really appreciate that.

After I hung up, I tried, but could not explain, why a friend from 20 years ago would feel the need to call and check on me, other than a divine intervention - nudged by God to help me walk through the valley that day. It's special when someone reaches out to you during troubled times, but when someone you don't know or haven't heard from for 20 years does it, there's a lot more depth to it. There are days when you need to be a brother's keeper, and there are days you need a brother's keeper in your own life.

Giving someone support and affirmation is what Daniel did on a regular basis to the down-and-out because he knew how much he needed it from others when he was down and out. Through these random encounters and acts of kindness, I was able to learn yet another aspect of Daniel's heart. It showed me, in a way, what it was like to be in the depths of despair, desperate for a thread of hope.

Although events like this which happened from time to time should be credited for getting me through some incredibly difficult days, it is actually my family that has provided the largest source of hope and support. Without them, I would be nothing but ashes and dust. On a daily basis, unconditionally, Carrie has stood by me and has been my source of strength when I had nothing left in my tank. Sometimes without even saying a word, her presence was simply enough to carry me through. She does more behind the scenes to keep our family together than anyone realizes, and I want to take a second to acknowledge that. I have leaned on her to be my communicator more times than I'd like to admit, but she has never complained or shut me out. She showered me with love and understanding when I needed it the most.

Carrie has been instrumental in maintaining and growing our relationship with Daniel's three boys, too. They are all three obsessed with her, and I can't blame them! She has a heart for those boys that is mesmerizing to watch. Carrie continually makes it a priority to stay actively engaged in their lives and consistently has the boys over for sleepovers, shopping trips, and adventures out into the woods. If it were just me here, I'm sure the boys would think I was just a boring old grandpa, but Carrie keeps me young and gives the boys the energy they need to feed their ever-growing and hyper minds. For that alone, I'm forever grateful.

Watching Dylan, Landon, and Gavin grow up is the ultimate thread of hope. They carry their father in their DNA and in their hearts everyday. I see Daniel come back to life in the little things they do. I see him in their personalities. I see him in their smiles and in their eyes. I see him in their curiosity and in their compassionate, giant hearts. When they're in the room with me, I feel like Daniel is too, and nothing else in the world can provide that for me, only them.

One of my biggest fears is that they will forget Daniel - that they'll move on with their lives and he will become a distant memory. To some degree, that is unavoidable. Daniel wouldn't want them to spend their entire life in continual grief, endlessly yearning for him. But I do want them to remember the real Daniel. I do want them to remember how much he loved them and longed to be the father his disease sometimes prevented him from being. Much of this book effort is for them. When they're old enough to wrap their minds around it, I want them to know the real story.

I've compiled a few stories below that I want Dylan, Landon, and Gavin to have etched in history forever. Memories that they will forever be able to look back on whenever they're having a bad day and miss their dad.

The very first memory is one of the best. The moment Daniel first became a father.

February 2007 - Wes was in the delivery room with Daniel as he welcomed his firstborn son into the world, Dylan Zachary Weidle. *"I've never seen anyone's face glow quite the way Daniel's did the moment he first laid eyes on Dylan,"* Wes told me. *"He was so proud and not at all hesitant to flash Dylan's baby pictures all around town right after he was born."* Much to Wes's luck, he was able to witness that same expression of love two more times with the birth of Landon and Gavin.

Wes also told me that he remembers being the stereotypical annoying little brother that wanted to be glued to Daniel's hip after Dylan was born. He spent many of the following days and weeks at Daniel's home watching him learn the intricacies of fatherhood for the first time.

Daniel didn't hesitate to change dirty diapers, although he may or may not have put a clothespin on his nose a few times. He didn't hesitate to get up in the middle of the night to rock his boys back to sleep after they woke up crying, and he didn't hesitate to sing nursery rhymes until he was blue in the face if it meant that his boys were happy and calm. Daniel was selfless in many areas of his life, but being a father illuminates that with the most direct light.

November 2011 - It was Landon's 3rd birthday and we had the boys over for the afternoon to celebrate. Landon loved tractors for the longest time, and so everything we did that day had something to do with tractors. I swear that kid could name every piece of heavy equipment at Weidle Corporation before he could even walk. We had picked out John Deere tractor rain boots and a little Carhartt coat for him. We had a cookie cake and stuffed our faces as we watched Landon opened his gifts. It was unusually warm for November, so we decided to take a hike at the Metro Park across the street from our

house. Hiking with the kids always seemed like a good idea at first, but it was almost inevitable that we always ended up carrying at least one of them back because they would end up too tired to walk! We meandered through the trails that day, stopping along the creek to throw rocks and walk across many fallen logs. Dylan was really into Spiderman at the time, so he pretended he was casting webs all along the trail while he jumped off logs, just like Spiderman would do. Landon's little 3-year-old legs got the best of him, so Daniel carried him on his shoulders the whole two miles back! But he didn't mind it one bit. I'm not sure who was happier - Landon for getting to ride on daddy's shoulders, or Daniel for just being able to have time with his boys. That was such a nice, peaceful day.

April 2012 - It was Daniel's 27th birthday. He just wanted to celebrate with his boys by his side. We all headed to Chuck E. Cheese's, which is a pizza/arcade venue. Daniel was just as big of a kid as his own and was all about this place! The boys arrived with a giant poster board birthday card that was strewn with candy and precious notes from

them. We spent a couple of hours playing games, eating pizza and cake, and just being goofy. Daniel was flying the airplanes, shooting the imaginary guns, and throwing skee-ball right alongside the boys. Dylan and Landon always brought Daniel joy and they loved being with him. Their laughter in his presence still echoes in my mind.

January 2015 - We were in the midst of a giant snow storm. Daniel and his girlfriend, Nova, came up to our house just to hang out as we were all a little stir-crazy from being snowed in. They brought Gavin, who was only about eight months old at the time, and we decided to get some photos of him in the snow for the first time. We bundled up and headed out to the back yard for Gavin's first snow day. I took a picture of he and Daniel, and it wasn't but two seconds before Daniel said, *"Now don't post that on Facebook, I don't have any hair gel in!,"* followed by that notorious smirk of his. Daniel was borderline obsessed with his haircut and always had it styled just perfect, but on this day in particular, it was not up to his standards. He didn't know this, but I posted it anyways because I thought it captured their happiness perfectly. That was a great day and typical Daniel behavior. We lounged, ate homemade cookies, and took turns snuggling with Gavin. When I look back at those photos, I remember that day so vividly.

December 2015 - This was the last time Carrie and I saw Daniel, and the last photo of he and Gavin together. It was taken the night before we left for Florida - just 19 days before Daniel passed. Daniel came up to our house as we were packing and getting ready for the RV trip the next day. Carrie had picked up Gavin from the babysitter to spend some extra time with him before we departed for what we thought would be

months in Florida. She was struggling with the thought of leaving Gavin as she had babysat him multiple days every week since he was born, and they had developed a special bond. She invited Daniel up for dinner that night to spend time together and say our goodbyes before the trip. Daniel came up as soon as he was off work, as he was never one to turn down a free dinner invitation! Daniel was rolling around on the floor with Gavin, tickling him into tears of laughter, and all of us were cracking up over Gavin's giggles. Gavin was asking for more every time Daniel pretended to give up. Daniel could never tell any of his boys the word *no*, so he would tickle him more and more! They were enjoying each other so much that night. Never in my wildest nightmares did I think that would be the last time.

Daniel would take on all the pain in the world if it meant that his boys were spared. Nothing hurts my heart more than realizing that Daniel's boys will grow up without their dad. Although another man will likely step up and take that role in their life, Daniel is irreplaceable. His heart and compassion are unrivaled. His boys will forever have a Daniel-sized hole in their hearts that no other man will ever be able to fill. With each precious baby boy that came into Daniel's life, his pride and his heart grew and grew. As Wes and I look back on Daniel's legacy, we will always think first of his children because that's what he would want. They were his world. And now, they're our world. They're our hope and our purpose for living.

Chapter 17

Through the Woods

"There is meaning and purpose in not surrendering in the face of loss, but instead working to bind up wounds, ease pain, and spare others what you have seen. Our obligation, our duty, is to ensure that something good comes from suffering, that we find some kind of gift in good-bye. Not to somehow, perversely, make the loss 'worth it.' Nothing will ever justify some losses, but we can survive, even thrive, if we channel grief into purpose and never allow evil to hold the field." - James Comey, *A Higher Loyalty*

If I have learned anything throughout the course of my life, it's that there is no way to escape the pain of this world. Life is unfair, bad things happen to good people, and good things happen to bad people. There is no way to run away from reality. And so as I sat in my grief and in my pain, I had a choice to make. I was either going to make my exit, or I was going to endure. It became obvious to me that the only way to survive this would be to face the storm head on, to let myself feel both the good and the bad, and to get comfortable with my loneliness. There was no way to bypass those symbolic woods, filled with thorns, and creatures, and darkness, and unpredictable elements. So if there was no way around it, I might as well camp out and accept my new normal. I might as well get acquainted with, and accept, the gnawing pain inside my heart because I knew it wasn't going anywhere. Except this wasn't so symbolic to me. The only place I have come to find solace is in the woods where Daniel used to spend much of his time, seeking solace. It gives me the peace and quiet my soul needs to sort out my emotions and allows my mind time to process and rest. It was through the woods, to my surprise, where I would come to lose my mind and find my soul. The story behind this unique piece of land, where Daniel and I both have experienced deeply personal moments, is quite remarkable.

The property itself has significant history. In the early 1900s, the Miami Military Institute, a private college and officer training academy, operated on this land. After the military institute closed, it eventually was purchased by the national chapter of the United Methodist Church. This organization developed the area into a christian youth program for summer camps and retreats. They set up a dozen or so campsites on the land and would bring in youth from the inner cities each summer for a 3-4 day experience in the woods. Because the land had already been utilized for military use and summer church camps, there were well established trails, and Daniel knew them better than anyone.

When the noise of the world became too great for Daniel, he would retreat to this specific parcel of land nestled on the outskirts of our small town. This was his therapy. I know the moments he spent there - the alone time, the quiet walks through the pines, and the sounds of nature - meant a great deal to him and calmed his aching soul. No matter what was bothering him, whether it be his own actions and demons, work responsibilities, or the demands of his dad, peace always awaited him in these woods. It was as if God had carved out his own hiding place, a refuge in times of trouble, just for Daniel.

Daniel was just a sophomore in high school when I purchased this 200-acre property. Within a year, he had already memorized the trails and property lines, and used it as his playground to hike and hunt. It wasn't a cheap purchase, but I knew that one day it would pay off and in the meantime, it was providing the two of us with a lot of happiness. There was a key section of this land that we didn't own, however, but I had my eye on it for years as it was the only thing between our land and the roadway. If I was able to acquire this, the opportunities became endless for possible property development.

In late November of 2015, I was working in the shop when Daniel came bursting through the doors in typical fashion, decked out in hunting gear from head to toe. It was obvious that he had come straight from the woods and I was expecting him to give me the ole "my deer got away again" story.

"Dad, guess what?! They just put a for sale sign out in front of the field!," Daniel exclaimed in giddy excitement.

I had no idea what he was talking about. *"Who and what are you talking about?,"* I replied, with a confused look on my face.

"The land on Stivers Road that you've been wanting! I came out of the woods from hunting and noticed the sign, it wasn't there when I went in!" He then proceeded to hand me the name and phone number listed on the sign as if he was expecting me to call right then and there to make a purchase. I was pretty excited myself, but decided to wait until

the following morning so I could go take a more thorough look at the details of the land before calling.

I took Daniel with me and we trotted through the three acre parcel. I had always envisioned the land as a residential development, and so I started to talk out loud with Daniel regarding my visions. I threw out ideas of where the road could come in and where the first house could be built. I noticed a change in his demeanor not long before he asked, *"Really, Dad? Is that all you think about?"*

That comment stung a bit because he was right. I backtracked our conversation and replied, *"You're right, I'm sorry. I'm just sharing the possibilities. We could do a lot with this land, that's all."*

I had a habit of jumping to development as I had done this numerous times in Germantown, not only because it's a smart financial investment, but because our tiny town had been stagnant in residential and business growth for decades. In fact, Germantown's population hasn't grown in 40 years and that was driving out many really smart and talented people. If we could help foster growth in untouched land like this, it would provide more opportunities for our young people and for our community.

I decided that this would be a great opportunity for Daniel to get some experience in business deals and land purchasing. I gave Daniel the green light to pursue the purchase and intentionally stayed in the background. I wanted him to take ownership of this because he was so passionate about it and it would teach him a great deal. I told him to give the owner of the land a call and ask a few basic questions - water source, gas lines, zoning, etc. I knew the answers already, but I was trying to put these things on Daniel's radar as important factors to know before buying land. I told him that if everything checked out, to make a cash offer, 15% under asking price. He did everything perfectly, but the owner declined. He wanted full asking price. I told Daniel to just give it some time and wait for the guy to come down. This was only about a week before I was scheduled to leave for Florida and pursue my pseudo winter retirement. Daniel never got the chance to see this through - another regret that I wouldn't be able to go back on.

One month after Daniel's passing, one of my first ventures out of the house was to the place where I felt Daniel's spirit would meet me. I wandered through the woods in search of Daniel's deer stands. I knew where each and every one of them were as I had went looking for Daniel in these same woods many times in the past whenever Daniel would disappear off the grid for too long. Carrie accompanied me, probably out of fear that I might otherwise not come back.

The first deer stand was in a forest of tall white pine trees, overgrown with honeysuckle taller than the average man. I fought my way through the brush and finally found myself directly underneath the place where Daniel had spent so much of his time. I immediately became overcome with emotion, fell to my knees, and just sobbed. In the middle of the woods, my cries echoed through the trees and my tears fell onto the earth, still half-frozen from winter. Carrie was right, I wanted to die right there. I didn't care anymore. If I was alone, I would have just laid down, let night fall, and freeze to death. Nobody else knew these woods or knew where to find me.

After about an hour, I managed to pull it together enough to start our way back to the car. Within just a few steps outside the overgrowth of honeysuckle, I noticed two natural rows of pine trees, lined up in a perfectly straight row headed due north. At that exact moment, I knew that I needed to clear the surrounding brush and open up the path between the pines so that others could access this beautiful niche of earth. What I had just experienced was spiritual, sacred even, and if I was the only one that ended up enjoying it, that would be okay, too. Either way, I had found my next mission and my next goal. I was going to transform these woods into a memorial for Daniel and a public park for others to rest in the tranquility that we so commonly found there.

The next day, I called my attorney and told him that I wanted to purchase the parcel of land that Daniel and I had tried to acquire three months prior. If I wanted to clear the path between all those pine trees, I would obviously need to own that land. I still wasn't up for interaction with the outside world, so I didn't even attend the closing or meet with the owner. My attorney handled everything, and as soon as I got the call that everything was final, I went to town.

Carrie and I began to cut the undergrowth ourselves in the midpoint of winter. She knew in her heart just as well as I did, that without something to focus on, something to pull me out of bed each day, I wasn't going to last much longer. It was bleak and bitterly cold outside, but it was nothing in comparison to the torture I felt inside my heart.

My first goal was simply to create a pathway which lead to one of Daniel's favorite places on this earth - his deer stand. I envisioned not just a pathway, but a spiritual and peaceful memorial in honor of Daniel. As each day went by, I felt a growing presence with me. No sooner would I finish one project, another one would pop up as if someone were trying to keep me busy and distracted. After the pathway

and trails were formed, I erected several life-size cedar log crucifixion crosses in key locations, created Teardrop Pond, and converted a 20-acre bean field into a native short grass conservation field, populated with over 300 pheasants and quail. Before long, what was once an overgrown wooded parcel where my son sought his peace, became a manicured refuge for others. Daniel's place of peace had now become Daniel's Peace Memorial Park.

Once I placed the Daniel's Peace Memorial Park boulder roadside, it became open to the public. Along the trails, visitors can stop along the way and look at shadow boxes filled with our family photos, along with Daniel's devotionals, handwritten letters, and some of his most cherished keepsakes. These items line the paths, which wind throughout this beautiful pocket of land.

People quickly began to come; they would just show up and explore. I've had countless visitors tell me, or post on Facebook, that the spiritual connection they felt walking this parcel was remarkable - supernatural, almost. One young lady that was battling depression would post a couple times per week about how she would visit the

woods while battling her own demons. We've also heard from parents who are helping their children fight addiction. Some have even brought their son or daughter to the park to share Daniel's story through the memorials and mementos scattered along the walking paths. The impact has been deep and vast, and every story inevitably brings a tear to my eye. Stories like this are why I went to such great lengths to make it a possibility, and I would do it a million times over to see other people find peace in the way in which Daniel did.

Daniel's Peace Memorial Park is located at 7500 South Stivers Road, Germantown, Ohio. It's now open year-round, 7-days a week from dawn to dusk. I invite anyone and everyone in the area to experience this at your leisure.

This parcel of land is where Daniel went when the noise of the world was too great for him to bear. He found hope and faith where there seemed to be none - in the wilderness. He was able to take it upon himself to sort through the trials of life in the alone time he spent there with God. Far too often, I also find myself struggling to drown out the noise of the world and the pain of his death. There is no way to go around it, to avoid it, or to hide from it. The only way out, is through. And so it's off to the woods I go, to lose my mind and to find my soul.

As I look back on the life of my son, I realize that he was a lost soul, but it brings me great comfort and great peace to know that he is now found.

In closing, I would like to speak directly to my firstborn son, the boy who captured my heart from day one, and will continue to be my purpose for living through to my last breath.

My sweet Daniel,

Everything I've done is for you. After we lost you, I became broken and shattered in ways that I didn't know possible. I knew deep down that I would never ever be the same again and I would likely never fully recover. So, I surrendered. I waved the white flag because the force of grief was monstrous. It wasn't the pain I surrendered to, however. I surrendered to a purpose greater than myself. I vowed to keep your memory alive and make the world a better place because you were a part of it. You taught me things that I hadn't realized in all my years of living, and even in death, you continue to teach me things. You taught me to fight, even when the odds seem insurmountable. You taught me to seek peace and solitude when it feels like the world is crashing down around me. And you taught me that love is bigger than anything else on this planet.

Everything I have done - from pounding on the door of a local pill dealer, to the medical malpractice case, to the passage of Daniel's Law, the creation of Daniel's Peace Memorial Park, and the writing of this book - was because you deserve it, son. You are worth it. As painfully uncomfortable and difficult as it often was, working for this higher purpose has kept me alive. I must make some sense of your death and of my pain. If the loss we endured didn't trigger positive change in the world to some degree, my will to live would simply dwindle away. Your story has, and will, continue to save others who have struggles just like you did.

You, my child, had a personality and a heart that were far too great and far too deep to selfishly keep boxed up in my memory bank. The world deserves to know you, and I hope your brother and I have helped illustrate that through the creation of this book.

Your legacy lives on through the memorial park, legislation, this book, but most importantly - the three brave, handsome, and loving little boys that you brought into this world.

I miss you every minute of every day, and I look forward to the day when we are reunited again. I'm proud of you, my son.

Love,

Dad

"Instead of asking why they left, now I ask, what beauty will I create in the space they no longer occupy?"

- Rudy Francisco.

For more information, resources, and ways to get involved, please visit

www.DanielsStory.org

References

1. American Society of Addiction Medicine. (2011, Apr 12). Definition of Addiction. Retrieved from https://www.asam.org/resources/definition-of-addiction

2. Kolodny, A., Courtwright, D.T., Hwang, C.S., Kreiner, P., Eadie, J.L., Clark, T.W., Alexander, G.C. (2015, Mar 18). The Prescription Opioid and Heroin Crisis: A Public Health Approach to an Epidemic of Addiction. *Annual Review of Public Health*. 36:559-74. Retrieved from https://www.ncbi.nlm.nih.gov/pubmed/25581144

3. Appleby, J., Lucas, E. (2019, Jun 21). Surgeons' Opioid-Prescribing Habits Are Hard To Kick. *Kaiser Health News*. Retrieved from https://khn.org/news/surgeons-opioid-prescribing-habits-hard-to-kick/

4. Blum K., Comings, DE. (2000). Reward deficiency syndrome: genetic aspects of behavioral disorders. *Progress in Brain Research*. 126:325-41. Retrieved from https://www.ncbi.nlm.nih.gov/pubmed/11105655

5. Brown, David. (2017, Sep 5) Opioids and Paternalism. *The American Scholar*. Retrieved from https://theamericanscholar.org/opioids-and-paternalism/#.XVmjgS2ZM6U/

6. Carren, Todd M.D. (2015). Lecture series. The Ridge Ohio Residential Alcohol and Drug Treatment. Retrieved from https://www.youtube.com/channel/UCpG5ibbZPL2T7_-RUH6rCeQ/videos

7. Centers for Disease Control and Prevention. (2016, May 3). 1 in 3 antibiotic prescriptions unnecessary. Retrieved from https://www.cdc.gov/media/releases/2016/p0503-unnecessary-prescriptions.html

8. Cleveland Clinic. (2016). Combating the Opioid Epidemic. Retrieved from https://www.youtube.com/watch?v=bkdOH2HC_xM

9. Dowdell, J., Girion L., Lesser, B., Levine D. (2019, Jun 25). Special Report: How judges added to the grim toll of opioids. *Reuters*. Retrieved from https://www.reuters.com/article/us-usa-courts-secrecy-judges-special-rep/special-report-how-judges-added-to-the-grim-toll-of-opioids-idUSKCN1TQ1N5?utm_source=applenews

10. Ebert M.H., Loosen, P.T., Nurcombe, B., Leckman, J.F. (2018). *CURRENT Diagnosis & Treatment Psychiatry (3rd edition)*. McGraw-Hill: Lange. ISBN 978-0-07-142292-5.

11. Edney, Anna. (2019, Mar 28). FDA Chief Lays Out Vision for New Pain Pills to Replace Opioids. *Bloomberg*. Retrieved from

https://www.bloomberg.com/news/articles/2019-03-28/fda-chief-lays-out-vision-for-new-pain-pills-to-replace-opioids

12. Families Against Narcotics. (2019). Video Library. Retrieved from https://www.familiesagainstnarcotics.org/video

13. First Call. (2019). Films. Retrieved from http://www.stoptheshame.info/

14. Fowler, J. S., Volkow, N. D., Kassed, C. A., & Chang, L. (2007 Apr). Imaging the addicted human brain. *Science & practice perspectives.* 3(2):4–16. Retrieved from https://www.ncbi.nlm.nih.gov/pmc/articles/PMC2851068/

15. Goldstein, R. Z., & Volkow, N. D. (2002, Oct). Drug addiction and its underlying neurobiological basis: neuroimaging evidence for the involvement of the frontal cortex. *The American Journal of Psychiatry.* 159(10):1642–52. Retrieved from https://www.ncbi.nlm.nih.gov/pubmed/12359667

16. Gottlieb, S. (2019, Feb 26). FDA Statement. Retrieved from https://www.fda.gov/news-events/press-announcements/statement-fda-commissioner-scott-gottlieb-md-agencys-2019-policy-and-regulatory-agenda-continued

17. Heinzerling, K. G., Lamp, K., Ober, A.J., Vries, D. D., Watkins, K. E. (2016). Summit: Procedures for Medication-Assisted Treatment of Alcohol or Opioid Dependence in Primary Care. *Rand Corporation.* Retrieved from https://www.integration.samhsa.gov/clinical-practice/mat/RAND_MAT_guidebook_for_health_centers.pdf

18. Henry J Kaiser Family Foundation. https://www.kff.org

19. Hirsch, Ronald. (2016, Apr 6). The opioid epidemic: It's time to place blame where it belongs. *KevinMD.* Retrieved from https://www.kevinmd.com/blog/2016/04/the-opioid-epidemic-its-time-to-place-blame-where-it-belongs.html

20. Joseph, Andrew. (2018). Opioid prescribing fell after clinicians told their patient had died of overdose. *STAT News, Boston Globe Media.* Retrieved from https://www.statnews.com/2018/08/09/opioid-prescribing-medical-examiner-letters-overdose/?utm_campaign=trendmd

21. Keilman, John. (2016.) Almost all doctors routinely overprescribe pain pills: survey. *The Chicago Tribune.* Retrieved from https://www.chicagotribune.com/news/breaking/ct-prescription-painkiller-overuse-met-20160324-story.html

22. Lawlor, J. (2016). CMS drops pain questions from patient satisfaction surveys. *Portland Press Herald.* Retrieved from https://www.managedhealthcareconnect.com/article/cms-drops-pain-questions-satisfaction-surveys

23. Levine, A. (2017). How the VA Fueled the National Opioid Crisis and Is Killing Thousands of Veterans. *Newsweek Magazine*. Retrieved from https://www.newsweek.com/2017/10/20/va-fueled-opioid-crisis-killing-veterans-681552.html

24. Lopez, G. (2017, Dec 21). The opioid epidemic explained. *Vox*. Retrieved from https://www.vox.com/science-and-health/2017/8/3/16079772/opioid-epidemic-drug-overdoses

25. Mcgreal, Chris. (2017 Oct 19). How big pharma's money - and its politicians - feed the US opioid crisis. *The Washington*. Retrieved from https://www.theguardian.com/us-news/2017/oct/19/big-pharma-money-lobbying-us-opioid-crisis

26. Mole, Beth. (2016). CDC just says no to opioid prescriptions opioids for chronic pain. *Ars Technica*. Retrieved from https://arstechnica.com/science/2016/03/cdc-just-says-no-to-opioid-prescriptions-for-chronic-pain/

27. Mozes, Alan. (2016). Most Doctors 'Overprescribe' Narcotic Painkillers. *HeathDay News*. Retrieved from https://www.webmd.com/mental-health/addiction/news/20160325/nearly-all-us-doctors-overprescribe-addictive-narcotic-painkillers-survey#1

28. National Institutes on Drug Abuse. (2018). Common Comorbidities with Substance Use Disorders. Retrieved from https://www.drugabuse.gov/publications/research-reports/common-comorbidities-substance-use-disorders/introduction

29. National Safety Council. (2019). Prescribed to Death. Retrieved from https://stopeverydaykillers.nsc.org/video

30. O'Donnell, N. (2017, Nov 8) Va Secretary on Opioid Crisis. *CBS News*. Retrieved from https://www.cbs.com/shows/cbs_this_morning/video/rKFRVhhQWEn_JaA5dwAcjj2j0Zw1zgLP/va-secretary-on-fighting-opioid-crisis-we-can-do-more-/

31. Ohio Alliance for Innovation and Population Health. (2019). Years of Lost Life: Overdose Deaths 2009–2018. Retrieved from https://docs.wixstatic.com/ugd/89e8f1_6f36fea2f1894e46aed077a0627237f2.pdf

32. Ohio Department of Health. (2017). 2017 Ohio Drug Overdose Data: General Findings. Retrieved from https://odh.ohio.gov/wps/wcm/connect/gov/5deb684e-4667-4836-862b-cb5eb59acbd3/2017_OhioDrugOverdoseReport.pdf?MOD=AJPERES&CONVERT_TO=url&CACHEID=ROOTWORKSPACE.Z18_M1HGGIK0N0JO00QO9DDDDM3000-5dcb684c-4667_4836_862b_cb5eb59acbd3-moxPbu6

33. Parvaz, M. A., Alia-Klein, N., Woicik, P. A., Volkow, N. D., & Goldstein, R. Z. (2011). Neuroimaging for drug addiction and related behaviors. *Reviews in the Neurosciences.* 22(6), 609–624. Retrieved from https://www.ncbi.nlm.nih.gov/pubmed/22117165

34. Physicians for Responsible Opioid Prescribing. (2019). Video Archive. Retrieved from http://www.supportprop.org/resource/video/

35. Raymond, N., Spector M. (2019, Mar 26). Purdue Pharma agrees to $270 million settlement in Oklahoma opioid case. *Reuters.* Retrieved from https://www.reuters.com/article/us-usa-opioids-litigation/purdue-pharma-agrees-to-270-million-settlement-in-oklahoma-opioid-case-idUSKCN1R70CH

36. Ross, Casey. (2017). Med School Reputation Tied to Opioid Rx Rate. *STAT News, Boston Globe Media.* Retrieved from https://www.medpagetoday.com/PainManagement/PainManagement/67141?xid=nl_mpt_DHE_2017-08-09&eun=g998142d0r&pos=1

37. Sack, David. (2017, Jun 22). A Doctor's Most Dreaded Patient: The Addict. *PsychCentral.* Retrieved from https://blogs.psychcentral.com/addiction-recovery/2014/05/a-doctors-most-dreaded-patient-the-addict/

38. Schumaker, Erin. (2016). Surgeon General Vivek Murthy: Addiction Is A Chronic Brain Disease, Not A Moral Failing. The way forward includes needle exchanges and calling addiction what it is: a medical condition. *The Huffington Post.* Retrieved from https://www.huffpost.com/entry/vivek-murthy-report-on-drugs-and-alcohol_n_582dce19e4b099512f812e9c

39. Science Daily. (2015). Opioid and heroin crisis triggered by doctors overprescribing painkillers. Retrieved from https://www.sciencedaily.com/releases/2015/02/150204125945.htm

40. Smyth, J. C. (2016). Pain care lobby gave $3.5M in Ohio as opioid deaths climbed. *Associated Press.* Retrieved from https://www.cincinnati.com/story/news/2016/09/18/pain-care-lobby-gave-35m-ohio-opioid-deaths-climbed/90623876/

41. State of Ohio v. Purdue Pharma, Teva Pharmaceutical Industries, Endo Health Solutions, Johnson & Johnson, Allergan. (2017, May 31). Common Pleas Court of Ross County, Ohio. Civil Division. Retrieved from https://www.ohioattorneygeneral.gov/Files/Briefing-Room/News-Releases/Consumer-Protection/2017-05-31-Final-Complaint-with-Sig-Page.aspx

42. Substance Abuse and Mental Health Services Administration. (2015). Clinical Use of Extended-Release Injectable Naltrexone in the Treatment of Opioid Use Disorder: A Brief Guide. Retrieved from https://store.samhsa.gov/system/files/sma14-4892r.pdf

43. Swartsell, Nick. (2018). Federal Judge in Ohio Allows Massive Opioid Suit to Go Forward. *City Beat*. Retrieved from https://www.citybeat.com/news/blog/21038046/federal-judge-in-ohio-allows-massive-opioid-suit-to-go-forward?fbclid=IwAR14ImsZs_99UnIzMTJeZe9cSyQzuBjloKIleUtm7H4vTlmN2mquFTgMjmE

44. The Center for Disease Control and Prevention. (2018). Opioid Overdose. https://www.cdc.gov/drugoverdose/epidemic/index.html.

45. The Center for Responsive Politics. Data on Campaign Finance, Super PACs, Industries, and Lobbying. www.opensecrets.org

46. The National Academies of Sciences, Engineering, Medicine. (2019). Medications for Opioid Use Disorder Save Lives. Consensus Study Report Highlights. Retrieved from https://www.nap.edu/resource/25310/032019_OUDhighlights.pdf

47. The Ohio Channel. (2017, Mar 29). Press Conference - Battle Against Drug Epidemic. Retrieved from http://www.ohiochannel.org/video/press-conference-battle-against-drug-epidemic

48. The Ohio Legislature. 132nd General Assembly. Senate Bill 119. Retrieved from https://www.legislature.ohio.gov/legislation/legislation-summary?id=GA132-SB-119

49. United States Drug Enforcement Agency. (2019). Drug Scheduling. Retrieved from https://www.dea.gov/drug-scheduling.

50. Vestal, Christine (2016). Few Doctors Are Willing, Able To Prescribe Powerful Anti-Addiction Drugs. *Stateline*. Retrieved from https://www.pewtrusts.org/en/research-and-analysis/blogs/stateline/2016/01/15/few-doctors-are-willing-able-to-prescribe-powerful-anti-addiction-drugs

51. Whitaker, Bill. (2019, Feb 24). Did the FDA Ignite the Opioid Epidemic? *60 minutes, CBS News*. Retrieved from https://www.cbsnews.com/video/opioid-epidemic-did-the-fda-ignite-the-crisis-60-minutes/

52. Whitaker, Bill. (2019, Jun 30). Opioid Crisis: The lawsuits that could bankrupt manufacturers and distributors. *60 minutes, CBS News*. Retrieved from https://www.cbsnews.com/video/opioid-crisis-attorney-mike-moore-takes-on-manufacturers-60-minutes-2019-06-30/

53. Winters, K. C., & Arria, A. (2011). Adolescent Brain Development and Drugs. *The Prevention Researcher*. 18(2), 21–24. Retrieved from https://www.ncbi.nlm.nih.gov/pmc/articles/PMC3399589/

54. World Health Organization. (2018, Aug). Information sheet on opioid overdose. Retrieved from https://www.who.int/substance_abuse/information-sheet/en/

Made in the USA
Monee, IL
24 July 2021